MAN ENOUGH

JUSTIN BALDONI

MAN ENOUGH

MAN ENOUGH

UNDEFINING MY MASCULINITY

JUSTIN BALDONI

HarperOne
An Imprint of HarperCollins*Publishers*

Names and identifying details of various individuals discussed in this book have been changed to protect their privacy.

FIRST EDITION

Designed by Terry McGrath

LIBRARY OF CONGRESS CATALOGING-IN-PUBLICATION DATA
Names: Baldoni, Justin, 1984– author.
Title: Man enough : undefining my masculinity / Justin Baldoni.
Description: First edition. | San Francisco : HarperOne, 2021.
Identifiers: LCCN 2020052732 (print) | LCCN 2020052733 (ebook) | ISBN 9780063055599 (hardcover) | ISBN 9780063055605 (trade paperback) | ISBN 9780063055612 (ebook)
Subjects: LCSH: Masculinity. | Self-actualization (Psychology) | Sex.
Classification: LCC BF692.5 .B36 2021 (print) | LCC BF692.5 (ebook) | DDC 155.3/32—dc23
LC record available at https://lccn.loc.gov/2020052732
LC ebook record available at https://lccn.loc.gov/2020052733

ISBN 978-0-06-305559-9
ISBN 978-0-06-314444-6 (signed ed.)
ISBN 978-0-06-314446-0 (BN signed ed.)

21 22 23 24 25 LSC 10 9 8 7 6 5 4 3 2 1

For my dad.
For my son.
For all those brave enough to start
the journey from their heads to their hearts.
You are enough.

CONTENTS

PREFACE

When I started being more open publicly about my journey with masculinity, I often used the phrase "redefining masculinity." I wanted to start a dialogue and create a new conversation around how we can expand the definition of masculinity to include more of us and more parts of us. At the core of that was a deep need to know that I was included, that I wasn't alone, that I had permission to be who I was—driven, sensitive, resilient, ambitious, impulsive, stubborn, emotional, fallible—and yet still belong.

All the messages surrounding what it means to be a man in this world created a box—a definition of masculinity—that to fit into forced me to wage war against myself. Not only did I have to numb my feelings, I also had to sever myself from them. Not only did I have to ignore my insecurities and shame, I also had to insult them. Not only did I have to put on a mask, but also I had to put on a full suit of armor to protect myself from the incoming attacks. But eventually, after learning how to navigate the battlefield and dodge the attacks, I realized that a suit of armor does nothing to protect you from the attacks being launched from the inside, that redefining masculinity only expands the room between myself and the armor—it doesn't take the armor off.

I want to take the armor off.

I don't want to redefine masculinity.

I want to undefine masculinity.

I wish I could say this journey has been fun. It hasn't. But then again, I've never written a book before, and from everything I've heard, nobody really finds it fun. It's actually quite the opposite, in a weird yet good way. Like when you've had three bites too much of that rich chocolate cake and now feel sick to your stomach but also emotionally fulfilled because it's chocolate cake. In some ways I've found the process therapeutic, and in others just strange, messy, and uncomfortable. I uncovered traumas I didn't know I had, let alone had big feelings about. I wrestled with my reasons for writing this book in the first place and honestly with whether I should even be writing it at all.

As the days, months, and years went by, I found myself constantly going back, rewriting and updating my views and opinions as they changed in real time. I think that's why this has been such a tricky and difficult experience for me—how can I write a book about my experience and thoughts around masculinity when I feel like my experience and thoughts are changing and evolving every single day?

In the entertainment industry, we often joke that a movie is never done, it just gets released. But what about a book? How the hell do other authors do this? Words are forever. I can't take them back if my opinions or views change. If my thinking evolves, if I learn or read something that changes my perspective or challenges my understanding, I can't just go back and update this book—a book that at this point has become a living, breathing, almost human thing in my life akin to a child. So I have learned to come to terms with the understanding that while this particular book may be done, my learning and growth is not. And so long as I am breathing, it never will be.

This is not a memoir, but it is a personal exploration that attempts to frame my perspective using oftentimes uncomfortable (at least for me) personal stories on what it's meant to be a man and also what it has the potential to mean if we approached manhood a little differently. Because it's so personal, it forces me to brush up against the codependent part of me that wants everyone to like me, accept me, and think what I have to say is "profound" and "interesting" and all the other words of affirmation that will come in one ear and go out the other because no matter how much I'm applauded, I'll struggle to really believe it. But I'll have no problem believing the other ones—the negative ones, the mean ones, the ones that reinforce that I was right, that maybe I shouldn't have written this book. The ones that force me to ask myself the question, What do I really have to offer?

I've learned through therapy that I question my worth because underneath the question is a statement, a belief that for some reason has been held, formed, brainwashed, projected onto me and socially reinforced in me every day of my life for as long as I can remember. That belief is that somewhere, deep down, who I am, as a man, a friend, a son, a father, a brother, a husband, an entrepreneur, an athlete, an X, is just simply . . . not enough.

ENOUGH.

ENOUGH.

ENOUGH.

Enough of what? How much is enough? How do we know if it's enough? Who even decides what enough is? By whose standards am I even comparing myself to?

Sometimes I wish we could—just for one day—be real with each other. Just one day. To say what we mean and mean what we say. I wish we could expose our innermost guarded and protected secret dreams and fears. A day of vulnerability, of openness, of true freedom where we show up just as we are—beautiful, complicated, messed up, and perfectly imperfect—and watch as our biggest weaknesses become our greatest strengths. A day where not just the people but all the leaders and nations on earth do the same. Where for once we realize that not only do we all have no idea what the hell we're doing here, but that more than anything, if we are ever going to figure it out, we need to lean on each other to do so. Now odds are this dream will never become a reality, but it doesn't mean you and I can't model it, that we can't practice it and, like any other socialized behavior, start the socialization by passing it down to future generations, even if we aren't perfect at it.

"Perfect." I don't think I've ever liked that word. But "imperfect," now that's a word I like. There's something about it that has always drawn me in, something I've always connected to. Ironically, it's also become a word I use a lot as a goal in much of my work. Whether it's the way I shoot my films or the messiness of how I try to use social media, there's just something about imperfection that recently has become a goal of mine. Maybe it's because for so long I felt like I was not enough and creating a goal of imperfection became a way for me to cope with, and accept, my own imperfections. Or maybe it was the realization that true perfection is unattainable, and as a believer in God, a higher power, the universe, I believe that perfection ironically exists in the imperfections. Then one night in a conversation with my wife, Emily, I realized what I had missed had, ironically, always been there from the start, and all I had to do was look at the damn word. I'M PERFECT. Being imperfect was the very thing that in fact made me perfect. Even the word itself was telling me. So if our imperfections lead so many of us into this feeling of lack, of not being good enough or enough as it relates to our work, our friendships, and romantic relationships, then maybe it's time we rethink what being enough even means.

We need to. We *have* to because:

Enough is enough.

So why now? Why this book? Well, because I *need* this book. Badly. I needed this book as the ten-year-old boy who was shown porn for the first time long before his body or mind was ready for it, likely paving new neuropathways linking images of naked women to happiness and false feelings of self-worth. Images that he would later use to attempt to fill voids in his life—voids that, when he was not aroused and in the moment of using porn, would be replaced by shame. I needed this book as the eighteen-year-old freshman in college who felt the need to prove his masculinity by hooking up with as many girls as he could, without any regard for their feelings or attachments in the process. And as the twenty-year-old who didn't know how to say he wasn't emotionally ready to have sex for the first time, and as the twenty-five-year-old man who was heartbroken and so financially broke that even if he could have afforded to eat for that month after he learned that he was cheated on, he wouldn't have. I needed it as the twenty-nine-year-old who had finally found the love of his life, staged one of the most elaborate proposals of all time, and then also found himself having cold feet for no other reason than what society was telling him would happen to him once he got married. I needed it as the thirty-one-year-old who was about to have a daughter and had no idea what to do or how to raise her because he realized that for most of his life, despite believing in equality, he had not treated women with the respect he knows they deserved, both socially and romantically. And I need this book as the thirty-six-year-old man who is typing these words right now, who now also has a son and desperately wants to raise him to be not just a good man but a good human. And I need this book as the son of two loving parents, who despite deep affection and love still finds himself feeling the frustrations and annoyances from his childhood when in their company, even while knowing he will regret wasting that precious time with them one day when they are gone. I need this book for every other year that I have been alive. Even more, I need this book to heal from those formative years where the other boys first taught me—scratch that—*enforced* the rules of masculinity, and handed me my first script that told me what was okay, what was not okay, and set the rules for how I must act to become a man. These rules stacked on top of each other over time, creating a suit of armor that I would wear for decades. An armor that I didn't even know I was wearing, and because I didn't know, I had zero tools that could assist me in removing it. An armor I continue to wear today, and still struggle to take off even as I write these very words.

So, while on the one hand I am questioning my worth and what I have to offer to this very nuanced, polarizing, confusing, and scary conversation, I still have to try no matter what that voice says. I have to try for my own story and for my children, whom I pray become better than I am in every way—more compassionate, empathetic, and emotionally intelligent humans who know their worth and who speak their insecurities and fears into the world, knowing that by doing so it removes them from the dimly lit basement of their hearts where shame grows like mold.

I have to try for my helpmate, the mother of our children, my wife, Emily, whose radical patience, love, and acceptance have made me feel safer setting off on this journey of self-discovery that feels equal parts isolating and terrifying. Watching her ability to dive deep into her own wounds, trauma, and pain to understand herself more has been nothing short of awe-inspiring and an invitation for me to do the same. I have to try to know myself more, to dig deeper and love myself more so that I have a deeper and wider capacity to know and love her more.

My family deserves the best of me, and yet because of the war that exists within me as I wrestle with my own masculinity, at times they don't get the best of me. That's why I am trying so hard now.

I have to try for our community, our culture, our world. There are serious issues that men are facing that frankly just aren't talked about enough, from addictions like opioids, porn, and alcohol to depression and suicide. And there are also serious issues that men, at much higher rates than women, are causing, from violence to sexual assault and rape, and, when it comes to white men in particular, mass shootings and serial murders.

This book is part of me trying. And if my journey of discovery and the subsequent realizations that flow from my heart and onto these pages can be beneficial to you, my new friend and reader, then maybe it can also ripple out from the both of us and be therapeutic and eye-opening for our families, communities, and—who knows?—maybe even the world. The Buddha said that thousands of candles can be lit by a single candle. If one candle can be lit by reading this book, then I can only imagine the thousands of lives we can collectively touch, and in some cases even save, as we begin to realize that deep down, you and I and all of us are enough just as we are.

MAN ENOUGH

INTRODUCTION

I'm not sure if there is anything really revolutionary in this book. Unique maybe? But let's get real. This whole thing is a messy, vulnerable exploration of manhood written by someone who sits at an intersection of power and privilege and who historically probably wouldn't willingly choose to get this vulnerable, as there would seemingly be no benefit. Why try to tear down the walls in a system that has benefited me my entire life? I think partly because I know it's right. Partly because I feel a deep responsibility to. Partly because I am now a father and I believe our children are our main source of hope and they deserve a better future. And partly because I feel I'm stuck in the matrix and really, really, really want to get out.

This book is about my own struggles with being "enough," particularly about a definition of masculinity, about being a man, that rests on being X enough. Now, "X" can mean anything. For many men—for me—it's meant being enough of all those traditionally alpha male traits: strong, sexy, brave, powerful, smart, successful, and also good enough as a father and as a husband. I am not saying these things are negative, or that we shouldn't aspire to be these things. That is not what this book is about. Being a "good enough" father or "good enough" husband can be pretty damned wonderful—but "good" is subjective, and we've got to stop trying to prove how "good" we are and just be it, live it, revel in it, and celebrate it without putting others down in the process.

So let's get a couple of things straight: I'm straight. I'm also cisgender. And white. While I will share the experiences of other men throughout the book, it is largely based on my experience and therefore I write from the lens I was raised in. Throughout this book, when I say "men" (or any form of the gender) I am including anyone and everyone who identifies as a man, and when I say "we" I am including myself in that group. This book is not a comprehensive course on gender studies, nor is it a case for the gender binary. Also, and perhaps most important, this book is absolutely NOT an attack on men or on masculinity. I believe men are good: inherently, intrinsically good. That YOU are good. And there are tons of aspects of the traditional definition of masculinity that I connect to and that I'm grateful for. I'm 100 percent not ashamed to say I love being a man. I am also not apologizing for being a man. But that is not to say that I won't be apologizing for the ways in which my interpretation of masculinity has hurt those around me. Those positive traits that have been associated with being a man—traits such as being resourceful and accountable, honest and trustworthy, loyal, a present father and husband, or even down to simply being strong, smart, and brave—are all good traits that I aspire to live by. But they are also traits that I believe every human should aspire to live by; they are not traits unique to men. They are universal. The key is not the trait. It's that voice in your head, in my head, that tells us we aren't X *enough*. Enough is enough. Enough with enough.

Call me naive, but I believe that overall, humans are good. And it is from that deeply rooted, foundational belief that this journey, and this book, begins and ends. I am not pushing any partisan belief system or agenda here. As a registered Independent, I don't subscribe to any political ideology, and though I absolutely vote and participate in elections, I don't talk publicly about who I am voting for. In my life I do my best to have empathy and compassion for those I don't agree with or who don't agree with me. So if I use a word that triggers you or makes you think I am pushing a political agenda on you, I ask you to keep reading, as I assure you I am not. My desire to be private and not participate in partisan politics stems largely from my personal faith.

As a quick reference, the faith I practice and will at times refer to in this book as it relates to the choices I have made is the Bahá'í Faith. If you are uncomfortable with religion, or maybe even reading a book from someone who practices a religion different from yours, then just imagine any quotes or analogies I throw out coming from either the "universe," an activist you like, or your own religion. I don't share my faith in an effort to convert or change your beliefs, but in sharing such personal stories, I write from what I know, what guides me and my decisions, and for me, faith is central to all I do and who I am. Bahá'ís essentially believe in the unity of all religions and the eradication of prejudices of any kind. We believe in the oneness of humanity and that every soul on Earth has been created noble and has its own relationship with God. That said, this is not a book about religion, and in fact, many in my own faith may find its content confrontational and uncomfortable. And for that I say, good! One of the fundamental beliefs of the Bahá'í Faith is the independent investigation of truth. We all must find what is true for ourselves and not ignorantly follow any faith or teaching without investigating it for ourselves. If there is a purpose to faith, I believe it to be the unification of the human race, and that our mission as humans (if we choose to accept it) is to simply be of service and create unity wherever we can. Perhaps one of my favorite aspects of my faith is the practice of unconditional love, nonjudgment, and the fight for gender equality and racial justice. As a Bahá'í, I am asked in my daily life to be a "defender to the victims of oppression" in whatever form that takes and to never exert my beliefs on another individual as God's love and mercy are far exalted beyond my limited reptilian brain. So even if I don't subscribe to a belief or ideology or lifestyle myself, it's my duty as a human to love and to rush to defend anyone who is being unjustly treated or oppressed. All that to say, as it relates to our country's political system and my ensuring this book does not jump into what is currently considered "woke" for the sake of wokeness, all I aim to write about are my beliefs as they relate to my own experiences as a man. I believe that more than anything right now we must find a way to stop the "otherizing" of our friends, family, and neighbors due to ideological and lifestyle differences, and instead find the common, human ground of empathy, respect, and love. It is from this place that I believe, as it relates to this book and masculinity, that we have to separate the masculinity conundrum from political agendas to do the nuanced self-work and necessary healing to successfully create space for the conversations to be had. The victims of masculinity, when it becomes unhealthy, as it has for so many of us men, are not just our friends, wives, girlfriends, and partners, but also ourselves. It's me, it's you, it's the men we interact with daily who are suffering and may never admit it. It's the hundreds of thousands of good, hardworking, kind, and loving men who take their lives each year because their pain has become too much to bear and they feel it's the only way out. It's the millions of others who suffer from depression and can't or won't or are unable to see a therapist. It's our own brothers, teammates, coworkers, and fathers, and for some of us, it's our sons. It's from that place of wanting to help stop and prevent so much unnecessary pain and suffering that I attempt to write this book.

Why Me?

Look, I got lucky. I grew up privileged, middle class, and in a home with parents who love each other, their children, their community, and the world fully. Now, they weren't perfect; they came with their own set of complicated and deep wounds, history, and trauma, without much guidance on how to heal that in themselves. But there was love. Always love. I'm so damn blessed to have been, and to continue to be, so loved. And even still, when I look back on my childhood, right beside all of the abundance of love sits the belief that something is lacking, the belief that I was lacking, that I was missing the mark.

But not necessarily because of something my parents said or did. I never felt like I was failing in their eyes. And it's not because of our faith; in fact, as Bahá'ís we believe that each of us is noble. As it turns out, that mark I was missing was the invisible, impossibly high and unachievable mark of masculinity: the mark of being a man. It wasn't enough that I was born and identified as a man, or that I walked and talked like a man—the world was telling me I was missing the mark, and because of it, I wasn't a man. It was as if the bar were set too high and I couldn't reach it, or more like the box was built too small and not all of me could fit inside it.

For as long as I can remember I've been an emotional and sensitive boy wrapped inside an energetic, testosterone-filled, creative tornado that can't sit still and needs to be physically doing something all the time. Sports were both my meditation and my medication. As I grew into my teenage years, I thrived in competitive sports but at the same time felt like I didn't fit in with my teammates. I was bullied, picked on, and celebrated, while simultaneously bullying and picking on other guys. One minute my teammates were making fun of me or calling me "Balboner" (good one, right?), and the next I could be tackled in celebration for scoring the game-winning goal or helping break the school record anchoring the four-by-one-hundred-meter relay team. One day I could be chased down and tied to a goalpost on the soccer field by the upperclassmen, and the next I would be tying someone else, someone younger than I was, to the goalpost. I was a confused and conflicted kid mostly because, like many male teens, underneath it all, I felt a mounting sense of urgency—pressure—to be accepted, to be one of the guys. So I taught myself to suck it up, play it off, be cool, and effectively hide my emotions and dismiss my feelings in an attempt to fit inside a box that was built long before my friends and I were born. I began putting on the armor that I eventually would forget I had on, armor I would think I needed to function as a man in this world.

Over the next decade, this complicated and confusing relationship I had with my masculinity manifested itself in broken relationships, poor choices, immense pain, inner conflict, and tons of wasted time, but most importantly, it manifested itself in shame. It was from this place of rising shame that I began the long and tumultuous journey to figure out how to get from my head to my heart, the journey from inside the box to inside myself. The journey of becoming man enough. To human enough. To just being fucking enough. But maybe the problem isn't that I wasn't and am not "enough," but that "enough" is a myth, a mirage, always eluding our grasp, always just out of reach, always receding toward the horizon. That feeling of "if only . . ." that this concept of "enough" produces has put so many of us in a trap. If only I were stronger, faster, smarter, richer. If only my biceps were an inch bigger, my dick an inch bigger, my brain forty points more on an IQ test. If only I had more money, more friends, more stuff. If only I did this, or had this, or was this, then it would be enough. Then I would be enough. And yet it never is. And it never will be.

An Invitation

If you are here to learn about the history of masculinity and how we got here, how to fix your life, or how to be a certain way to impress someone, then you picked the wrong book. This isn't an academic treatise or a motivational self-help book. I don't need to tell you to start your day off with a victory by making your bed when you wake up in the morning, although I love those books and always thought that my first book would be just that. But instead of writing a motivational book, I am writing an invitational one. I am sharing my story in hopes that it invites you into yours. I am asking questions of myself in hopes that together the collective "we" can ask those same questions. Like, "Why did I say that?" "Why did I react that way when she said that to me?" "Why the hell am I so pissed?" "Will they ever find out I'm full of shit?" "Why am I unhappy when my life is awesome?" "Why did I keep asking after she said no?" And the hundreds more questions I have asked myself over the course of my thirty-six years on Earth. To this day, asking questions of myself is the tool I use the most to dig deeper, to learn, to discover, and to navigate roadblocks on the path from my head to my heart.

If you had told me a few years ago that I would be writing this kind of book, with a focus on masculinity, I would have laughed. Not at you, but at the prospect of me. After all, it was only a few years ago that I even began my public and private journey to explore masculinity. The truth is, none of it was planned, and it still boggles my mind that we live in a world where simply by changing our Instagram bios, we can stumble onto our purpose. Here's the short version of how I got here. After my daughter, Maiya, was born, I found myself with a lot of thoughts, ideas, and questions and nowhere to really share them. So, like many, I turned to social media and used it as a public diary of sorts. Instead of just posting pretty pictures and sharing the highlight reel of my life, I wrote long captions and waxed poetic about life and love. I talked about my wife and how in awe of her I was, and got real about marriage and the challenges that come with it, as well as all the hopes and dreams I had for my daughter.

It didn't take long for various (female-facing) press outlets to pick up my posts and to quickly label me as a feminist fighting for gender equality. In fact, it happened so quickly that I hadn't even realized that's what I was or was trying to do. At first this was honestly just me sharing my heart, but it became clear that while men take up our fair share of space in the world, the sharing of hearts and feelings was an area that could certainly benefit from having more men in it. Shortly after, I decided to go all in and create the show *Man Enough*, where I gathered a bunch of friends together and had public conversations on camera that I had never seen men have—conversations I wish I had had a chance to watch as a young man. When I started asking those questions of myself a little more publicly, that's when I got the big call: the invitation to do a TED Talk. But not just any TED Talk, a speech about masculinity at TED Women. The invitation alone was more than humbling; it was daunting, and one that I wanted to turn down. My wife was pregnant, my son was due just a week before I would be scheduled to give the talk, and I was acting full-time in *Jane the Virgin*. My first instinct? Say no. What do I have to offer? I should step back and make space for a woman, right? It is a conference about the power of women, after all, and a woman I'm not. I wanted to turn it down because I was at the beginning of my journey, not the middle and not the end, and I was not ready to share my thoughts because I didn't even know what thoughts were! At the time, so many people were putting me on a pedestal like I had some secret ingredient that could help men become better, and that in turn could help women, but that pedestal made me extremely uncomfortable because I was honestly just doing the bare minimum yet that was still separating me in some ways from other men. I was so confused; how could I help other men when I was having a hard time even helping myself? And more than anything else, I was aware the higher that pedestal gets, the harder the fall. I hate pedestals.

But what's most true is that I wanted to turn it down because I didn't think I was good enough.

Boy, did that feel familiar. I had spent the better part of my life becoming good friends with that feeling of inadequacy. I knew it well—what it felt like, what messages it told me, how it always traveled with shame. And I had started learning what it had to teach me. For me, fear, inadequacy, and shame are the ultimate challenges; they are invitations to lean in, to get closer, and to practice being comfortable in the uncomfortable.

What did it look like to lean in? In this situation, it meant saying yes to a TED Talk when shame and fear wanted me to say no. And that "yes" meant that I was also telling myself it was okay to not have all the answers, it was okay to not have read all of the research, and it was okay to be learning in real time.

It was enough just to be me. To speak from where I was in that moment in my journey without offering any solutions, just my story.

And yet I wanted to quit multiple times and almost did, because I felt that the risks were greater than the rewards. I was nervous I would actually hurt the women's movement by saying something wrong or offensive, plus I knew my work was with men and not women. I also knew that few men would even find the talk unless a woman in their lives showed it to them. It wasn't until I finally reframed doing the talk as a challenge to myself—was I man enough to take this risk?—that I actually committed to not quitting. How messed up is that? To use a term historically used to put down and keep us in a socially constructed box, a phrase that encourages unhealthy competition, unhealthy relationships with other men, and ourselves. To use that same phrase to get myself to show up for a talk where I dismantled and repurposed that phrase to challenge men to be better than I was being in that very moment. But that's okay because it taught me what I knew I needed. It taught me that my socialization, my baggage, the programming and lessons that have come from all over the world and have been ingrained in me for as long as I can remember weren't my fault and could be used for good as well if we are willing to say yes to the invitations. The poison when repurposed can also become the medicine.

I just realized that I'm talking a lot about a speech that you have probably never seen. Since so much of this book is inspired by it, here is my 2018 TED Women Talk in a nutshell:

- As a man I realized much of my masculinity was performative, and for years I had been acting and pretending to be a man I'm not.
- I believe in the "radical" idea that women and men are equal.
- As men we shouldn't be afraid of the parts of us that society deems "feminine," aka "weak."
- Much of what I learned as it relates to performative masculinity I learned from my dad, who I realized learned it from his dad. Or I learned it from my male peers, who learned it from their dads. We pass down scripts generationally. We must break the cycle.
- As men we need to use our strength and bravery and other traditionally masculine traits to explore what's in our hearts. Basically, all the other parts of ourselves we probably wouldn't put on our résumés or social media profiles. Things such as being sensitive, vulnerable, and good listeners.

- Let's just shut up and finally listen to the women in our lives.
- Oh, and my dad, whom I secretly resented for years because of his predisposition to sensitivity, is also the reason I learned how to use my heart in place of my fists as a boy and now as a man. So while he's not perfect, which I will unpack in later chapters, he's pretty damn special, and I couldn't be more grateful he's my dad.

The Power of Story

Well, I did it. The feedback was instant, and it was *mostly* very encouraging and affirming. From women. Men? Not so much. But it was nuanced, because women were sharing it publicly, writing comments publicly, sending it to men publicly. Women were outspoken in their applause, but I noticed an interesting phenomenon, one that I called out in the talk itself: where were the men? Men weren't out publicly sharing or commenting (and if they were, it was usually to put me down). The positive, life-altering responses from men were all happening in private. They were in my direct messages, my private messages, and in emails: teenagers telling me it was the first time they felt like there was a place for who they were; a sixty-year-old man saying he could for the first time articulate what it felt like to be disowned by his gender. Men wrote pages of text sharing their deepest, most intimate feelings and fears. Men said they finally felt seen, and in feeling seen, they felt free. But this was only a portion of the men. By the time the message reached the others, it had been misconstrued, taken out of context, and weaponized as political.

I distinctly remember the night the two-minute video TED had posted of the most passionate part of the speech went viral (by that I mean it had upward of fifty million views in a matter of days on the platform). After getting tons of texts and calls from family and friends that instantly gave me anxiety, as I knew that with massive amounts of love comes, at times, an equal or greater amount of hate, I hesitantly logged into my Facebook knowing what I was about to find and saw that I was getting tagged in many of the reposts of the video by random men. Unfortunately, many of the men who were tagging me were doing so to publicly criticize me. It took me right back to being that kid who desperately wanted to be liked by the other guys, and I knew I had two options: to close the app and try to ignore the hate or to genuinely try to understand what men didn't like about the talk. I chose the latter. After all, I can't preach about getting comfortable in the uncomfortable without being willing to hear the feedback from the very audience I was trying to reach. After scrolling down past all the women who were heaping praise, I landed on the first post by a male. He was a white man, living in the Midwest, and had shared my post with a warning to men, essentially using me as an example of what's wrong with "The Left" and how I am attacking men. I decided to write him privately to try to understand what it was about the talk that rubbed him the wrong way. I could tell by his post that there was a good chance he didn't actually watch the full talk but was making an assumption after watching the portion of it that TED posted. Surprised by my message, he responded politely and admitted to not having seen it but felt like he could gather "what I was saying" from the clip he did see. I asked him kindly to watch the eighteen minutes and consider having a longer conversation with me, as many of his comments alluded to me being a "man-hating" feminist and apologizing for being a man. I explained the "why" behind my talk, that it was about using our strong attributes as tools to dive deeper into ourselves, and about how much my father influenced me. After watching it he wrote me a long message apologizing for his post, then immediately posted a public apology and asked his friends who had joined in on the public bashing to watch the full talk before condemning it. This interaction, and ones similar to it, gave me massive amounts of hope. I found that men, when confronted and lovingly challenged in private, were not only more than willing to listen but, even more inspiring, were open to doing the necessary self-work to become the most honest, virtuous versions of themselves. My deduction: most men, regardless of our actions and beliefs, what side of the political aisle we sit on, want the same thing. We want to become the best version of ourselves possible, to simply become better men. That is what kept me going. And that is why I am writing this book.

Our stories may be individualized, but there is a universal thread that connects us. And every single man I know has had countless experiences of feeling like we don't fit in. My story is a buildup of decades of experience trying to fit into the man box, trying to wear the suit of armor that made me man enough, until I became so weighted down by who the world told me to be that I didn't even know who I was.

The power of my story isn't in the details, although this book will dive deep into the details of my experience. The power is in the invitation. It's in the opportunity to hear something in my story that reminds you of something in your story and invites you to lean into that, question it, and reframe it. The power lies in the invitation to believe that **you are not alone in your struggles, emotions, or fears.** You are not alone in this box—this constricting set of socially constructed identities that have pressed and pressured us into thinking we have to think, act, and be a certain way to be man enough.

The Risk

I am admittedly a bit scared of finishing this book, having it published, and then launching it into a public space to be openly criticized. There is innate risk in vulnerability by its very definition: the quality or state of being exposed to the possibility of being attacked or harmed, either physically or emotionally. This book is an exposure of parts of me and my feelings that I have struggled with talking about and, as a result, long felt shame around. This isn't an airing of my dirty laundry, or a confession of sins, but hopefully it's an exposure of my humanity—a humanity we all share.

And it will be just that: an exposure. I'm diving in, heart first, and I share it with you in the most authentic and sincere way I can, because I know no other way. The risk of being harmed, or ridiculed, or cut off from my gender (the gender that part of me still, despite this whole process, wants to be accepted by) is real. But in this case, the rewards far outweigh the risks because what's even scarier for me than being called names or being bullied online is spending another thirty-plus years afraid of knowing who I really am, knowing only who the world tells me I'm supposed to be.

The Hope

I want this book to feel like a trusted friend—whether you are a man who, like me, feels like you've been trying for too long to fit in a box that's too small, or you are a woman or nonbinary person who wants insight into how masculinity has affected not only your life but also the lives of the men you know and love. I want this book to serve as an invitation to begin, or continue, on your own exploration. There is no right way. That is the purpose of undefining something. It opens that thing up to interpretation and exploration. It creates space and allows for creativity. And where there is creativity, there is love.

I want this book to be a companion on your journey as you navigate the long and tumultuous path from your head down to your heart, arming you with sincere human truths that will bring some relief to the long-held cultural belief that you have to be X enough to be man enough.

Most importantly, I want this book to restore in you the belief that you are good, inherently and intrinsically good, and that who you are, as you are, is enough.

CHAPTER ONE

BRAVE ENOUGH

What It Really Means to Be Brave

"Jump, Boner! Don't be a pussy!" I'll never forget hearing Tim shout from the freezing water below, where several of the guys laughed and called me out for hesitating to take the leap. The river raged twenty feet down from where my skinny, thirteen-year-old body shook with its own raging undercurrent of dread as my legs clutched onto the side rails of the bridge. I'm pretty sure that at that point, my balls were living somewhere between my belly button and my chin, so if he had instead yelled, "Grow some balls!" I imagine they would have been difficult to find.

What Tim and the other boys didn't know, and what I refused to tell them before I climbed onto the side of a perfectly good bridge, is that I'm scared of heights when not secured by windows and guard railings and the various protections we build to keep people safe so they don't slip or fall off the very thing I was about to willingly jump off of.

So what did I do? I held my breath and did what most young boys do when their manhood is questioned. I manned the hell up and jumped. But only after starting and stopping myself like ten times, which only got me teased more. Eventually, though, I did jump. And while I'd like to think I looked like the Rock escaping from an enemy's attack, or jumping from a burning building and effortlessly falling into the water only to reemerge even more badass than before, I definitely didn't. If you had been watching, I'm guessing it would have looked more like a screaming pencil falling into the water at a weird angle. But hey, I did it, right?! But not because I was suddenly struck by a bolt of courage and inspired to face my fears. Not because I'm a real man. Nope, I jumped because more than being scared for my physical safety, I was scared of being seen as a "pussy." Let me translate that into the not-so-secret language of masculinity, the rules that govern our very existence. To a young boy, being called a "pussy" means being seen as weak. And I was more scared of being seen as "less than," as inferior, than I was of missing the three-foot opening of rock-less water and paralyzing myself. Yep, it's that intense, simply because in the language we young boys and men speak to each other, being a "pussy" means being a girl, which means not being a man, or at best, it means you're a very weak man, which is absolutely rooted in sexism. We don't even take the time to pause and think about how the normalization of using these words as teasing or harmless fun unconsciously affects the way we see and treat the girls and women in our lives. Even though we all knew plenty of girls in our class who had jumped off that bridge, other boys knew that calling me a pussy or a girl for being afraid to jump was the quickest way to get me to actually jump. Language is powerful, and it affects us in ways we don't realize. As a boy, and even now as a man writing this, I'm either on one side of the term or the other, so to my thirteen-year-old brain, being called a girl meant only one thing: I was not a man. So when I jumped, it wasn't because I was brave, but because I was terrified of being seen as "less than" just for experiencing real emotions. I was terrified of admitting I was terrified. Welcome to the clusterfuck of a young boy's mind and the rational and irrational process by which we make decisions.

Little did I know at the time, this would be just one moment in a string of thousands that reinforced a dangerous and confusing message about bravery and masculinity: acts of bravery aren't judged by ourselves internally, but are completely dependent on external factors and judged by whether we are living up to the unwritten expectations of what most men (and women) see as brave. In other words, if we aren't inherently risking our lives physically, then we aren't being brave. For some reason, at an early age many of us start to associate bravery as actions that could cause us physical harm. I mean just think about all the young people risking their lives to take epic Instagram pics or the crazy stunts people are pulling to go viral on TikTok. We live in a culture that thrives off consuming content and heaping praise on people who risk their lives for popularity's sake. This is no different than what it was like for me growing up, except that social media was simply your reputation, and "likes" were measured by whether you had anyone to hang out with on the weekend. Now, given the fact that after I jumped, my friends shouted, "Yeah, Boner!!!!!" (I still have no idea why that became the name they called me, for some it was "Balboner," "Boner" for short), I learned that praise from my peers (even if it's rooted in an insult-based nickname) when overcoming my fears was more validating than the fear itself. This is a dangerous line because, while I absolutely believe in conquering nerves and fear and diving into the very things that scare us, I also believe in doing them not for external validation and accolades but for internal validation, which needs no celebration or praise. When we are taught, as young boys, to distrust our feelings and to disregard our fear and unease, we immediately start to associate those feelings with weakness, and in our egocentric young brains, that weakness becomes associated with our worth. Our self-esteem plummets as we begin to wonder why we are "different," since it appears that no one else has these problems—these feelings—that we do because the social constructs we adhere to prohibit anyone who feels them from sharing. And yes, my use of the word "problems" is intentional, because to myself, and to many young boys and even men, feelings of fear, anxiety, and shame are all seen as problems to overcome instead of emotions to feel.

Speaking of shame, here's an embarrassing story that ties back to the genius nickname I was given in school. I was twelve, and like most twelve-year-old boys I had absolutely zero control of when my body would decide to have an erection. Half the time it was happening, I wasn't even aware until it was already at midday salute. But because it's never talked about in school, and as a young boy no one prepares you for those few years of uncontrollable erections that come exactly when you don't want them to, we start to feel embarrassed and ashamed of our own bodies. We can't talk to anyone about it because we think it's only happening to us, and we start to wonder if we are abnormal. Oh, and if God forbid anyone in school caught us with an erection, or making that awkward adjustment where we hunch over and shove our penises up into our waistline to twelve o'clock, then we would be made fun of forever just for having a completely normal and changing testosterone-filled body. So I was twelve, and I was going to the mall with my sweet aunt who was visiting (who is extremely Catholic, conservative, and very, very, very modest). I was wearing bright yellow windbreaker pants that were easily three sizes too big for me, and when it was windy, they looked more like an unpacked parachute than joggers. As we were getting out of our Chrysler minivan, my aunt made a (serious) comment about what was in my pants and that I had to take whatever I had shoved in there out because it "sure isn't funny!" I had no idea what she was talking about until I looked down and realized that I did in fact have something in my pants but taking it out wasn't an option. Cue the silence. That horrifying, awkward silence. I stared down in shock and embarrassment as I felt like I had been betrayed by my own body. My aunt, not knowing what to say or do, quickly looked away, and like the kind Catholic midwestern woman she is, I think she pretended it never happened. I remember her saying "Oh. Okay! Let's go!" and walking away while I, ashamed and humiliated, adjusted myself and waddled over to catch up with the rest of the family. I never spoke of the incident again and I've never told that story. Until now.

The thing is, we are all so much more alike than we are different, but because we as boys are socialized to not share or talk about anything that could potentially be used as a weapon against us, we are forced to suffer in silence. Whether it be our changing bodies, a learning disability, a struggle at home with an alcoholic or abusive parent, or what can seem like a trivial thing, like being stuck twenty feet above a river on the side of a bridge because we are too scared to jump and too scared to admit we are scared, the very moment we start to otherize ourselves for being different, or not being manly or brave enough, we fail to realize that the reason we feel so alone is because the other boys have learned what we will soon learn—how to suppress our emotions.

So what was the main lesson I learned that fateful day on the bridge? That my sense of myself as a man didn't come from within, didn't bubble up from some inner core of manliness or innate worthiness. There was no Jedi hero's journey moment where the Dark Side was conquered and, in an epic demonstration of bravery, I stood up to my biggest fears and slayed the bad guy. Nope, manhood was something that was going to be conferred—or withheld—by other guys. It's that simple and that complicated. If they said I was a (insert heteronormative insult here), then that's what I was. If they said I was a dude, I was a dude. This meant that my "man card" relied on my ability to perform, and they were the audience and also the critics. It meant pretending that I didn't have the feelings I had, and also pretending that the feelings I didn't have were actually the ones I did. It's called acting. And I got pretty damn good at it.

What's in a Word?

To be clear, when I talk about masculinity and offer bravery as a defining trait, I'm not talking about how we celebrate the nurses and doctors who risk their lives on the front lines or the firefighters who run into burning buildings, nor how we revere our military service people as heroes or applaud anyone in any line of work who rushes toward danger with little regard for their own life. This concept of bravery, and the applauding of this kind of bravery, is not wrong or toxic in any way. The folks who live these professions and put their lives on the line for our freedom and safety are, without a doubt, real-life heroes! I am not saying that we should stop applauding these men, women, and nonbinary people for their acts of heroism. I am not saying that they should be considered any less courageous or brave. However, what I would love to see is a broadening of the definition of standards that men can uphold and traits we can exhibit that exist outside of physical feats or acts of heroism. I'd love to create room for all the ways in which bravery manifests itself in each of us, in the ways that we take risks, not just with our bodies, but also with our hearts.

I'm a big fan of Brené Brown, PhD, a research professor and author who explains courage in the most astute and necessary way:

> In one of its earliest forms, the word courage had a very different definition than it does today. Courage originally meant "To speak one's mind by telling all one's heart." Over time, this definition has changed, and, today, courage is more synonymous with being heroic. Heroics are important and we certainly need heroes, but I think we've lost touch with the idea that speaking honestly and openly about who we are, about what we're feeling, and about our experiences (good and bad) is the definition of courage.

In my late twenties, before I was ever aware of Dr. Brown's work, I instinctually began to honestly and openly examine, and even question, what it meant to be a brave man. As I started to look at my behavior of disconnecting from my emotions and the nuanced way it established itself in my psyche, I felt this pull to question, for myself, if I would ever be brave enough to honor how I felt. But the truth was that I didn't even know what I felt—hell, I wasn't even sure if I knew how to feel, much less how to honor the feelings that bubbled up.

It is this not knowing, this emotional paralysis, that author and scholar bell hooks considers a real blight on men's sense of self, and I couldn't agree more. In her groundbreaking book *The Will to Change: Men, Masculinity, and Love,* hooks writes:

> The first act of violence that patriarchy demands of males is not violence toward women. Instead patriarchy demands of all males that they engage in acts of psychic self-mutilation, that they kill off the emotional parts of themselves. If an individual is not successful in emotionally crippling himself, he can count on patriarchal men to enact rituals of power that will assault his self-esteem.

Pretty intense, right? But it rings true for me. To be accepted as a man, I first had to learn to suppress the parts of myself that other men would think were "unmanly." And if I didn't do it on my own, you better believe there would be another man—who was also wanting to be accepted—to do it for me. You see, long before I was taught to view girls as property, as a commodity; before I learned that I should be mean to the girl that I have a crush on, as a way of showing her I like her; before I was taught that it's impossible for boys and girls to be "just" friends, that there is no way they can have a platonic relationship because if sex isn't involved, then what's the point? Long before these and the many other unspoken rules that I will begin to unpack in the chapters ahead rooted themselves in my brain and cemented themselves in my actions and behavior, the foundation had already been laid upon the repression—the killing of—the emotional parts of me; my feelings. The road between my head and my heart wasn't simply riddled with speed bumps and short detours around a roadblock here and there. The road dead-ended at a steep cliffside, and deep in the abyss below was my heart.

Let me be clear that the damage this causes women is inexcusable. The messages that this behavior sends to women is reprehensible. From calling boys "girls" or "pussies" as an insult, to the wage gap, to rape culture (which many men don't believe exists) and domestic violence, we live in a culture that not only slights men for being what we have dubbed as feminine but also puts down women, physically and emotionally, in the process. This is not a liberal or a conservative opinion. This is what is actually happening. The work to undo and repair this damage is monumental. At first I thought that this work—the work of repair and equality—was where I should start if I wanted to be helpful. I thought I needed to dive in and research and educate myself on women's rights and connect with leaders and organizations to help advocate for systemic change for women. But the deeper I dug, the more I realized that this form of activism would be in vain, would lack authenticity, and would ultimately prove to be futile if I was not also doing the work of connecting with myself, being aware of and advocating for my emotions, and changing my behavior—not just talking about it, but actually taking the journey from my head to my heart. In other words, I don't believe women need another man jumping on the "woke" bandwagon, wearing a feminist T-shirt, and tweeting and speaking out about social issues who isn't willing to start by doing the hard work of introspection and self-reflection. I believe the world needs men to show up, not in big ways, but in hundreds and thousands of little ways, ways that don't produce "likes" on Instagram or create social clout but instead create a better, more equitable, more just world. That work doesn't begin with an audience; it starts in the mirror, with an audience of one.

The Influencers: Family and Friends, Bullies and Boys

Where do we learn this stuff? To generically blame "society" for how we've come to focus too heavily on physical conquests when discussing "masculine bravery" feels a little too vague and easy. When we say things such as "socialization," that isn't enough for me. And keep in mind it's not just us men who have been influenced by society; it's also women; it's all of us.

Socialization is the idea that we are shaped and molded by the places where we live and grow—schools, workplaces, families, sports teams, etc. Schoolyards can be like little factories, taking the raw materials of children whose personalities and traits range all over the place, and molding them and shaping them to represent whatever today's current definitions of gender norms and expectations are. We don't necessarily learn this from the formal curriculum—though we do learn the falsehood that men did all the exploring and inventing and building that created modern society. But while we may not literally read that in our history books, we mostly learn and absorb it through an informal curriculum—who gets called on, how our teachers look at us, speak to us, reward and discipline us. And then we learn it even more informally, when the teachers aren't looking, when we have a few minutes to ourselves, as kids—on the playground, in the locker room, in the lunch line, after school playing sports or doing theater.

Speaking of theater, I first fell in love with performing in middle school when I got the chance to play the emotional and quirky best friend of Romeo (Mercutio) in *Romeo and Juliet*. I actually auditioned to play Romeo—mostly because he got to kiss the girl and I had never been kissed—but of course that role went to Luke, the popular, tall jock with the blue eyes and blond hair who couldn't act to save his life. I swear I'm not still bitter. In the end, I got to play two roles—Mercutio and Paris—which meant I got to die twice. This would be a skill I would lean on early in my career with the award-winning, made-for-TV movie *Spring Break Shark Attack*. But I digress. Unlike in high school, in middle school I didn't have to choose between performing in the school play or being an athlete. I was actually encouraged to do both, but that all changed when I was a freshman in high school and wanted to try out for the school play. Having been a veteran actor in middle school, landing supporting roles in multiple seventh- and eighth-grade productions, I thought I would be able to take my well-honed skills into the big leagues of high school. Little did I know that if I wanted to audition for the fall play, I would have to give up soccer, the sport I had been playing since I was five, and the sport that I thought would be my ticket to college. And the spring play was out of the question as well, since spring was reserved for track and field and I was assured I would make the Varsity team as a freshman, which was a big deal. The irony of this false choice is that had I picked theater over soccer, I would have more than likely been met with a different style of masculinity, as the boys in the theater program were more open and in touch with their sensitive, emotional sides. They were generally considered nerds, choir boys, or theater geeks, and they would eventually be the guys I sought refuge with later on in high school, when I was tired of trying to fit in as the jock I very much became.

During my junior year, I started using my dad's fancy new home video camera that he bought to film my soccer games, to confess my undying love for girls I liked via the sacred act of lip-syncing in boy band music videos—a skill that would have for sure made me a teenage TikTok influencer if it existed back then and one that would serve me well when I proposed to my wife eleven years later. While the deeply moving and very unsexy performances of NSYNC's "God Must Have Spent a Little More Time on You" and the Backstreet Boys' "I Want It That Way" were fun and self-deprecating ways to try to get me out of the "friend zone," what they really did was help cement my place there. But more than anything, making these videos also allowed me to connect, and become friends with, the theater guys who also found that creative performance helped them express their thoughts and emotions. To this day I still feel sad about how the system of false choices makes young people, and in my case, a young man with talent in both sports and on the stage, choose between these two avenues. I often wonder what high school would have been like for me if I didn't have to choose, if I had theater as a creative outlet then. Later in high school, I found ways to express my creativity, whether it be through our fun and ridiculous school assembly dance performances or as a local DJ at the radio station, but it wasn't the same.

My first year in high school was scary as shit—the girls were older and gorgeous, the guys who dated those girls all played sports, while the theater kids got picked on and had sodas thrown at them when they walked to lunch. So, of course, I chose sports over theater. Think about this for a second: how many great athletes have secret dreams of becoming action stars, writing books or poetry, playing the piano, starring in the school musical, or in my case dying (twice) onstage in *Romeo and Juliet*? And how many physically talented musicians, writers, and performers could have also kicked ass on the soccer or football field? What unwritten rule of masculinity says we can't do both?

The irony here is that four years after choosing sports over theater, I would tear my hamstring during my senior year and lose it all. All that hard work—four years of endless practices, of putting up with the assholes and bullies as an underclassman, the upperclassmen who subconsciously want to inflict the pain they suffered when they were younger to experience a false sense of power. What was it all for, anyway? The depression that followed my injury was led by the feeling that it was all for nothing. What if I had made a different choice? What if I felt like I had a choice? What if I had just said fuck the social status, fuck being "one of the guys," fuck trying to be popular and liked? What if I felt encouraged and empowered to explore ALL the things that were interesting to me, instead of having socialization and fear choose for me?

While the systems in schools sometimes made the choice for me, I'm even more aware of the ways in which my personal relationships shaped my sense of myself as a boy and as a man. At the core of those relationships were my parents, and outside that innermost circle were my classmates—both male and female.

I was lucky in those early years to be raised in a family where my sensitivity as a boy was validated and affirmed. My mother was the spiritual backbone of the family. She was, and is, strong in her opinions, a brilliant creative (she's an artist and a clothing designer by trade), super loving and affectionate, and also a little bit kooky in the best way. My father was emotionally available, supportive and nurturing, and between him and my mom, I was doted on with more love and affection than I could ever ask for. And although my dad had been taught to suffer in silence, to feel his own difficult feelings alone, he attempted, without even realizing it, to teach me otherwise. (I will get into the complex, challenging, and also beautiful and awesome relationship with my dad later.)

Simultaneously, however, school taught me the ABCs of what it meant to be a brave boy, and eventually a man, through the eyes of my classmates. When the lessons on the playground contradicted what I would learn at home, I felt confused, conflicted, and ultimately isolated from the boys I desperately wanted to be friends with. And so, what initially made me feel secure in my father's love also sadly caused a part of me to resent him as I grew up.

The conflict between home and school became painfully obvious to me when I was about ten years old and we moved from the progressive, coastal city of Santa Monica to a small, conservative town in Oregon. Here I was in a town where men worked with their hands and chewed tobacco and where, at one point, a third of the students in my small elementary school class were related (not fully a joke). Some of the other dads were loggers, some were truck drivers, others were carpenters, blue-collar to the core. Their sons weren't far behind and were being prepped to follow in their fathers' footsteps.

My dad was, and still is, an entrepreneur to his core. He is a businessman and a creative genius who uses his heart as much as he uses his brain. It's something I admire deeply and find myself replicating now as a grown man, but that's not what I wanted to learn from my dad when I was growing up. I wanted a dad who was like all the other dads in that small town—one with set hours who knew what he was going to get up and do at work the next day, or one who could chop down a tree with an ax or light a fire with a few sticks and a rock. I actually don't even really know why I wanted that because I loved what my dad did (and still does) for a living. If I were to dissect the real feelings underneath it, it had to have something to do with the other dads looking and acting more like the tough men in movies: grittier, less clean-shaven and manicured, with dirty hands and big forearms, whose idea of a relaxing night was a six-pack of beer, some pizza, and some peace and quiet (aka, don't ask him anything because the game is on). While there is nothing wrong with that, not all men fit that description, and my dad certainly didn't. See, my dad didn't teach me what the other dads taught their kids. He couldn't build a fire without a lighter, and he didn't own a gun. We didn't hunt or fish on the weekends. In fact, my dad would later tell me that he went hunting *one* time with his uncle and he had to shoot a squirrel and it was "the absolute worst thing ever" and that he would never wish that pain on anyone. So it comes as no surprise that not only did I not know how to hunt, but I also didn't know how to throw a punch or what to do if someone threw a punch at me.

The first time I remember confiding in my dad and asking him for help was when I was about thirteen years old and was getting bullied by a few kids in middle school. They would get in my face and start pushing me, trying to get me to throw the first punch. They would push me while someone stood behind me and held their foot out so I would trip backward. They would throw stuff at me and tell me they were going to jump me or "beat my ass" the next day. I would find myself walking through school with my head down, doing whatever I could to not be noticed, just so I wouldn't have to be publicly humiliated or physically threatened. It was terrible. It was not the first time this had happened, but it was the first time I felt genuinely scared. I thought about it all the time and had anxiety going to school, as I felt completely alone not having anyone there to stand up for me. So one night I asked my dad to help me learn how to defend myself. My dad always told me that his dad (my grandfather) was a Golden Gloves boxing champion in college and that he had taught my dad how to throw a punch when he was younger, so it made sense to me that those lessons could be passed down one more generation. Well, the lesson lasted about two minutes and ended with me accidentally landing a pretty massive right hook to his jaw as he was stepping in to help me with my form. Even though my dad took it on the chin "like a man," I could tell it hurt him, and hurting him hurt me. The lesson ended as quickly as it started. I felt terrible, and the irony was palpable. There we were, two sensitive guys trying hard to act tough, desperately trying not to show the other how sensitive we actually are. What my dad didn't know then was just how disappointed I was. On one hand I had never hit anyone before, so just the feeling of my fist connecting with his jaw awakened some sort of primal instinct in me that made me feel powerful. But on the other, accidentally hurting my dad and seeing him cover it up and put on a tough face also ripped my heart out. I still wanted to learn how to fight, but I knew then that my dad wasn't the right person to teach me. I think this is one of the first times I really noticed how confusing it was to be a boy trying to figure out how to be a man. And I am one of the lucky ones; I have a living and present father who was willing to take a punch to help his son. So while I was confused, disappointed, and angry that I felt my own dad wasn't man enough to teach me how to kick another kid's ass, looking back, that memory is also one of the sweetest things ever. Just typing those words helps the resentful boy in me heal as I dissect that memory and come to cherish the fact that my dad is such a beautiful and kind man. But at the time, it didn't help me in the schoolyard, which quickly became a classroom, albeit an anxiety-inducing one, where I would learn what it took for me to be accepted by the other boys—what it took for me to be deemed good enough, tough enough, strong enough, brave enough, man enough. And it all starts with one simple rule: don't show your emotions.

Now from the outside, it may not have seemed like I, as a city kid, had a lot in common with the country boys in Oregon, but there was one undeniable thing every one of us could relate to: no one wanted to be labeled a "pussy," and the way to avoid that was to follow rule number one. Having grown up in two distinct, and in many ways diametrically opposed, places, I've come to learn that, whether I or the other boys were white-collar or blue-collar, low, middle, or upper class, that lesson seemed to pretty much reach all of us. And frankly, whether on the beaches of Santa Monica or the logging mills of Oregon, for an empathetic kid like me, the message of not showing my emotions was a death sentence. I cried easily (in private) and could find myself amused or excited by the simplest things, like when the classroom caterpillar spun its cocoon and hung in the corner like Batman (I still get excited when I see a caterpillar spin a cocoon). I loved to laugh at mundane things and make loud obnoxious jokes, but I was also easily hurt. None of these qualities paved the way to acceptance from the other boys, so I quickly became an outsider who was bullied for being "soft." Even at a young age, long before I could articulate any of it, to feel disowned by my own gender felt like a death. And in some ways, maybe it was. Maybe it was the first death (of many) to my ego.

By this point, as they so often did, many of the girls in my class had welcomed me in. This is a pattern that would continue throughout my life. While I initially reveled in how it felt to be accepted, it was short-lived as the girls' acceptance only fueled the boys' case for my rejection, which I believe was rooted in our society's internalized homophobia. If you ever want to cement yourself as a "pussy" or be called "gay" or a "homo," the irony is that you don't actually have to have romantic or sexual relationships with other boys, you simply have to have *feelings* and friends who happen to be girls.

Here is a sample of the unwritten rules and lessons that I remember, broken down into simple "don'ts":

Don't be friends with girls. The boys will call you gay.

Don't be too nice to girls. If you're too nice to girls, you're sensitive, and that means you're also gay.

If you get kicked in the shin playing soccer at recess, don't cry. Don't even let them know you're hurt. If you cry, you are a girl. Or gay. Pick one.

If you get picked last for basketball, laugh it off loudly, and proudly say something that is self-effacing, or better yet project overconfidence, because that's what everyone else does.

And whatever you do, don't cry. Because if you cry, then you are a girl. Or gay. Again, pick one.

If the boys ask to see your nails, don't hold your hands palms down with your fingers straight and slightly spread apart. Because every boy knows that real boys, real men, hold them palms up, curling their fingers so their nails show. But if you don't know, and you show them your nails the "wrong" way—the way a girl supposedly would—and they start laughing and making fun of you and calling you gay, don't show them that their laughter hurts your feelings because that also means you're gay.

If you climb halfway up the rope swing in PE class before realizing that you're scared of going any higher, don't let them know you're scared. Instead, blame it on chafing. Boys respect a boy who looks out for his dick. (Also, what's with me and heights?) But if you don't blame it on something, be prepared to be called a girl. Or gay.

The foundation of every single lesson? Don't show emotion, and never talk about how you feel, otherwise you're a girl, or you're gay, which really means you are disowned from your own gender.

I hope your heart hurts a little (or a lot) reading that list. I hope you can start to see the pain we are causing millions and millions of boys, and the damage we are doing in the process to girls, along with anyone who doesn't identify as straight or is confused by their own sexuality. To have the most supreme insult for one gender be the identity of another is harmful and wrong on many levels, and it isn't a far leap to see why depression and suicide numbers are so elevated for teenagers on all sides of the gender spectrum.

In this minefield of aggression, the conflict began between who I was, how I felt, and who the world—no, sorry, who the boys—told me I needed to be, and what followed was the killing of my emotional self, the destroying of the path between my head and my heart. And if it did that to me, a heteronormative boy, I can only imagine what it was doing to girls and to boys who were gay.

> *I can remember speaking to a 12-year-old boy, a football player, and I asked him, I said, "How would you feel if, in front of all the players, your coach told you you were playing like a girl?" Now I expected him to say something like, I'd be sad; I'd be mad; I'd be angry, or something like that. No, the boy said to me . . . , "It would destroy me." And I said to myself, "God, if it would destroy him to be called a girl, what are we then teaching him about girls?"*
>
> —Tony Porter

A New Challenge

In my midtwenties, I lost everything that I had been using to prove to myself, and to others, that I was man enough. I didn't have the nice, fast car, or in my case the '76 fully restored custom Bronco I had bought from my first TV series and had to sell because I ran out of money. I didn't have a girlfriend anymore because she went off to shoot a movie for two weeks and fell in love with her costar. I couldn't book an acting job to save my life, and the house I bought was dangerously close to going into foreclosure. My masculinity was having a full-on quarter-life crisis, and the only emotion that was okay to express was anger, but all I wanted to do, and all I could do, was cry and ask for help.

What's interesting about this particular point in my life was that the male friends I had cultivated were actually very similar to me and had very similar upbringings. I reached out to them. I needed them. But those friends couldn't be there for me every day and didn't have the emotional vocabulary or patience to hold all that I was feeling without giving me advice or telling me what I needed to do. So I ended up spending most of my time with the most emotionally available and accepting people in my life: girls, who had become women and who still welcomed the outlier. I began learning from them what it meant to be vulnerable, how to feel again, and how to risk sharing those feelings with other people. These were not lessons that were lectured to me, but they were examples of behavior that were modeled and shown to me.

What did I learn during *this* time? Well, I expected—or at the very least hoped—that I would learn that underneath it all, I was fearless and brave.

Instead, what I really learned is that I am afraid—a lot.

And a decade into this journey, that is still true. I am afraid of not providing for my family, not being financially secure. I am afraid of losing my kids, my wife, my parents, my loved ones in some sort of accident or in a way that's beyond my control. I believe wholeheartedly that death is like birth and that we are merely inches away from a new life through death, and yet I am afraid of dying. I'm scared of not living up to my potential and being forgotten, scared that if something happened to me, my wife would meet someone else and he will be more of a man than I am and be able to give her all the things she longs for that I fall short of. I am afraid of losing my relevancy, of messing up my next movie and going to "director jail," of gaining weight or not aging well (whatever that means) and then not getting any work as an actor because it had never been my talent that got me the work for all these years but my looks. I am afraid that I will be seen as an imposter and everyone will find out that I've just been faking it this entire time and really have no idea what I'm doing or how I even got here. I am afraid that I am failing as a father and husband and friend, that my kids will grow up resenting me because I am doing too much and am too focused on my career and not able to give a hundred percent of myself to anything, and yet ironically the only thing I truly care about succeeding at is being a present father, husband, and friend. I am afraid of the fact that I am so afraid. Oh, and I'm still afraid of heights.

But of all the things I am afraid of, here's what I know to be true now: I can be afraid and I can be brave at the same time. They are not mutually exclusive. In fact, as my therapist once told me, I can only be brave if I deal with and confront my fear. If I'm not afraid, there is no such thing as bravery. But the bravery conflict only arises when I live inside the false choice that I have to be one or the other, when the truth is that I can be both. I can also be afraid and not let that fear be the driving force of my life. I have the ability to put fear in the back seat, turn the music up louder, and enjoy the road without it influencing any or all of my decisions. What I now believe and live by as it relates to fear is this: be afraid, be fearful, honor those feelings when they come up, but don't dwell on them or let them consume you. Because it's one thing to feel fear, and it's another thing to let it win. And call it traditionally masculine, but I like to win.

The Ultimate Test, the Realest Reward

About four years ago, I put this lesson to the ultimate test. I had been going through a lot and found myself feeling lonely and in need of some help. I was struggling with something and I didn't feel comfortable talking to my wife about it, and at the time I didn't have a therapist. So I reached out and invited my closest guy friends to get together with the hidden intention of risking vulnerability—of putting my shit out there and saying, "I am struggling, and I need help." Of course, I didn't let on to that in the beginning, so instead I framed it as needing to escape and have a guys' weekend in Mexico. Yep, I was so afraid of being vulnerable that I felt like I had to take them out of the country as a means of coercing them into showing up, just so I could share.

There were multiple times throughout our first couple of days together that I felt like I had an opportunity to start sharing, but each time I found myself stuck. Instead of saying, "Hey, can we get real for a minute?" I opted for "Let's go for a run or workout"—proving again that tearing down my physical muscles in the name of growth was much easier than opening my heart in the name of growth. When our last night rolled around and I was staring my commitment to be vulnerable in the face, while staring my guy friends in the face, I was finally going to share. But ironically, one of the other guys broke the ice by sharing first. That moment, and the twenty-four hours that followed, were hands down the most scared and most brave I had felt in years.

As I fumbled through what I was struggling with, admitting what was difficult, shameful, frightening, I felt the visceral weight of shame begin to lift, and to my surprise my other friends jumped in and began sharing what they struggled with too. It was as if my vulnerability, along with my even more brave friend, was an unspoken invitation for them to share their deeper selves. Outwardly, my friends and I had been living out the lessons we had learned on life's playground. We had been rejecting what had been deemed feminine and weak. But secretly, knowingly or not, we had each been waiting for permission to express ourselves, to be seen, to be heard; we had been waiting for a safe space to feel our feelings. It was this realization, this longing for permission, that made me double down on my radical path of self-discovery and growth and begin to take that journey from my head to my heart.

In case you are wondering what I was struggling with that caused me to set up this whole guys' trip in the first place: it's porn. And while it may seem like a non-issue for some, for me it was looming large and occupying too much space in the back of my mind, and I had no idea how or who to talk about it with.

So, I took off my armor, piece by piece. And while the first piece felt nearly impossible to lift, I noticed that the more I shared, the lighter my armor became, and the easier it was to remove. That night I shared that my relationship with porn was unhealthy, and that I desired more control over if, how, or when I used it. That I was afraid to talk to my wife about it because I didn't want her to feel that I was looking at images and videos of naked women because she wasn't enough for me. That I felt shame, and I felt dirty, and I felt like a bad person. That so many younger people around the world and in my faith looked up to me but sometimes prayer wasn't strong enough to stop the pull of porn, especially when I was having a hard day or dealing with pressure and stressors in my life. I was using it as a coping mechanism to calm my mind, and I felt hypocritical because, on one hand, I was building a reputation as a man who spoke up and out on behalf of women and gender equality, who was learning about social justice and the effect porn has on rape culture, yet on the other hand, I couldn't fully control my own use of it, especially on days when I felt like I wasn't enough. In response, my friends shared their personal pain as well. One friend struggled with infidelity that was rooted in the pain of being molested by a family friend as a boy. Another struggled to break the cycle of emotional abuse and toxicity in relationships that stemmed from the emotional abuse he suffered at the hands of his father. Other friends shared their own struggles with porn. While it took us three days (or more than thirty years) to get there, when we finally did, the emotional floodgates opened.

It's amazing to me now how similar we were in what we didn't say, what made us feel ashamed, and how that shame, or fear of being shamed, was such an organizing principle of our performance of manhood. Boys grow into men, yes, but in some ways we always feel ourselves to be on that playground, always feel afraid someone is going to call us weak and not man enough. We craft our armor against it like medieval knights, but if you've ever tried on one of those chain mail suits of armor, you know that not only are they so heavy and confining you can barely walk, but they also end up cutting us off from the outside world and completely preventing true intimate connection to others.

One of the ways that I have begun reconstructing the path from my head to my heart is by creating experiences that force me to be vulnerable. If there's something I am experiencing shame around in my life, I practice diving straight into it, no matter how scary it is. If shame thrives in silence and isolation, then the opposite must be true: shame dies in speaking up and in community. So I asked myself: am I brave enough to be vulnerable? To reach out to another man when I need help? Am I brave enough to dive headfirst into my shame? To be sensitive, to cry whether I am hurting or happy, even if it makes me look weak? Am I brave enough to be a man who honors his feelings (even when my actions are at times contradictory to them)?

This is the kind of bravery I want to make room for.

The kind of bravery that includes an alcoholic going to his first, or five hundredth, AA meeting.

The kind of bravery that includes a man who was abused as a child, and who then became abusive, getting the help he needs.

I want bravery to include the young man who tells his roommate that he is struggling with depression and thoughts of suicide.

And the man who didn't think he was ready to be a father, who abandoned his family, but realized his mistake and comes back to apologize and do the hard work needed to earn their trust.

I want us, as a community and a culture, to applaud the bravery of the veteran who comes home from war and walks into a therapist's office to care for his mental health.

I want bravery to include the twentysomething man who speaks up to the guy in the bar who is speaking down to women.

And I want it to include the husband who had to leave his career to care for his partner who is battling cancer, the son who put his promotion on hold to take care of his father who has Alzheimer's, and the man who, on top of working fifty hours a week, serves as a caregiver for his brother—a role he has had most of his life.

I want it to include the group of thirtysomething men who had to go out of the country, to a remote area, just to get into their own hearts.

I want bravery to include any boy or man of any age who is courageous enough to take the journey. Maybe one day, a skinny, barely-a-teen boy will stand twenty feet above a river, holding on to the side of a bridge for dear life, knowing what he feels, knowing that it is brave to honor how he feels, and he will make the choice to jump or not based on what his heart tells him—and not what will happen to him if he doesn't.

CHAPTER TWO

BIG ENOUGH

The Body Issue: From Head to Toe and All Parts Between

It's 11:00 p.m. and I'm eating a bowl of cereal and potato chips while weighing in at a healthy ten pounds heavier than usual. It's also smack dab in the middle of a global pandemic, and I'm carrying the weight of needing to finish postproduction on *Clouds* (my next film), while closing down one company and launching another, all the while trying to keep my family sane and safe and show up as a husband and dad. No big deal, right? You would think if there was ever a time to be a little extra kind to myself and my body, now would be it. After all, on the scale of importance, a six-pack and broad shoulders fall a few notches below everything else that comes with a global health crisis. Yet it's not that simple. My confidence and energy have, for as long as I can remember, been linked to the way I feel about my body and the way I perceive how the world sees me.

Before I deep-dive into this chapter I want to be very clear. One of the things I love most in life is health and fitness, yet it's also one of the areas that has become so confusing for me. I believe deeply that our physical state influences our mental state, and I believe in the incredible power of movement to both reinvigorate and heal. When I am feeling low-energy, or down emotionally, tapping into my body and getting in a great workout or working up a sweat has been a lifesaver for me and will continue to be. But that's not what this chapter is about. As much as I believe that my mental health, energy, and confidence are tied to how my body feels and functions versus how it looks, it doesn't change the fact that men have begun to experience what women have been experiencing for, like, ever. Today, men are no longer being rewarded for simply having functional bodies, instead, we are being rewarded for having big, muscular, defined, and aesthetically pleasing bodies. If this wasn't the case, more diverse bodies would be represented in the entertainment industry, and fitness influencers would build a following based on what their bodies can do versus what they look like. We would see a wide range of normal bodies on the cover of health and fitness magazines, instead of fitness models who too often use extremely unhealthy measures to attain a body that is glorified as the epitome of strong and fit. On the other hand, as I said, I am a firm believer in the mental and physical benefits of working out and eating well, but unfortunately it's not, and never has been, that simple or reductive for me. The relationship I have had with my body has been complicated and confusing, and I believe that I share that complicated relationship with many men in America and, more than likely, the world.

My body has been both a blessing and a curse. If you're ripped and strong, then chances are other men want to look like you, and many women (and men) may want to be with you. But that's not always a good thing because of a little thing called envy. Envy is not to be mixed up with jealousy. My mom would always tell me the other guys picked on me because they were jealous (which now, as an adult, I don't believe to be true in most situations), but I do believe we sometimes pick on and bully others when we are envious. And what do men do to other men they resent and don't like? We police them and make them feel terrible about themselves. We bully, talk shit, spread rumors, and manipulate to boost our egos and to bridge the gap. And all the while, we secretly want that very same quality in the person we are putting down. Think men are simple? Think again. We are more complicated than you realize.

In middle school and high school, I was generally one of the better all-around athletes, but I definitely wasn't the coolest. Call it being a "beta" or whatever you want, but all young boys go through periods where we follow whoever tends to be the most dominant (which generally means whoever is the biggest jackass with the loudest mouth). Young boys and men tend to be drawn to follow whoever feels the most "alpha" in their approach to making other boys feel weak or less than. This happens because we are all secretly insecure about something, and we overcompensate for our weaknesses by exercising dominance over other boys who may have more obvious weaknesses, in an attempt to make ourselves feel strong (i.e., envy). But because I know how it feels to be on both sides of this coin, I have a bit of an issue with the whole alpha/beta movement and method of thinking in general, as I worry it ends up doing far more harm than good—not just to other men, but to ourselves. I have zero issue with wanting to be a strong man, or even raising a boy to be strong emotionally, as the world is a scary place and being able to withstand the tests and trials, pain and disappointment, that life will throw at each of us is an important survival skill, but not just for young boys—for kids of all genders. Of course, I want my son to be able to get back up when he falls down, to wipe his tears away after he cries them and keep going. To stand up and defend against injustice when he sees it, and to step in on behalf of someone else who is being bullied or oppressed. But I would never raise him to kill off his sensitivity or drown out his empathy in the process. I believe a man can do both. Just as I believe women can and in many ways have historically done this better than men. But that's contradictory to this alpha/beta methodology, at least how it seems to be practiced and spoken about today.

In the West, there has been a growing movement among men focused on stopping what they call the "feminization" of men. The basic belief is that every strong civilization that has ever existed has needed strong masculine men to survive and flourish and that the patriarchy isn't a socially constructed thing—it's just the way God made us. The belief is that our system is part of the natural hierarchical organizational process of humans and animals and that the men have been benevolently extending and granting rights to women and protecting them for thousands of years. There are countless offshoots, subgroups, and beliefs held by many of these men, but essentially one of the core beliefs is that men are divided into two categories: alphas and betas.

What I find ironic about the alpha/beta classification and debate is that it takes its roots from science and ethology, the study of animal behavior, yet is supposed to apply its findings to humans, and often men in particular, as a means of helping a man succeed in both his career and his love life. In a fascinating article titled "Do Alpha Males and Females Actually Exist?" author Eric Devaney describes how in ethology the term "alpha" refers to an individual with the highest rank in a social group. And what's one of the key benefits that come with being the most badass or powerful member in the group? Sex. According to Devaney, the benefits of being an alpha include first dibs on sex with the females of the group, first dibs on food, and grooming from the other members. Harvard professor, primatologist, and expert on the "alpha" phenomenon Richard W. Wrangham told Devaney, "In primates, the alpha male is the one who can literally beat up every other male. So the position depends on physical violence." He goes on to say that discussing humans as alphas can be inaccurate: "In primates there is almost always just a single dominant hierarchy, i.e. the one based on violence. But in humans a single group can have multiple hierarchies, such as those based on skill in sports, scholarship, social skills, etc." So what makes someone an alpha in one social hierarchy could theoretically make him a beta in another, especially as humans are divided into millions of different social circles and hierarchies to begin with. Take one of the most badass MMA fighters in the world—the king of his circle, worth millions of dollars, and widely respected by people around the world—and put him in Tanzania in the Maasai tribe, where men possess technical hunting and survival skills, and suddenly your alpha by all definitions is considered a beta. An alpha in the gaming community would more than likely be a beta in a group of athletes. And an alpha athlete is probably a beta in a community of intellectuals and PhDs, where intellect is valued over physical prowess. See where this is going?

What I also find odd is that while every animal group has its own version of the alpha/beta hierarchy, humans, and especially men, often bring up primates (apes) and wolves to get their point across. But even in wolves, the idea of the lone wolf or the alpha wolf has been debunked and proven false by none other than the original author who made the term mainstream, L. David Mech. Mech is arguably one of the world's foremost experts on wolves and has spent forty years studying them in both captivity and the wild. He has written eleven books and is the founder of the International Wolf Center. In the article "The Myth of the Alpha Wolf," Kara Lilly points out that in Mech's 1970 bestselling book, *The Wolf: The Ecology and Behavior of an Endangered Species,* he discusses a biologist from the 1940s who had been studying wolves in captivity and who first used the term "alpha wolf" in reference to the biologist's "observation that male and female wolves seemed to compete to become dominant within their group." After Mech's book became a massive success, the idea of the "alpha wolf" went mainstream and continues in pop culture today. The problem that Mech discovered was that wolves behave differently in captivity than they do in the wild, and the "alpha wolf" actually doesn't exist. This bothered Mech so much that he has spent the better part of the last forty years publishing articles and debunking the confusion around the myth of the alpha wolf and has even gone so far as to try to stop his publisher from printing more copies of his original book. How bizarre is it that as men (and people in general), we can read something, find a way to make it fit our own narrative, and even despite scientific articles, studies, and the author himself proving the theory wrong, continue to adapt it into social movements over sixty years later. I am continually amazed by the audacity of our species.

So to clear things up, here are the facts as Mech explains them. In the wild, wolves form family units similar to the family units we see in the world today. In those units, the "alpha" male is simply the dad and the "alpha" female is simply the mom, and the others in the pack follow their lead, but not because the dad and mom physically overpower the others, or exercise dominance, but for the same reasons my kids follow my wife and me—because we are the parents, and they love us. So if anything, it can be said that wolves are organized by alpha males *and* alpha females because the way they organize is by who reproduces, not who is dominant. Sounds a lot like wolves have figured out gender equality better than we humans have. But I digress. . . .

In my life, I have been both the perpetrator and the victim of bullying. In school, I had seasons where I tried to be the alpha, yet I often fell into being more of a beta, all the while experiencing being the victim of both. And if you end up being on the receiving end of someone who puts you down to lift themselves up, you often then end up engaging in that same behavior or policing someone else to make yourself feel better so that the abuse can stop. As boys, we do this when we know it's wrong because the consequences feel far worse if you don't. This behavior spreads and perpetuates the message that the last thing you want to be is the guy who defends the kid being picked on because it's a short trip right back to the bottom.

One of my first memories of how this relates to my complicated relationship to my body is when I was about twelve years old. My club soccer team was playing a tournament out of town, and as young boys and athletes, we were always shirtless and running around in next to nothing. I was never self-conscious about my body as a younger kid because all of us boys on the teams more or less looked the same. But that changed when puberty hit. After a postgame hot tub in the motel where we were staying, I found myself in front of a mirror with Matt and Sean, two of the guys on my soccer team who would have considered themselves the alphas. They were examining their emerging abs and teasing each other about pubic hair. I, in my skinny preteen, shirtless body, was a few feet away, watching their interaction when suddenly they turned, looked at me, and jokingly asked me where my abs were and started making fun of me for being a bit behind. Instantly, a knot of inadequacy grew in my stomach. For them, and probably for any adult nearby, it would've looked like a moment of seemingly innocent, lighthearted teasing—kids just being kids, boys just being boys. Interactions like these would play out in similar scenes over the course of my life, and I would eventually play both parts. But every fire needs a spark, and more than twenty years later, I remember that moment as a pivotal one in the complex, nuanced, and often very unhealthy relationship I have with my body today.

Sometimes I wonder how so many of us men are even able to act as normal as we do. Just thinking about the playful, although often truthful, teasing that we engage in at the expense of our self-confidence makes me wonder if this could be one of the reasons why the fitness and supplement industry is worth the billions of dollars that it is today. And while it may be relatively new to me, women know all too well how the dominant culture creates judgments about bodies and then profits off them. Magazines and books telling men how to transform ourselves keep hitting number one, and male plastic surgery and liposuction have been growing exponentially year after year. And while this may have just been one of thousands of little paper cuts, where other boys commented on or teased me about something that meant nothing to them, it did mean something to me. A cut is a cut, and even if it's tiny, everyone knows a paper cut can sometimes be as painful or even more so than a larger wound. These paper cuts have done far more damage than I ever allowed myself to realize. Over time, they have compounded into a secret and unhealthy relationship with my own body that has been rooted in proving that my body was good, strong, or big enough—not to impress girls or women, but more to try and prove my worth to other boys and men.

Truth be told, I feel that same knot of inadequacy I had way back then growing in my stomach as I write this. But because of that knot, I am tackling this topic as close to the front of the book as I can. If I want to walk the talk, then I have to be willing to dive into shame and insecurity; I have to be willing to sit with what is wildly uncomfortable for me to sit with; and I have to be willing to risk rejection from outside voices in an attempt to find acceptance from inside my own head.

And what are those outside voices saying? They're telling me that as a Hollywood actor who gets paid to take his shirt off (read:

gets paid to stay "in shape"), who can mostly fit into the historically narrow definition that our culture has come up with for physical attractiveness, I have nothing to offer to the conversation on male body image. And not only that I have nothing to offer but also that I do not have the *right* to contribute to the conversation because of my privilege.

My rational mind sees their point. My rational mind is acutely aware of the privilege I have simply for having the genes and resources that I do. And yet, under whatever amount of muscle definition I think I have or do not have, is a little boy who feels like his body will never measure up, a young adult who struggled with terrible body image, and a man who, to this day, suffers from a problem that he helps perpetuate.

It's complicated; it's nuanced; it's even, at times, embarrassing. And it's real. So let's dive in.

Body Image Basics

What even *is* body image? How does it differ from our appearance? While shooting episode three of the first season of *Man Enough*, I got to sit down with Dr. Roberto Olivardia, who is a clinical psychologist at Harvard Medical School, and get answers to some of these foundational questions. Dr. Olivardia laid it out simply for me by explaining that appearance is objective, such as brown eyes, six feet tall, and dark brown hair, whereas body image is more about how you *feel* about your body. So our body image is completely separate from our appearance and is intricately tied to our perception of our body, our attitude toward our body, and how we think other people see our body. This explains why people who, for whatever reason, society has deemed "beautiful," "perfect," "hot," or "#bodygoals" can still have a very unhealthy body image. How we look and how we feel about how we look are completely separate from each other.

Dr. Olivardia also explained to me that research into male body image—men having a relationship with their body—didn't really emerge until the early 1980s. As a man who definitely thinks about my body outside of its function, who has feelings and a warped perception of it (and who has for a long time), this shocked me. But Dr. Olivardia explained that prior to the shirtless advertising that began in the early '80s, there was the Marlboro man, who had a definite ruggedness to him, but he wasn't a jacked, muscular guy. It was this new advertising approach, coupled with the Hollywood stars of the time (Schwarzenegger, Stallone, Van Damme, etc.) and the accessibility to anabolic steroids that provided a platform for the messages of muscularity and masculinity that still plague my psyche to this day.

It's not that men didn't have bodies, or that men didn't actually look at their bodies; it's just that prior to the 1980s, men tended to see their bodies as "natural," not as objects of the "gaze." For thousands of years, women have understood the power of the male gaze—the power of men to objectify women, hold them against a specific standard of beauty. Naomi Wolf's 1991 book *The Beauty Myth* was a colossal bestseller because she talked about how women's magazines reinforced this idea that women's bodies were constantly being observed and therefore were a never-ending project. But men?

In 1985, the *New York Times* published an article in their "Science Times" section with the headline "Women Unhappy with Body Image." The article went on to "discover" what feminists and therapists had been discussing for years—the frightening rise of anorexia and bulimia among teenage girls and young women. Pretty obvious reading it nearly four decades later.

The article's subhead read, "Men Tend to See Themselves as Just About Perfect." What's changed in the last four decades? Not women's perceptions of their bodies, despite nearly half a century of discussion and debate. No, it's that we men most assuredly do NOT see ourselves as "just about perfect." Far from it.

Fun fact: here's something else I learned from Dr. Olivardia. When G.I. Joe was first introduced in 1974, he stood five feet, ten inches. He had a thirty-one-inch waist, a forty-one-inch chest, and twelve-inch biceps. Strong and muscular, yes, but still possible and not very far off from my own measurements. Flash forward to 2002, and G.I. Joe was still five feet ten, but his waist had shrunk to twenty-eight inches, his chest ballooned to fifty inches, and his biceps bulged to twenty-two inches, close to the size of his waist. If he were a real human, he would be unable to touch his own shoulder, let alone execute an impossible special ops mission and save the planet. Can you imagine how hilarious that *South Park* episode would be? G.I. Joe parachutes in to stop a bomb from detonating, but he can't reach behind his back to get the tool from his belt because his biceps are too big!

Actually, I think it's all Tom Hintnaus's fault. Don't know who he is? It's okay, I didn't either. Dr. Michael Kimmel, who is now in his late fifties, told me all about Tom and the effect he had on men across the country when Dr. Kimmel was younger. Tom was a former Brazilian Olympic pole vaulter who is known for modeling in a 1982 Calvin Klein underwear ad. Dr. Kimmel told me that from the moment that billboard appeared in cities across the country, American men of all ages suddenly "knew" what the ideal male body was. And they started comparing themselves. And they started coming up short.

I was born into that culture, just two years after that ad first appeared. I've never known any other world.

Muscles, Messages, and Masculinity

"Where are your abs?" The question was followed by that preteen laugh that, as a filmmaker, I would have shot in slow motion and extreme close-ups with a slowed-down, almost evil laugh coming from my supposed friends. Those four words said teasingly to me may have been the first time I consciously equated my muscles with my manhood. Even though I had been obsessed with Van Damme and Stallone, and even at four years old had asked my parents to buy more spinach so I could get big muscles like Popeye, those were guys on the TV, cartoon and action heroes. They weren't the guys I competed with and against in my real life who were now making fun of me. The message was clear: if I lacked muscles, I lacked manliness; if my muscles didn't measure up, then I did not measure up. This whole notion of our muscularity being a barometer for our masculinity is often referred to as the "Adonis complex." It is perpetuated in men's fitness magazines and in the entertainment industry (including the porn industry), and it has now become a way to make money and have influence on social media. Before a boy is picking up a fitness magazine or logging in to Instagram, he is absorbing the same message when the chubby boys, the scrawny boys, and the girls are getting picked last in gym class, when he goes to the movies to see his favorite action star kick ass and get the girl, and when he sees the girls ogling over those said action stars. The message is introduced subconsciously at a young age: ripped and muscular = powerful, strong, confident, manly, cool. Too chubby = slow, lazy; too scrawny = little and weak; girl = not a boy and therefore weak. This list goes on and on.

As we've already pointed out, in our culture we have often placed a higher value on men's physical feats, which also means we place a higher value on physicality and muscularity as a means to measure masculinity. Tragically, this results in little to no value placed on male bodies that fall outside of what we think represents strength and fitness. This is probably most often experienced by boys who are considered overweight, along with boys who are part of the disabled community, through relentless bullying and harassment.

Another event burned into my psyche from my childhood occurred when I was about ten years old and I was the new "city kid" who moved from LA to Oregon. I had no friends, and my Jewish-Italian features, especially my "Roman nose" and massive eyebrows, stuck out in our rural, small town. Even though I was a skinny kid, I was athletic and subconsciously knew I could try to prove my worth as the new kid via anything sports related. But I took it one step farther—farther away from my own body's abilities (worth) and made it about someone else's body (worth). I'll never forget it: in a desperate attempt to be accepted during a game of kickball in PE class, when a boy who was overweight stepped up to the plate, I stood in the outfield and shouted, "Let's go, fat ass!" and laughed at my own joke just as other boys would later laugh at my lack of abs.

Even at ten years old, I had taken in enough of the messaging about our bodies to know that the one boy who would be below me on the man-enough ladder would be the boy who was overweight. I had taken in enough of the messaging to know that if I tore him down, it would build me up.

How fucking cruel.

A teacher checked me hard that day, which completely took me by surprise, and as a sensitive kid, I took her words to heart. But my words had been spoken, and while I don't think he heard what I said, it doesn't matter because *I* heard it. I wish I could wrap my arms around the boy I bullied that day and apologize to him. I also wish I could wrap my arms around the ten-year-old version of myself and remind him that he is more than enough just as he is, and that everyone else is too.

We men do this thing where we assess our perceived place on the man-enough ladder, whether it's in the boys' club on the playground or the boys' club in the boardroom, and then we attempt to climb up the ladder by stepping on the man we perceive to be on the rung below us. Often the boy or the man on the lowest rung is the one whose body is farthest from what society has deemed as a "normal" representation of physical strength. One look at a men's fitness magazine and the headlines leap off the cover: "Three Exercises to Be a Better Man," "Lose Your Gut to Make Good Sex Great," "Six Weeks to Your Perfect Bod," "Big Arms Fast," "Better Body for Better Sex." In fact, I still remember one *Men's Health* article that has stayed with me for more than fifteen years. The title read something like "Wide Shoulders, the #1 Body Part Women Agree Is the Most Important." And as a guy with relatively narrow shoulders, it might as well have read "Justin, You Are Not Enough." I have so much empathy for people of all sizes, and especially those in the disability community, who grow up in America. The strength it requires to have self-confidence and feel good about yourself in a world that is bombarding you with messaging that literally tells you the opposite is something that should be congratulated and celebrated. All in all, the message is clear, and it sells as companies profit off our insecurities because it's been programmed into our brains from a formative age: for men, our masculinity is measured by our muscularity. And if you want to be a better man, then it's your duty to build a "better" body.

What is a better body? Let's fire off some of the themes/messages around male bodies:

- The coveted inverted triangle, where the shoulders are broad and muscular, and then the torso tapers down to a slim waist.
- Big and toned arms. But don't skip leg day.
- Men should be tall, or at the VERY least, taller than the woman they are with. If they aren't tall, they better be able to pull a semi, or deadlift a small Japanese car. Or be rich. Having money wins over everything.
- Chiseled chest. Men shouldn't have man boobs.
- Bigger is better when it comes to hands and feet because apparently that's an indication of a bigger penis. And a bigger penis is the ultimate measure of a bigger man.

Protection and Power

There is another layer to this messaging I want to tackle, but as with this whole topic, I feel like a toddler trying to talk about quantum physics. Part of the nuanced messaging drilled into boys as we grow up is that muscles and strength also mean protection. On the playground they mean you can beat up another boy or defend yourself from a bully. On the soccer field they mean you can overpower your opponent, and on the football field it's often the factor that determines whether you even get to play. But the other message of protection—the one I always thought was healthy—was that by being strong, I could protect not only myself but also the women in my life and eventually my own family from the attacks of other men.

But this is a good thing, right: the innate desire to have a strong enough body to be able to protect my loved ones, especially my wife? Recently, I had the honor to speak with Dr. Susan Brison, renowned professor for the study of ethics and human values at Dartmouth, as she dug even deeper into a message that's so normalized that most of us men consider it healthy.

Dr. Brison has a unique perspective on what it means to need protection from a man. One morning while on a walk in a neighborhood she had passed through many times before, she was followed by a neighbor, raped, beaten with a rock, and then left for dead near a creek. Her road to recovery was long and slow, and to this day she deals with the physical and emotional effects of her attack. Brison released a book titled *Aftermath: Violence and the Remaking of Self* to educate and help other survivors recover both emotionally and physically from their abuse. After Dr. Brison told me her devastating story, I didn't know what to say. So many things were running through my mind, yet all I could do was apologize to her on behalf of men. As I've said before, I have spent my life longing to be accepted by my own gender, yet at that moment I felt disgusted and betrayed by it. As I apologized, I couldn't help the feeling bubbling up inside me that I wished I could have been there as a man to protect her. I imagined catching this man mid-act and beating him to a pulp. I imagined being the hero who could save her from the last twenty-five years of physical and emotional duress, of night terrors and the fear of just existing in the world as a woman. My body tensed up and I noticed I was clenching my fists, yet my demeanor stayed relatively calm and collected. I apologized for the fact that she as a woman couldn't even go on a morning walk without this happening, a feeling that far too many women have every single day. So later in the conversation, when I told Dr. Brison about my desire to be able to protect my wife from potential attacks like the one she faced, she took a breath, looked at me like she could see through me, and then powerfully replied, "I'm a mother—I get the protective instinct—but women shouldn't need to be protected by their men from other men. It's connected to the view that women aren't seen as fully human, fully worthy of respect, but rather potentially prey for some men, and then it becomes the job of other men to rush in and protect them. I don't want to be protected. I want to be left alone. I want to be able to walk down the street safely." If I didn't know what to say before, I definitely didn't know what to say after that. This rocked me. How, at thirty-four years old, had I never heard this? Then it hit me. My wanting to be big and strong, my protective instincts and anger in reaction to her story were just that, a reaction. What if our wanting and needing to be strong to protect the women in our lives is a reaction to the fact that we haven't and aren't doing enough to prevent violence from happening to them in the first place? What if our physical strength is simply a Band-Aid on the bigger problem? A problem that exists within our culture, and with masculinity as a whole. A problem that has brought me to writing this book in the first place. If we are trying to get bigger and stronger, if we are trying to learn self-defense and survival skills, if we are buying guns to protect our families from intruders, or buying pepper spray for the women and girls in our lives, or offering to walk them to their cars at night, then there's a pretty damn good chance that we are really late. The work to protect the women we love must begin with ourselves first, and then with the men in our lives. Dr. Brison was absolutely right: no woman should need to be protected by a man.

I had become so acclimated to the message and behavior of being able to protect a woman with my physical strength that I viewed this as a positive trait without digging into the nuance of how problematic it is, and without noticing the burden that women carry while we as men (even well-meaning men) vie for power and compete with each other in the name of protection. So let's be real, fellas. It feels good to be able to walk a woman to her car, or to know that we could kick another guy's ass for attacking her or crossing a line, right? There is a perpetual fantasy that many men have (including myself) of rescuing and saving the women we love, which is undeniably more about us than about the women we purport to protect. We have to ask ourselves the hard question: are we doing it for them, or in some fucked-up, unconscious way, are we actually doing it for us?

This dynamic of equating our bodies with power and protection comes up outside of the heteronormative scripts as well. As part of the *Man Enough* show, I got to sit down with incredible men from all different backgrounds and talk about personal topics that you don't usually (or ever) see men talking about. During our episode on body image, two of my friends, actor Javier Muñoz and trans activist/fitness model Aydian Dowling, shed light on how the messages of muscularity and masculinity have manifested in their own personal stories within the gay and transgender community.

Though different in detail, there is still a commonality of our physical strength, or our *appearance* of physical strength, equating protection and safety. Javier explained that the first pressure of appearing more muscular, and therefore more masculine, for gay men is safety. He said, "In the eighties and nineties, growing up in NYC, if I was by myself and in certain contexts where maybe I wasn't welcome, my survival instinct clocks the situation and says 'Am I small enough that these guys feel they can start something with me, that they can take me? Or am I so big and aggressive that they are going to have to think twice?'" As a transgender man, Aydian echoed this by sharing, "When I transitioned into male, it was like 'Okay, I am going to start working out,' because if I go into a bar and that guy over there doesn't like my choices, if he sees that I'm muscular, maybe he will think twice about coming at me."

Another layer of this protection for both Javier and Aydian came from feeling "less than" for so long, and as a result, they felt pressure to live up to the standards of traditional masculinity. So there's the protection of the body in the form of physical safety, and an attempt at protecting the heart from being further lessened as a human. I mean it makes sense, right? If men are going to pick on you and make you feel less than, then why wouldn't you want to change your body to be able to protect yourself to discourage future insults and attacks?

Finally, there is an aspect of health that men in the gay community feel an added pressure to display. As a man who is HIV-positive, Javier experienced other men in his community being incredibly cruel toward him because of the stigmas attached to the condition. Because weight loss is associated with the transition of the virus from HIV to AIDS, there became this need to maintain a certain physical physique so that you always look healthy (and therefore could be a suitable partner).

Our ability as men to display that we can protect ourselves or our loved ones comes from a deeper place of being able to protect our power from a perceived threat. When I really dig into it, for me, it actually comes from an insecurity—a fear of being overpowered or having another man either hurt my family or take Emily from me. The world has always told us that, as men, we need to have power, and then we need to protect and maintain it. It's central to the messages of our worth as men, and the backdrop of thousands of movies and television shows. And what's one of the easiest, most efficient ways to assert yourself as powerful and strong? By having a body that is muscular and fit.

And yet if this is the way to power, then why do I feel—why have I always felt—so powerless when it comes to my body?

Maybe it's because bulking up one's body at the gym is not the same thing as actually being strong? Maybe because "looking" strong is not a way to be strong, but a way to pretend to not be weak? Maybe looking powerful is the best way we've found to pretend to be powerful—even if inside we feel weak.

Man in the Mirror

My insecurities around my body and appearance started young, and I don't think that it's a coincidence that the first memories of my body image issues are intertwined with my memories of seeing pornography. We will tackle that in a later chapter, but I do believe that what you consume is what you compare. As a young boy and teenager, long before the days of social media, I was consuming men's fitness magazines, sports magazines, and porn, all the while consciously and subconsciously comparing how my body did or didn't measure up to the images I saw, which of course translated into how I did or didn't measure up as a man.

To this day, when I look in the mirror, the first place my eyes go to are my shoulders. One of the unconscious factors that determines if I wear a particular shirt that day is whether my shoulders fill it out. If they don't, then I won't wear it. As a scrawny kid, I used to wear two T-shirts at once to make my shoulders look bigger than they were because I was always hyperaware of how narrow my shoulders were in comparison to some of the other guys, especially the older, popular guys, and the men I was seeing on TV and in the media.

My identity and my worth were constantly wrapped up in how I perceived my body. I can look back at myself in high school and see what little sense of self-worth I had relied solely on my abilities as a soccer player and sprinter on the track team. When I tore my hamstring and could no longer participate in those sports, I fell into my first bout with depression. But instead of heading to a therapist's office to dig through it, I did the manly thing: I headed to the weight room in an attempt to bury it.

At eighteen, when I lost all control and my college future was uncertain, I sought control, power, and worth by becoming hyperfocused on my body. But I wasn't hyperfocused on the health of my overall body; I was hyperfocused on the size of my muscles. I was subconsciously telling myself that if I got bigger, if I got stronger, then maybe I would win over that one girl or show the guys at school that I was an alpha; if I got bigger and stronger, then I would be happier, or at the very least, less unhappy.

So I hit the weight room, and I hit it hard. I became obsessed with gaining muscle and at one point put on twenty-five pounds of muscle, which for a six-foot-tall skinny kid was a big feat. But it wasn't enough. It was never enough. When I looked in the mirror, I didn't see what everyone else saw. I didn't see a teenager who was so jacked that he was accused of being on steroids. I didn't see the six-pack. When I looked in the mirror, I still saw the skinny kid whose abs weren't visible enough, whose shoulders didn't fill out his shirts enough, who should probably try harder and put in more hours to gain more muscle. Wake up earlier. Push harder. Be better. It's never enough, and it never will be. I never will be. Just like now, when I look in the mirror, while yes, I still have muscles, I see an extra layer of fat over where a more defined six-pack used to be. If only I could go back to having the body I didn't appreciate back then. One time, after hearing me comment negatively on the way I looked, my dad told me that one day I will look back at that same photo and wish I still looked that good. There's a one-hundred-percent chance that one day I will say the exact same thing, thinking back to my body today. So why can't I just appreciate and love my body as it is?

It wasn't until a few years ago that I learned that this is part of body dysmorphic disorder, which Dr. Olivardia explained as "body image disorder in which people have a very distorted perception of a part of their body. So it could be their skin, their height, their hair, their muscle." In fact, muscle dysmorphia is a more recently recognized form of body dysmorphia that occurs almost exclusively in men. No matter how big I got, it was never going to be enough for me because deep down, underneath any superficial facade of confidence, I saw my muscles through the distorted lens of body dysmorphia.

Ironically—or maybe not so ironically—my physical transformation wasn't enough to gain the acceptance I was seeking from other guys either. The same guys that teased me about being skinny were now giving me shit for being too muscular. It went from "Where are your abs?" to "Jesus, Baldoni, put on a damn shirt!" I went from wearing two T-shirts to appear bigger to being ridiculed anytime I took off my shirt (no longer plural) because suddenly I was flaunting my abs. Here's the thing about guys: it doesn't matter what side of the equation we are on, we police each other. All the damned time.

Shouldering the Weight of Worth

Intricately intertwined in my relationship with my body is my career in the entertainment industry. Although as I joked on the TED stage, you may have recognized me from my earlier roles of "male escort #1," "photographer date rapist," or "shirtless steroid-using con man" (God, I hope the sarcasm translates here), I got my first big job in my early twenties on the show *Everwood*. It was my first time being a series regular, which is the coveted holy grail of gigs for any actor, let alone a brand-new actor. The role was set up to be an interesting one. I was playing a medical student named Reid Bardem who struggled with depression and who lived with one of the main characters (Chris Pratt), was a new love interest to the female lead (Emily VanCamp), and became a nuisance to the male lead of the show and her soul mate (Gregory Smith). I had been acting for less than a year at this point, and let's be honest, I wasn't that good. But I was ripped and considered attractive by industry standards, so while I got the part, it wasn't one that would go the distance. Shortly after I landed the gig, the network announced it could potentially be the beloved show's final season. That meant the producers had only half a season to wrap up the entire arc of the series. So that news, mixed with my subpar acting chops and the blowback from fans about my character getting in the way of the main couple, meant one thing: Reid had to go. I found myself with fewer and fewer lines, while also coincidently wearing less and less clothing. My character was often shirtless and would literally be working out half the time I was on-screen, more than likely to justify why I was in such good shape, but also because I don't think there was much else for my character to do, or that as an actor I could handle. I ended up as largely comical relief and even remember doing a scene in which I was doing push-ups in the background while studying as the two main characters talked about something serious and even commented on my strange behavior. Now as a producer and director, and since having become close with the *Everwood* producers themselves through the years, I understand why it happened and how these were circumstances beyond everyone's control. But for my twenty-year-old self, who was already insecure as a man and as an actor, being the random, shirtless guy doing biceps curls on an intellectual, well-acted drama was tough to swallow, as I already felt like I wasn't enough as I was, and it just further cemented the false belief that my value came from my body. But hey, I was blessed to be working, and it made me money, right? My body, looking the way it did, helped make me money. But at what cost?

What people didn't know about the shirtless medical student was that behind the scenes, the guy playing him wouldn't eat carbs for weeks before he had to be shirtless in front of the camera. He would be at the gym for hours a day and not drink water on shoot days so he could look more ripped. He was subconsciously depressed, lonely, and obsessing over muscle mass and body fat percentage because he felt his only value on the show (his job, his source of income) was solely dependent on his physical appearance.

I wish I could tell you that ten years later, after quitting acting to dive into directing and producing deep and meaningful content, I had worked through some of this. I wish I could tell you that after spending years making documentaries about incredible people living with terminal illnesses, I gained some perspective in regard to my body's real worth—my real worth. I wish I could tell you that as I went on a spiritual journey in my twenties and dove headfirst into my faith, I really grabbed hold of the belief that I have a body, but I am not my body. But I can't. Yes, I know it and understand it to be true, but I still struggle. I know this because ten years later, when I fell back into acting, I found myself in the exact same situation on the set of *Jane the Virgin*. But this time the pressure felt heavier as I was the lead male on a global phenomenon, working alongside an award-winning acting juggernaut, with social media and the new fad of slow-motion GIFs weighing in on my worth.

The only difference ten years later was that my body could not keep up with the grueling workouts and intermittent fasts while also building a business outside the show and putting time and effort into my new marriage. And just like before, I found myself having anxiety when I had to be shirtless. I confessed my anxiety to friends in each department who would get the scripts a week before we actors would, and then text me if I had to be shirtless in a particular episode.

So there I was, years after my first TV job, newly married and about to become a dad, repeating the cycle, yet this time I was at least aware of it and with a partner who was witnessing it firsthand.

It was in this space of becoming more aware that I started examining the conversations I was having inside my own head, picking apart the messages I tell myself in my darkest moments and bringing them to the light. In the Bahá'í Faith, Bahá'u'lláh says that "man should know his own self and recognize that which leadeth unto loftiness or lowliness, glory or abasement, wealth or poverty." By being brutally honest with myself, about myself, I knew that I had a lot of internal work to do around the relationship I had with my body, and it all came to a head in season two of *Jane the Virgin,* when I tried to really practice being vulnerable by being open about my struggles with various people and castmates. It started with me saying something simple like "I'm feeling kind of insecure, and I don't want to take off my shirt next episode." The response? Wait for . . . yep. Laughter. "Oh, shut up." "Poor you and your six-pack." "Are you joking? I would do anything to look like that." While it might have been well-intentioned and even weirdly complimentary, it triggered that same sense of policing I had felt when I was younger, and it resulted in feeling more of the same pressure I was trying to release.

Javier Muñoz echoed a similar experience when he shared that prior to the *New York Times* review for *Hamilton,* he was very comfortable in his skin. And then the review came out and the very first sentence was "Hamilton is sexy on Sundays," referencing that Muñoz was Lin-Manual Miranda's alternate on Sunday and was noticeably more muscular than Miranda. He made it clear that he was not complaining about the positive remark, and at the same time he was very aware of the impact it had on him. Suddenly he found himself thinking, *Okay, I won't be having pizza tonight, let me cut this [or that] out of my diet.*

The message is the same: our body determines our worth. Our muscle size, penis size, shoulder size, and waist size carry the weight of our worth. And if our body falls outside of the mold society has constructed as "hot/sexy/fit/attractive," then we are seen as "not enough." At the same time, if our body falls into that mold (where there is *definite* privilege that comes with fitting in it), then we are good—then *I* am good, even if I am standing in front of you telling you that I am struggling. It is the message of comparing—of sizing up, measuring up, and manning up. It is a message that causes me (and so many others) to suffer, and as I have learned, it is a message that I help perpetuate.

I Am Part of the Problem

I started taking inventory of my thoughts and actions in regard to my relationship with my body. This was kick-started in large part thanks to my wife, who while compassionate to my struggles, was also pretty damn tired of hearing me complain about myself. It's thanks to her that I started to realize just how often I was talking to and about myself in a negative way. So naturally I started listening. When did I notice myself talking shit about my own body? What was I saying? What triggered me to feel worse about my body? When I look in the mirror, do I look for the flaws first? What helped me feel good about my body? The more conscious I became of my thoughts and actions, the more frustrated I became with the systems in place that perpetuate the messages that often lead to unhealthy body image, body dysmorphia, and eating disorders.

It's when I realized that I still had that teenage boy inside me who was seeking validation and acceptance, that I could begin to reframe some of the messages that boy had received about his body from TV shows, magazines, and his peers. But as soon as I began to try to reframe those messages, I realized that my career as an actor—the roles I was taking, the superficial prison I had created for myself—was perpetuating them. On one hand, in my personal life I was beginning this journey to (hopefully) find a level of body acceptance that I had never known; but on the other hand, I was taking off my shirt on TV and literally creating the same images that triggered my insecurities as a boy. These opposing things were happening in real time, and there was nothing I could do about it . . . except talk about it.

Ironically, or fatefully, in the middle of writing this chapter and tackling this conflict, an essay titled "How We Ruined the Dad Bod," by Gianluca Russo, was published on *GQ*'s website. *GQ* is the quintessential men's magazine, and it's one I've always wanted to be in (*just* maybe not in this context). The essay dives into the origins of the phrase "dad bod" and how it was coined to celebrate what a "real, average working man looks like." The dad bod quickly gained cultural acceptance as it "let all men know that, despite a lack of abs or chiseled shoulders, they could still be loved and found attractive, and that they shouldn't feel any lesser for not being as defined as Instagram influencers with thighs so thicc they could suffocate you. . . . It told men they could enjoy life without the constant strain of having to hit the gym; that they need not reach for unrealistic ideals that might not even ever be attainable." Even though at times the dad bod is used to publicly poke fun at men who once had more defined muscles and who were now carrying extra pounds around their midsection, the foundational message of it represented male body positivity, and it was a message I could get behind and needed. And to really epitomize my personal conflict, it was a message that, according to the essay, I helped ruin.

"Recently, TV shows have confused dads with, well, *daddies*. Though small screen patriarchs were once joyful, laid-back Average Joes, they've now transformed into ripped, muscular heartthrobs like Milo Ventimiglia on *This Is Us*, Mark Consuelos on *Riverdale* and Justin Baldoni on the recently concluded *Jane the Virgin*." The essay goes on to discuss how these *daddies* on TV are working against the body positivity movement and intensifying the pressure on men to have a body that looks a certain way to be a man of any worth. "Because it's impossible to ignore these men's muscular—and often shirtless—bodies, real world fathers may forget that that's not realistic, which can lead them down a path towards extreme dieting, exercise addiction, and generally toxic habits."

Fuck. And *no shit*. Because guess what? That "daddy" on *Jane the Virgin* is a real-world father who has been on that path of extreme dieting, exercise addiction, and bad habits to show up on your TV screen looking the way he does. And on filming days when his insecurity is too much to bear, he makes human choices, disguised as acting choices, to cover his midsection because he's convinced that piece of pizza is going to be noticeable to the viewer, the director, and to the person who signs his paycheck. Want an example? If you feel like rewatching *Jane the Virgin*, look for shirtless scenes in the last few seasons and often you will find that I use props or a shirt to at times hide areas I am insecure about.

So the cycle continues: I crave the acceptance that the dad bod message invites, I do a TED talk on masculinity, start a show having real conversations about body image and my insecurities, crave to be included in a magazine that every day men buy because of course I still want to be liked by men, and yet the character I play ruins the dad bod, and I finally get written about in that magazine for perpetuating the problem that I am being vulnerable and open about an attempt to help men navigate. All in a day's work.

I'm tired. I'm so damn tired of it. I'm part of the problem, and I'm also suffering, and those two things are not exclusive. So at the very least can we start talking about it?

Changing the Conversation

The only way to change the conversation is to start having the conversation. We have to talk about these things and bring those deeply rooted messages out into the open so we can dissect them and reframe them. But where do we start?

Dr. Olivardia suggested that everyone could benefit from beginning to take a mindful assessment of their body image talk. We all do it, and this internal monologue either promotes a positive body image or perpetuates a negative one. Some examples of negative self-talk are, "Oh if this was just a little more of this, or that was bigger or smaller or . . ." It's talk that is not affirming, talk that constantly feeds us the idea that our body is not good enough on some level. A huge part of mindfulness and meditation is simply being aware of what you're feeling and how your body is feeling at this very moment. The majority of the day our thoughts run wild on autopilot, and we so rarely stop to notice what and how we are actually feeling. If we practice this idea of mindfulness as it relates to our own self-talk, it will help us take a massive step in healing.

As we start being more mindful of this internal dialogue, we can begin to change the conversation we are having with ourselves. For me, it made sense to look toward my children to help me change my dialogue. With my kids, I focus on what their bodies allow them to do. "Look how your legs help you run so fast!" "Your arms are working so hard on the monkey bars!" If I catch myself talking shit about my own body, I pause and find a way to infuse that same principle of gratitude and function that I share with my kids. I try to find gratitude for my arms for being able to throw my son up in the air, or I'll try to appreciate my legs for allowing me to invoke the "Running Man" (my version of the bogeyman) to chase them all over the house. But let's be real: most of the time my wife overhears me saying something negative about my body, or sighing while looking in the mirror, and then I will quickly try to recover and pivot.

Another simple practice I've introduced is complimenting one part of my body when I look in the mirror, instead of doing what feels normal, which is criticizing multiple parts of my body. I don't always succeed at this, but I try! I think of the wise words Emily often tells me when she catches me being hard on myself. She'll say, "Be nice to my husband." So I'll attempt to bring some of her radical acceptance of me into my own self-talk. I'll compliment my hair, my eyes, and sometimes even how my ass looks. I mean, I have a pretty nice ass. Why do I feel weird typing that as a man? Anyway, despite the awkwardness of it all, just like I've gotten used to taking cold showers every day and getting comfortable in the uncomfortable by sitting in a tub filled with forty-degree water, I am trying to get used to the awkward feeling of being nice to myself as well. Who would have thought radical cold exposure would be easier to adapt to than radical self-acceptance?

After assessing the way we talk to ourselves internally, we can begin to look at how those conversations lead us to action. When our body talk is negative, we might find ourselves overexercising, restricting food that our body needs, binging and purging, or using stimulants, fat burners, anabolic steroids, or high doses of HGH (human growth hormone). If you're like me, you also may find yourself consuming images (through social media and entertainment) that, while meant to inspire you, trigger you into a negative conversation with your body and the feeling that you aren't enough as you are. Anything that clearly isn't about health anymore is an indication that there might be something that needs healing in the way we see ourselves.

Recently I have been coming to terms with the fact that my body doesn't move or look like it did when I was twenty. It takes an extra day of soreness for my muscles to recover, and if I don't warm up, I am much more likely to pull a muscle or throw out my back just picking up my kids because of all the damage I've done to my body over my lifetime. That acceptance has been pretty awesome for me, as I have been able to adjust my expectations of myself as they relate to my overall health and why I want to work out in the first place. I'm now realizing that what I want more than anything else is a body that works, a body that moves without pain and that will last as long as possible. I want to be able to teach both of my kids how to throw a punch when they're in high school, like my dad did for me (except I'll duck when they swing at me), and to be able to kick their asses on the soccer field (if they choose to play sports).

Now that I'm in my thirties, a healthy and functional body is more important to me than a ripped one, so adjusting my expectations means also adjusting my Google searches, my social media, and my self-talk and making sure that I am consciously countering both the external and internal messages that love to remind me of everything I am not. It starts with each of us, with changing the conversation we are having with ourselves and challenging our actions to follow suit.

The Why Ladder

One of the tools I utilize the most to help check myself is the concept of the why ladder. It's about taking a brief pause and asking myself why, and then why again, and then maybe why again. It's not just something I do for my exercise and eating habits; it's something I try to use in all areas of my life. It's about climbing the why ladder as a way to check, and challenge, my intention. So as it relates to my body, it might go something like this: I feel the need to work out, but before I hit the gym in our garage, I ask myself why. Why do I want to work out? Because I am feeling stressed and I want to release some of that energy from my day. Why? Because I know that my mind and body are connected and when I move my body and sweat, I feel better. Or maybe another day the answer is that I want to work out because I want to be stronger. Why do I want to feel stronger? Is it to feed the hero mentality that's wrapped in my masculinity—the mentality that says I need to be able to protect a woman from another man? Or do I want to be stronger to be able to keep throwing my kids in the air and have the stamina and the health to keep up with them? Or is it more about being stronger so that I look "good" or "better"? And being 100 percent honest, some days my why is because I just need to set a damn goal for myself even if it's as superficial as losing a few pounds of fat so I can see my six-pack again. But as superficial as that goal is, the exercise of asking why is a good practice because it helps me understand what is really going on and what I'm potentially covering up. For example, I haven't been working out as much, and I want to look better and feel stronger. Why? Maybe it's because I want to be big so I can protect my wife and family, or maybe because I am feeling a bit insecure that I'm aging. Why? Because I'm worried about how I'm going to pay my mortgage next year if the next movie I direct bombs, and I need to stay fit because I still hold the false belief that my value as an actor in Hollywood is dependent on how good I look versus how skilled I am as a performer. So now that I know I'm wanting to look better because I'm insecure, I can start to address the real reason, while choosing to work out because I want to, not because I feel I have to.

The why ladder isn't about perfection; it's about being curious and being mindful about my actions. More often than not, asking three whys generally gets me to the truth of the matter, and chances are my motivations are never really the things I think they are. Asking why is about being inherently curious about myself and using that curiosity to gather information to help me dissect, observe, and reframe the messages in my head. It also doesn't have to be a long process; one "why" can get you there and the mental check can happen in seconds. At the end of the day, it's simply about being accountable to and honest with yourself and then not judging the answer. Even if your reasons aren't coming from a healthy place, even if they are emotional, it doesn't mean you shouldn't work out; it just means you are one step closer to understanding yourself and the real reasons why you feel the way you do about yourself. Awareness is everything.

The awareness gained from using the why ladder has helped me begin to find balance and ease with my relationship with my body. Even though I am still far from healed, I've made progress. Before, I would have not eaten for twelve hours because of my anxiety about looking a certain way on a TV, whereas now I have times where I fast for health reasons instead of solely superficial ones disguised as health reasons, which inevitably ends up benefiting my physical and mental health as well. As part of the Bahá'í Faith, every year we engage in a nineteen-day fast when we abstain from food and water from sunrise to sunset (roughly twelve hours). There is a reason that fasting has been ordained in the major religions of the world for thousands of years, and it was never about making sure we looked good or that we had a six-pack. Fasting is about detachment and purification, and this past year was the first time in twenty-one years of fasting that I was actually okay with losing muscle mass and weight. It's also the year I enjoyed more of the spiritual benefits than ever before. My mindset went from trying to fast spiritually while also worrying about a physical deficit, to truly detaching and focusing on a spiritual surplus.

The why ladder has given me a practical way to get to the root reasons of why I do what I do, and in that I am able to keep myself in check and keep the messages that I am feeding on, as well as the messages that I am feeding to my kids, more aligned with what feels most pure, healthy, and sincere for me.

What are those messages that I want to be most true in my mind and my actions? I have this body, but I am not this body. I have the body of a man, but my body doesn't determine my worth as a man. My body does not need to be man enough to be enough; who I am, who God made me to be, as I am, is enough.

CHAPTER THREE

SMART ENOUGH

Why I Don't Have Every Answer and Why That's a Good Thing

It's 5:00 on an extra-warm, muggy New Orleans morning, and it's the first day of principal photography (shooting) of my directorial debut, *Five Feet Apart*. I've been working on this for almost two years now. What started as an idea I believed in had to transform to become an idea that everyone believes in. Oftentimes I've felt like P. T. Barnum trying to sell an idea that deep down I didn't even know I could pull off. I had to convince the people in power of my worth and value and that I'm not just that guy on *Jane the Virgin* or whatever they know me as. At this point in my life, I think I've been known as the shirtless guy on *Everwood*, the proposal guy, the guy who makes those inspirational *My Last Days* documentaries about people who are dying, the shirtless guy on *Jane the Virgin*, and then most recently the TED Talk guy. But I had never really been known as the filmmaker/director guy. Ironically, out of all of those professional labels, perhaps the one that would mean the most to me is the label of filmmaker. I've always wanted to be a director. Ever since I saw *ET* when I was six years old and then later got a chance to stand behind Mr. Spielberg himself in line when my dad took me to see the grand opening of the *ET* ride at Universal Studios Hollywood. I've always wanted to tell stories like Mr. Spielberg—stories that make people feel like I felt as a young boy. I wanted to capture people's attention and open them up to a world they didn't know existed, a world where they could be reintroduced to life and maybe even their own humanity. This was my chance to finally prove my worth.

After years of convincing studio executives in Hollywood that I am capable and ready to take their money and turn it into a beautiful piece of art (that will, in turn, make them more money), I am finally here. Today is day one of twenty-five of *Five Feet Apart.* So on this muggy morning on what should be one of the most exciting and thrilling days of my life, why am I not excited? Why am I full of anxiety and fear that I'm about to make a massive mistake? Why am I struggling to figure out what to wear? Why am I questioning myself, my intelligence, my capabilities? Well, while I have been trying to convince all those people for years that I am worthy and capable, that I am ready to make a movie and lead hundreds of people to victory and win at the box office, that I am enough . . . it turns out I forgot to convince myself.

In school, no one ever called me "book smart." I was an antsy kid who literally couldn't sit still at a desk (and still can't). I got average grades in high school, never was a good test taker, and attended college on a partial athletic scholarship for approximately three minutes before getting my heart broken and dropping out to pursue acting full-time. And while I know now that book smarts don't equate to intelligence or to the ability to be an effective leader, that is not the message that was prevalent in the education system in which I grew up. As a result, I consistently felt dumb or less than when it came to my ability as a student, which translated into feeling dumb as a kid outside of the classroom and eventually dumb or less than as a man on a movie set or inside a conference room.

Where do those feelings lead for me and many other men? Overcompensation.

Ever meet a man who was clearly not good at something but acted like he was the foremost expert in the world on the subject? You don't have to answer.

Over the course of my education I had to constantly look for ways to keep up with the class. I remember many times when I felt really smart just because I finally knew the answer to the question, only to realize that it was an easy question and everyone knew the answer. Deep down I wanted so badly to excel at school and to be seen as a smart kid because I knew that the things I really wanted to do in my life required intelligence and not athletics, but the truth was that the way in which my brain learned and processed information was counter to the constricting box the standard public school curriculum was putting me in. More than likely I had, and still have, some form of undiagnosed ADD (attention-deficit disorder). I say undiagnosed because despite my teachers suggesting over and over again that I may have it, my parents never actually got me tested. In some ways it was good they didn't. They also never sat me down and asked me, "What's wrong with you?" or treated me like I was less than because of my troubles or inability to focus in school. That doesn't mean that I didn't get grounded a few times for talking back to teachers or lying to teachers by telling them my dad was a lawyer and he was going to sue them—unfortunately, a very true story (no one got sued). If anything, my parents built me up so much and at times gave me an unrealistic idea that I could do anything (which I now realize isn't totally true) and tried to reinforce the idea that I just needed to apply myself. Instead of this message, I wish they had just told me that I was enough no matter whether I succeeded or failed—that's the message I needed and that could have served me as a child and especially now as an artist.

What I wish I knew then, and what I know now, is that ADD is not a deficit or a disorder at all, and if we choose to shift our perspective, it can even become an advantage. At least that's how I am choosing to look at it. And while I am in no way comparing my struggle with theirs, I have many friends in the disabled community who feel a similar way about their unique set of gifts and challenges and have inspired me to apply a similar mindset. What got me in trouble as a child and what led to countless and embarrassing parent-teacher conferences for my parents, has ultimately become one of the things that has helped me build companies and create successful films. I have to believe that part of my success has come from the ability to multitask and to perform highly doing multiple things at once. But too much of anything is never good, especially when it comes to a lack of focus or even a surplus of it. Of course, at times my restlessness drives me crazy and I wish I could be more like the people who can sit and meditate for hours. I also have to appreciate and understand *my* mind and body and the way I was created. We all have different strengths and weaknesses, but unfortunately too many of our systems apply a one-size-fits-all model. In education, if you don't learn the way the system teaches, then you tend to exist outside the norm and are given a diagnosis with the word "disorder" in the name. Know what a word such as "disorder" or "deficit" does to a young person? It makes them feel less than, like something is wrong with them and that they aren't enough, nor will they ever be. Just think about the way we treat folks who have disabilities as they grow up, and the language we use surrounding them. I have so much empathy for people in the disabled community who have been told over and over again that they aren't enough, who have had to fight twice as hard to be accepted or seen as normal when in reality it's the fact that they are different that makes them unique, and their perceived disadvantages create advantages and surpluses in other areas. In other words, their differences give them superpowers, like Daredevil. (Not the Affleck one but the Netflix one.)

As with any of these topics, the messages are mixed, confusing, and deeply ingrained. I often find myself living in the tension of the messages I received as a child and teenager—the self-talk, insecurity, and inauthenticity that go along with them—and the more inclusive messages that I have come to believe in my adulthood. These almost dual realities are pervasive. On one hand I know in the logical parts of my brain that I am smart and capable, but on the other there's the part of my heart where I still feel like that little boy in school who was always told he had a problem, that he was a troublemaker who needed to focus more if he wanted to succeed . . . if he wanted to be smart. This little kid always felt misunderstood and didn't know why. I live in the tension of being confident in my competence (and my capacity to continue to learn and grow) while simultaneously feeling like a fraud who doesn't deserve the professional opportunities I have worked my ass off for.

Back to that early morning in New Orleans as I was getting ready for day one of my first film. As I breathed through the anxiety and tried to conquer those feelings of inadequacy, I walked into the closet of the 1800s haunted craftsman we were renting and sifted through the clothes I had packed. (And yes, it was definitely haunted. If you don't believe in that stuff, I get it, but when your three-year-old starts talking to the little boy and girl in the ceiling and something grabs your leg at 2:00 a.m., you better believe you sage the hell out of the place just in case.) After digging through my clothes and low-key freaking out that I packed terribly, I decided to sport my usual T-shirt and jeans look. Then I backtracked and thought I should go for a more dressy-casual look as I am, after all, the director and producer and would be setting the tone for the rest of the crew. So I threw a blue collared shirt on over my T-shirt, thinking it would look clean-cut enough, but I kept my sneakers on so as not to push me over the edge of trying too hard. As I looked in the mirror, though, all I could see was that third-grade boy who couldn't keep up, who couldn't focus or understand math, and who overcompensated because of it—that little boy who just wasn't enough. The pit in my stomach grew as, on top of not feeling qualified to direct a movie, I was worried that my crew would see the weakness in me and intuitively not trust me. My mind raced. What else would work against me? Would the guys in the camera department see me as someone to make fun of behind my back and not as a skilled leader? Knowing that filmmaking is predominantly a hybrid of intellectual and creative skills, I did the only thing I could do to both make myself feel better and also ensure that I had every opportunity to make the best first impression I could with a group of 120 people whom I didn't know that well: I put on a pair of glasses with no prescription in them. My thought process was simple: if anything can help me look less like a guy who has been taking off his shirt on TV for the past decade and more like a man they can trust will make smart and creative choices, not crack under pressure, and get them home in time for dinner . . . it's glasses. It worked for Clark Kent, and maybe it would work for me. Welcome to my imposter syndrome.

The Mixed Messaging of Male Intellect

We've already established how the physical strength of a man's body tends to be valued much more than his mind, and how bravery is typically measured in physical feats and not necessarily in emotionally deep dives. The message as it relates to intellect starts early in social circles with the popularity and praise of the athletic boys, and the labeling of the smarter boys as nerds. The boy who knows the answers to every question the teacher asks is often teased for being a "know-it-all" or a "try-hard." The funny kid who cracks jokes and picks on the smart kid is going to tease himself for bombing the spelling test before others can beat him to the punch because he is actually dyslexic, and the athlete doesn't *seem* fazed by barely passing his final because his worth isn't tied to his performance in the classroom; it's tied to his performance in the game. The clincher is that the athlete knows that as long as he stays strong and good at sports, he will continue to be at the top of the food chain. It's one reason I think bro culture's invincibility complex has spread so far and wide and that young boys have figured out how to turn the phrase "try hard" into an insult to make boys excelling in the classroom feel less than.

The tension and pressure on boys and their value being tied to their perceived intellect are both subversive and yet so powerful. I remember feeling a sense of relief as I settled into being labeled a good athlete in middle school and high school. I didn't really need to be smart, and there was plenty of room at the table for me if I was seen as just an athlete. Of course, there were always exceptions, like a kid named Ryan, who was known to be both a standout athlete and an academic whiz and who was also extremely well-liked because he was kind to everyone. He was a young man of faith and character and rarely if ever engaged in gossip or bullying. I don't remember much about Ryan, as I didn't know him that well, but I do remember feeling really jealous of him. He seemed to have it all, and people talked about him like he was a unicorn. I wish instead of being jealous of him, I had tried harder to be his friend and had been humble enough to learn from him. He seemed to have the secret sauce of what it took to be good at everything, but it also makes me wonder what he struggled with. Knowing what I know

now, I know that it can be lonely when people assume you have it all together. Wherever he is, I hope Ryan is kicking ass at life and living in his bliss.

Okay, back to the year 2000.

I would have never been able to articulate it at the time, but being one of the athletic kids in school gave me an in—a sort of pass with other guys—and it let me off the hook for not being seen as smart in the classroom. Even if it wasn't something anyone was aware of, it helped me come to terms with it. I remember in high school only striving to get a decent enough grade to keep myself eligible for sports, and I had coaches, who were also my teachers, reiterating the same message by letting me turn in assignments late and retake tests or by not grading me as harshly in group projects as other students who didn't need to be eligible for a sports team. It's easy to see how the privilege of male physicality starts early and in unexpected places.

Similarly, Joel McHale, an American comedian and actor, was a good athlete growing up who went on to be a walk-on for the University of Washington's football team, but earlier in his childhood he had been diagnosed as a "slow starter," which he says is basically a diagnosis of stupidity. He repeated grades and could not read because of dyslexia (which wasn't diagnosed until decades later, when one of Joel's children was diagnosed with dyslexia). He said that his entire education experience was figuring out how to work the system so he could pass classes to be able to participate in sports.

At the societal level, men are just "supposed" to be smart, simply by virtue of being men. And if we're dumb, that's okay too because we've created a culture where forward progress is still possible simply by virtue of being a man, hence the term "failing up." Women are the emotional ones, but men, due to our capacity to cut ourselves off from emotion, are the "rational" ones, the smart ones, the problem-solvers. And believing is seeing: the world around me has always reinforced that because I am a man, I have a better chance to land in a position of power and that the sky is the limit, even if I am not as smart as the women I am competing against. As a man it's been culturally ingrained in me to believe that I naturally have the edge. It's not spoken, but it's programmed into us thanks to the media we consume and what we see in every arena—business, politics, science, you name it. We so easily mistake the outcome of male dominance (the oversupply of men in positions of power) for the "cause," which is the idea of gender inequality being "natural" or biological.

So as I was ingesting the message in the classroom and from my teachers that I wasn't smart enough, whether it was because I wasn't applying myself or because I wasn't capable, it didn't matter because I was also seeing mostly, if not only, men in positions of power and influence. This created a strange inherent sense of not only feeling smarter than I actually am, but also being *smarter than* just because I am, and identify as, a male. It's hard to explain, but if you are a man reading this and if you really check in with yourself, I believe you will find times in your life where you have felt this. It's also a feeling that is hard to notice, but the behavior that comes as a result is the giveaway. For me it's also the very thing that ends up leading to the phenomenon of "mansplaining," which if it were an Olympic sport, I would have probably medaled in three times by now. If you don't know what mansplaining is, or don't believe it exists, text or call a female friend and she will probably admit to you—if you are willing to listen—that you have probably done it to her once or twice. But if you want a fun example, here it is.

In high school, one of my teammates told two female classmates that girls and women had menopause every month and go through their period later in life (he had no idea he had it backward and had mastered mansplaining long before the term was coined).

So essentially, by definition, it's a man lecturing or educating a woman on something she already knows more about. Now, while I can't speak to exactly what was going through the guy's head, I can imagine that it had nothing to do with impressing the girls (which he clearly was not doing) and more to do with not being seen as wrong in front of us guys. I can remember conversations where my friends and I would talk in absolute circles trying to prove that we were right, when in reality none of our stances even made sense because we were just making shit up. To remember those times, I don't have to go that far back. I just need to think about the last conversation I had with my best guy friends. It's kind of just what we do. It's not about outsmarting the other guys, but on some subconscious level it's a competition to see who can out-bullshit the others or who will give in first. It's harmless and fun when it's with the guys, but we have to be mindful not to take that same energy and create unintended annoyance and hurt in the world.

The same dynamics of mansplaining remind me of how so much of trying to be man enough isn't at all about impressing women; it's about impressing other men. Am I strong enough, smart enough, whatever enough? Who gets to decide what enough is? And God help the one of us who goes over the line, who is too smart, too ripped, too much. It's that male policing again. Toe the line and you're safe; go too far and you're intentionally humbled. All. The. Damn. Time.

Along the same lines, what happens when a man is a professional athlete, superior in physicality over the average guy, and also wildly book smart? In other words, what happens when a man goes outside the script he's been given? The script that says if you're going to be a jock, you're not going to be smart? Richard Sherman graduated from high school with a 4.2 GPA, attended Stanford on an academic and athletic scholarship, graduated from Stanford with his degree before his senior year, and is one of the NFL's top cornerbacks of all time. Sherman is a brilliant intellectual who happens to be an exceptional athlete as well. So he obliterates the dumb jock narrative, and yet he's ostracized for it all the same. The critiques of him are not only rooted in racism; they intersect with the expectations of Black masculinity. Sherman's intellect is rejected because that's not what society expects from men as athletes, especially when they're Black, and it plays a role in how quickly he is dismissed and degraded by other men, especially those who are white. Because we are constantly sizing each other up, if a professional athlete clearly outsizes us in physicality, we tell ourselves that we are superior in intellect because he's just an athlete or a "dumb jock," but when he is also smarter than we are, we become insecure. We've already learned the natural response that many of us use to hide our insecurities: we put the person down so we can be lifted up.

While most people don't use the phrase "dumb jock" as much as they used to, the message is still prevalent every time you hear a commentator, whether they're on TV, via Twitter, or sitting next to you at the bar, tell an athlete that they should "stick to sports" or, as one reporter infamously told LeBron James, should "shut up and dribble."

But despite these male stereotypes constraining male athletes, I think overall we still tend to believe that we are smarter and more capable than women. This is probably due to a combination of a lot of factors, from how we are socialized to the people we have historically seen in positions of power. I don't think I can remember seeing a film when growing up that was marketed to me as a young boy or man that opposes this narrative, and I worry that it's this assumption of superior intelligence that has made us intellectually lazier in some ways than women because we don't have to work as hard to be seen or heard.

It's this convoluted, confusing, contradictory messaging that has told me time and time again that even though I don't feel smart enough, thanks in large part to my being a man, there is room for me to pretend I am. And where do I fake it the most? You might think it's in front of other women, but it's not. It's almost always in front of other men. We men know that it is other men who are constantly judging us, comparing themselves to us, seeking ways to kick us out of the "man club" while making sure that their spot is safe and that they might even move up a notch. Masculinity is always tested and proved to other men: that's the pecking order we rely on most for our self-worth. Sometimes it feels like we're just a bunch of roosters in "cockfights." I wonder where that pun came from.

Knowing Where North Is

While the messaging about being smart is often conflicting, there is one message that has remained consistent across personal experience and societal pressure: we have the answers. Whether it be in the TV shows or movies that we watch, or in my own family's home growing up, if you want to be a man of value, you have to be a man of resourcefulness. But not just any resourcefulness, your *own* resourcefulness—your own smarts, competence, and intelligence.

Look at MacGyver. (For you younger readers, he was the inspiration for the character MacGruber on *SNL,* and if you have never heard of MacGruber . . . thanks for making me feel old.) MacGyver can get himself out of any situation with a toothpick and some floss. Or James Bond, who is an analytical and multilingual strategist whose physical attributes are matched only by his intellect. He is smart and suave and somehow knows the exact temperature of a martini—but when he has to fight, he always wins, and if he doesn't, it's only because they needed to make a sequel. There are countless character references of the self-reliant male who doesn't ask for help because he knows all the answers. Even today, as I was in the gym and listening to a motivation mix that helps me get off my ass when I'm feeling low, a song came up that actually made me stop my workout as the chorus kept repeating, "I walk alone." I couldn't help but smile. As the artist sang, "Those who fly alone have the strongest wings," I also noticed myself nodding as it resonated with me. And that's where it gets confusing. There's truth to the empowering feeling of being a guy and making it all on your own. There's even a part of me that wakes up when I hear speeches or music that give me this primal chest-pounding adrenaline rush to push past my limits and do an extra rep. But taken out of context, this message can also be misleading.

That mindset of challenging us men to show up in the world and inspiring us to offer our full self without excuses or needing other people's validation is also the mindset that can hold us back from becoming the most full and happy versions of ourselves. It's what leads to isolation, depression, and disconnection. The confusing messaging that real men don't need help to solve problems and that we will always figure it out is both inspirational and damaging. Just as medicine in the wrong dose can become the poison, it's important for us to be mindful of our doses and ask ourselves why we are resistant to asking for help when a situation arises that could be made so much easier if we were just willing to put our egos aside and ask.

Let's get specific. What is one of the most stereotypically hated ways of asking for help, that we generally try to avoid at all costs? Asking for directions. Even those of us who do ask feel like a part of us dies when we reach that humiliating place of not knowing where we are, of not being man enough to know which direction we should be going. It's an easy laugh for a comedian to get because it's funny, but it's funny because it's also true. A study by TrekAce, which makes GPS navigational aids, found that the average British man will travel nine hundred additional, unnecessary miles over the course of fifty years. And even after realizing they are lost, only 6 percent of the men polled would check a map or ask for help. C'mon, fellas, that means that for every one hundred of us who get lost, only six are willing to ask for directions?! But I am also not absolved of this sin. Not long ago my wife and I were in the car, going someplace we had been before, and I got lost but refused to check the GPS and instead insisted I knew where we were. (Truth: I did not know where we were.) Oh, and by "not long ago" I mean last week. It's like there is this part of me that intellectually knows I don't know where I am but that needs to prove that I am a good navigator and don't need help getting places, *especially* places I have been before. Failure to get us there on our own in some weird, messed-up way equals failure as a man.

One of my oldest and best friends laughs when she tells me about her husband. Now, Renee comes from a family of especially good navigators. Her grandfather served in three wars as a navigator in the air force. He was the human version of the complex computer navigation systems we use today and one of the sweetest men ever. Renee confessed that she constantly gets annoyed with her husband when he doesn't know where he's going or makes a wrong turn on the way to a place they've been before. She, on the other hand, has a keen sense of direction and yet has also been subject to the messages about men needing to know where they are going. So instead of simply making it about how we are human and make mistakes, or how we have different skill sets, she realized that she was subconsciously guilty of making it about her husband's competency, that he was somehow less of a man because he made a wrong turn. Men may think we're making up the rules, but we often get a lot of help and encouragement.

We also get that encouragement from "history" (his story).

Enter Christopher Columbus—what revisionist history we have in him. This guy has been centered and sensationalized in our society, and our education system, for centuries for his navigational skills. We were taught in school that this brave and talented man, long accepted and revered by mainstream society, sailed across the ocean and discovered America. I even remember being so proud of my Italian roots because of what we learned about him in school. It is only recently that our society and education system have begun to deconstruct these long-believed stories and tell the truth about how he "accidentally" found America and was much more of a colonialist, rapist, and murderer than he was a brilliant explorer. In an interview with CNN in 2004, Patricia Seed, a history professor at Rice University and author of *Ceremonies of Possession in Europe's Conquest of the New World*, said, "We celebrate him because he's a guy that made a mistake but had good luck." She goes on to say that "Columbus miscalculated the distance between Europe and Asia." In glamorizing him, the message we send to men is that if getting lost worked for him, maybe it will work for you.

There is something in a lot of us men, and in a lot of the messaging about men, that feels like we need to know where north is and that our manhood depends on us somehow instinctually acting like we have a true north compass in our back pocket. But not just in the car that we are driving, or on foot in a new city but also in our own lives. I've been in relationships where my lack of having a clear direction for my life, even in my early twenties when the majority of people don't have one, was used as a measuring stick for what kind of man I was and what kind of life partner I would be. The critique was that I didn't have direction, and that translated into a critique that I wasn't man enough for my girlfriend because I wasn't a man with a plan, a man with the answers for the next twenty steps in my career. We have this idea—this standard—that we always have to have an idea of where we are going even if we don't really know, and that we have to figure it out on our own to prove our worth, our competency, as a man. The rhetoric becomes this: asking for help means you are incapable of helping yourself, which means you are helpless, and then a victim, and finally, weak. But I'm just going to say this: I would rather be okay not knowing which direction I am going for a short time than willingly going in a direction just for the sake of it and then waking up twenty years later realizing that I was lost the whole time. We must stop punishing ourselves and other men for having momentary bouts of feeling directionless. The policing and the pressure that mount on a man when he doesn't feel that he has direction or purpose can be debilitating to his mental and physical well-being. SO WHAT if we don't know where we are going or who we are today? So what if we are feeling lost? Every inhale needs an exhale before our lungs can refill. The bow needs to be pulled backward before the arrow can be shot forward. Some of the most important moments of my life have come from feeling lost or the realization that I was going in the wrong direction, and they are what ultimately led me to find my path, but not without a few bumps from society and this ridiculous hustle culture trying to shame me off that path in the process. I think one of the worst parts for us is that the very people we would want to ask for help when we are feeling our lowest, the men in our lives we love and respect, are the very men we don't ask because we fear we will lose their respect. What if we could find a way to let the men in our lives know that it's the willingness to ask for help in the first place that will gain us respect? How many lives could we save every day?

This isn't just a randomly held belief that the easy-to-blame male ego created on its own. These standards and stereotypes that we are trying to live up to are so imbedded in our culture we often don't even know they are there, much like my friend who found herself judging her husband's competency for making a wrong turn. A study led by Ashleigh Shelby Rosette, an associate professor at Duke University's Fuqua School of Business, showed that male leaders are judged more harshly, and perceived as less competent, when they ask for help. The same didn't hold true for their female counterparts. This validates exactly what Liz Plank says in her book *For the Love of Men* when she states that "while women are encouraged to ask questions, men are expected to pretend like they know everything even when they don't, even when it comes to large and existential questions about their gender and their lives."

Similarly, I bump up against this almost every time I am in a new city and approach another person to ask for directions (which is a part of my quest to "get comfortable in the uncomfortable" because yes, it still feels awkward for me to approach another guy and ask for directions or help). Will they give me directions? Absolutely. And many are super kind about it, but it doesn't lessen the resistance to getting myself to ask the question. As men it's easy for the solution to once again become "fake it till you make it" because who wants to be the guy who looks like a lost puppy looking at a map on his phone in the middle of the city? But here's a thought for all of us. What if the real answer is knowing that we can't get to where we really want to go without depending and leaning on others? What if our collective intellect, our collective resourcefulness, is the only way to become the best version of ourselves? What if the very thing we as a society deem as weak is really the very thing that makes us strong?

The Power of Mentorship

Intertwined in the messaging of male intellect and resourcefulness is this concept of the lone wolf—this ideal of self-reliance that views asking others for their support or expertise as a sign of weakness or defeat. It's confusing because we know from ethology that wolves prefer to travel in packs and that wild wolf packs are organized into almost domestic-looking mother- and father-led families. So it would seem that a lone wolf would actually be more of a lonely outcast wolf than a self-made alpha wolf who is slaying it at life. Like I touched on earlier with the song "Walk Alone" and the at times celebratory nature of us men making it completely on our own, the myth of the lone wolf survives on ego. But too often, at least in my life, my ego has led me to desolate isolation, and it's in that place of isolation that my feelings of shame and insecurity thrive.

Growing up feeling like I wasn't as smart as I should be had a silver lining in the sense that, from a young age, I learned that I would need help from others to get a good grade or be deemed smart enough. Because I felt inadequate on my own, it led me to having a lot of opportunities to ask for help, especially from teachers.

One of the more pivotal moments in my own relationship with my intelligence came in high school during my senior year when we were assigned to complete a big book report that would heavily weigh into our final grade. I was a fast reader but had trouble retaining the information I had read. This is something I struggle with to this day. While reading, my mind would wander, and I would play entire movies in my head and then realize I had just read three chapters and had no idea what had happened. Beyond that, I struggled to get my thoughts and ideas from my head onto paper. Not because I couldn't write but because the very act of sitting down to write felt like competing in an Ironman. As I asked for help, Ms. Reed took a completely different approach than most of my other teachers had. She didn't brush me off. She didn't make me feel bad for my shortcomings. She didn't extend the deadline because of sports, and she didn't go to her list of tutors who could help me with the report. She talked with me, listened to me, and challenged me to complete the assignment in a way that excited me. We brainstormed together and decided that the best way for me was a video book report. I didn't have to type, I didn't have to get my thoughts from my head to the paper, and more importantly, I got to tap into my love of creating, of videography, and of acting. Instead of a book report, I got to make a movie.

I received an A on that assignment, but more than that—so much more than that—I can tell you that it was the first time in the entirety of my formal education that I felt like I was operating in my genius. It was this epiphany where I began to realize that I wasn't dumb, I had never been dumb, I just learned differently from others. It was the beginning of the mental shift for me regarding my own abilities and intellect. That shift never would have happened had Ms. Reed simply followed the rules and insisted that the book report needed to be written in one way, and one way only. But it also wouldn't have been successful had I not been willing to ask her for help in the first place. This was my introduction to the power of mentorship. She was an expert and used her knowledge and experience to guide me in a way that empowered me to learn and more successfully complete the project than I could have done without her. By guiding me, she helped me become a better student, and without knowing it, she helped water the actor/director/entrepreneur seed that had been planted in me since I was a child. Finally, and maybe most importantly, she helped me begin to realize the power of mentorship, and of collaboration. (If you're curious, the book was *The Great Gatsby*. And my "report" involved creating an alternate ending, which I directed with my friends as actors in my backyard. That video also involved me being shirtless, so I guess taking my shirt off on camera has been a theme for longer than I realized.)

Asking for help, input, or advice is a muscle. Early on, I was given a lot of opportunities to exercise that muscle. And while of course there were times when it was uncomfortable and initially would make me feel dumber, I've come to learn that the initial discomfort is actually my ego. My ego always wants to remain comfortable, safe, and in control. My ego wants to have all the answers, to be self-reliant. My ego wants to stay within the scripts that we're given as children, as jocks, as students, as men. But by exercising that muscle—by tearing down my ego and allowing that muscle to grow in its place—I have not only become smarter, but I also have been able to do my job better, serve more effectively, and become a version of myself that I know I would not be capable of becoming on my own.

But just as all muscles need to be used and pushed to grow, so does the muscle of mentorship, of being the person who is asked for help, not just the one asking. Are we willing to help? Are we willing to share our expertise with the rookie on the job or the new kid in class? Are we willing to mentor and give advice, and as a leader, are we willing to be mentored and receive advice? Are we willing to ask for help or input from others? Or do we reject a request for help and not ask for it ourselves because of the scripts we've been fed, because of the idea that to be a smart man and a worthy leader, we have to get to the top on our own merit, with our own resourcefulness? By continuing to exercise the muscle of asking for help and also giving help, we are able to gain valuable information about ourselves, others, and the messages we've been told our whole lives. It's from that place of awareness that we can begin to reframe and rephrase the messages that are hindering our growth and preventing us from becoming the men we so desperately want and deserve to be.

Right to Be Wrong

For me, part of accepting and embracing the fact that I don't have all the answers also means having to look at my fear of being wrong and my knee-jerk reaction of defensiveness when I am corrected. I think most of us would agree that it feels good to be right and that being wrong, or being outsmarted in a discussion, or being corrected can often feel embarrassing and emasculating. For me, it instantly brings up that insecure kid who felt like he wasn't enough, and I find myself wanting to puff out my chest and assure the other person that not only am I enough, but also that I know more than they do. Actor and comedian Dax Shepard echoed a similar sentiment on his podcast, *Armchair Expert,* when he described himself as a "know-it-all" who was insufferable to be around in his twenties. Shephard, like McHale, also has dyslexia and spent much of his childhood feeling, and being told, that he was dumb. So it makes complete sense that his response would be to overcompensate because he has this complex, this insecurity, where he assumes that everybody he is talking to thinks that he's a dumbass.

I operated from that same place of insecurity my first day on the set of *Jane the Virgin.* I had been out of the acting realm for a few years, so I felt off my game. But truth be told, I often felt off my game in acting because I didn't have any formal training; I just kind of fell into it. Early in my career I'd go to these auditions or be on set with actors who studied acting and theater and had a knowledge base beyond mine, and I'd feel inadequate. But instead of letting that insecurity spur me to action and challenge me to grow, I buried it and pretended like I knew what I was doing and had been doing it my entire life.

So there I was, my first time back on a set as an actor. I had been directing documentaries and commercials the past few years but hadn't really acted in probably three years (especially not in a lead role), and I instantly ran into the perfect test of my ego. Enter Gina Rodriguez, the brilliant actress who played Jane. Gina is NYU-trained and one of the best actors I have ever had the privilege to work with. She understood scenes, dynamics, and techniques much quicker than I did. She's also a social magnet who can memorize lines by looking at them once and act any emotion on the spot. When you act opposite someone like Gina and haven't done it in a while, it can be pretty damn intimidating. With each passing episode I found myself getting more and more insecure about my own skills and knowledge of the craft while she carried the weight of not just being the lead on our show, but the new face and shining star of the network.

But instead of leaning into that insecurity, quieting my ego, and giving myself space to grow by asking for her thoughts and opinions about a scene or how I could be a better partner for her, I buried my insecurity and pretended that I was a seasoned veteran and even overcompensated at times by offering to help her. In other words, fake it till you make it—and thus I tried to make myself feel like I was enough.

However, as I continued on in my journey of masculinity, had my first child, and started to do a deep dive into practicing vulnerability and challenging the messages around men not being allowed to show weakness, I made it a point to challenge myself with Gina. It took me a long time, but I finally got the courage one night, in the final scene after an exhausting shooting day, to ask her how she saw the arc of the scene playing out for my character. I remember her looking at me in such a pure and kind way, almost silently congratulating me on overcoming all the barriers that prevented me from asking her sooner. She smiled and I intuitively knew that she had been waiting for this moment for a long time—waiting for me to come around and be willing to put my ego aside so we could elevate our collective art together.

What I didn't know then was that the simple act of letting go of my need for control and my desire to have all the answers would end up being the key that unlocked our chemistry, my vulnerability, and my creative freedom, not just as a man but also as an artist and as her scene partner. What resulted was an incredible, collaborative relationship and friendship that made our show and our scenes that much more interesting, dynamic, and emotional because it wasn't just me looking at them, but often it was us looking at them together. I was able to learn from her expertise and experience, which frankly was more often than not better than mine, and there were even a few times she was able to learn from me. That's the power of vulnerability.

I had to brush up against that discomfort, up against that message of masculinity that told me I needed to use my own resourcefulness, my own smarts, to be successful, up against the lie that asking for help would take away the fact that I earned my success. I had to lean into the discomfort of acknowledging, to myself, that I pretend to have answers when I don't. I had to lean into the discomfort that comes with admitting you don't know it all or that you were wrong. And look, I get it. The fear is real. I get that fear of being wrong. It sucks. And the hard truth is that in this day and age, we live in a culture that doesn't leave room for mistakes and is looking for any chance it can to collectively bring someone down for being wrong. But what I've learned is that being willing to be wrong, to ask for help, for directions, to admit sincerely when you've made a mistake and also admit that you don't know the answer, makes it that much harder to "cancel" you because you are effectively canceling yourself. By humbling yourself and sitting in the discomfort of your humanity, I believe something almost spiritual happens, and regardless of who you are, you become real and relatable. Every person on this planet can identify with the universal truths and feelings of being lost, making mistakes, and being wrong.

Now, that still doesn't mean I'm great at it. I still feel my chest want to puff up defensively when a friend approaches me to tell me that what I said was insensitive, or when someone I work with tells me that something I did rubbed them the wrong way. I can still feel that insecure boy who didn't fully apply himself and was "just an athlete" wince a little when I am directing a movie and someone has a better approach to shoot a scene than the one I came up with or suggests a method that I am unfamiliar with. But I am learning and reframing those triggers as invitations to actually become smarter, to become more of my best self, and to learn in the process. And if I had to attribute my success in the past six or seven years to one thing, I think it would be the willingness to learn.

Our Superpower

The one thing I know for sure is that I do not know. It's that simple. I've learned that I cannot be my best self by myself. Experiences are meant to be shared. Knowledge is meant to be passed down and around. And growth and pain are meant to become lessons to be taught to others so that pain can be avoided and collective growth can be achieved. I spent much of my childhood overcompensating for my insecurity of not feeling smart enough while simultaneously exercising the rare muscle of asking for help, and I truly believe that as a grown man, this combination has become my superpower, one that all men have the ability to develop. If I want to be smarter and more competent, if I want to be a better actor, director, and entrepreneur, not to mention a better husband, father, and friend, then not having all of the answers is actually and ironically a very good thing.

One of my deeper life's passions is finding a way to contribute to the way communities respond to those experiencing homelessness. Long before I ever had any sort of celebrity platform, I was volunteering and taking friends down to skid row, the epicenter of our nation's homeless epidemic. But as that platform began to grow, the opportunity for activism grew along with it. While my heart was always drawn to the community of people who are experiencing homelessness, if I am being transparent, I really knew nothing about the nuances of homelessness, let alone the systems of inequality and racism that combine to cause it. So when we created the Skid Row Carnival of Love through our nonprofit, The Wayfarer Foundation, I had some grand ideas of what kinds of services we'd be bringing to the event and to the people who live on Skid Row, and I was super excited to implement them. But what I quickly learned was that my ideas, though pure in intention, were not what the community actually needed. So, here I was again, faced with an option, to arrogantly insist that we stick to my ideas, or to detach from my ego and be open and willing to listen and learn from the very people and the community I wanted to serve. When framed that way, the answer is simple: detach from my ego, ask questions, listen, and learn.

It's hard to put into words, but there is an immense amount of freedom that I have experienced when I ask questions and admit what I don't know. It tends to catch people off guard, and at times they have even looked at me like I am testing them, like it's a poker game and my admitting I don't know is a ruse, a bluff, to see if they really know. But it's not. And what I've found is that it not only makes me more approachable, but it also makes me a better leader—a more empathetic, compassionate, kind leader.

The age-old myth that a leader must always know where he is going is just that—a myth. It's a lie that's been passed down for ages that has limited us not just as a gender, but also as the entire human race. Sure, a leader should always have a vision, but visions adjust and adapt to circumstances, and true leaders always lean on others for guidance and direction. And while there will always be times and circumstances where the collective whole must lean and rely on one individual (especially in the armed services and in matters of life and death), I believe the overwhelming majority of leaders could benefit from a more servant-leader approach that relies on the feedback and help of those they are leading.

I am also learning that I don't always have to lead, that sometimes it's better to invite another person to step into their genius and take over the wheel. It not only builds capacity but also shows a sense of quiet confidence that is far stronger than the kind of overcompensated confidence I had practiced throughout my life. From a business standpoint, it leads to a better product and builds capacity in your team. From an entertainment industry standpoint, it leads to more sincere, commercially relatable, and successful content. From a nonprofit standpoint, it leads to serving people more effectively. From a human standpoint, when I value people enough to know that I can learn something from everyone, it leads to valuing myself enough to know that I don't need to have all the answers to be smart enough, that there is an easier road that leads to more fulfillment, connection, and friendship if I quiet my ego and listen.

The best part is that this superpower is available to anyone and everyone. Women have been using it as long as there have been women. There's no shortage of it, and I believe that the more of us men who discover it, the faster our dreams will be realized and the happier—and the smarter—I believe we will all become. It's no coincidence that two of my favorite comics—both *X-Men* and *The Avengers*—are collective stories about individual superheroes who must come together for the greater good to defeat a common enemy. Oftentimes in the comics, as in life, the worst situations come from ego and superheroes not being willing to ask for help. But the truth is that when they are on a collective mission, they are stronger together. If we could only realize that we are already superheroes in our own right, we would see that our true power as men actually lies in our ability to ask each other for help.

CHAPTER FOUR

CONFIDENT ENOUGH

Confidence in a Sea of Insecurity

If you had met me in high school, chances are you might have described me using adjectives like "cocky," "arrogant," or "overconfident." At face value, I was outgoing and loud, and it was often said that I was full of myself. Nothing hurt me more than hearing that said about me.

"Full of himself." What a strange expression. If anything, in high school and into my twenties, I was the exact opposite of full of myself. I was empty of myself and full of everyone else. I'd pick up pieces, mannerisms, phrases, opinions, tips, and tricks from the guys I perceived as confident—the guys who were popular, whom girls liked, who were well-spoken, and who had social capital. So when it would be brought to my attention that I came off as overly confident, it felt so foreign because I was well aware of my deep-seated insecurities and lack of confidence. So much of my personality was put on and performative. I can look back now and almost see this play out and feel so much compassion for myself. Other people might have seen an arrogant teenager who would assertively interject himself into conversations and make stupid jokes about everything. What they didn't see, what I managed to keep hidden, is that the same kid would go home at night, exhausted from pretending all day—pretending not to be hurt by the jabs his friends made about him, pretending not to feel sad that the girl he liked just saw him as a friend, pretending that finding food in his braces at the end of every day wasn't embarrassing, pretending to be confident when he had no idea how confidence even felt below the surface. Luckily I had a mom who understood from her own experiences what it was like to be bullied, left out and made fun of, and she always gave me the space to cry—to feel whatever I was feeling. I'm so grateful for her and her ability to listen, while also reminding me of parts of me that were good but not always visible to others because I felt the need to conceal them.

In Glennon Doyle's brave and powerful book *Untamed,* she describes in detail a moment she considered not even putting in her book, which she wrote in an effort to liberate women by being vulnerable and sharing the parts of herself that she spent her life concealing. She uses the term "golden" to describe the high school students who get selected to the homecoming court each year—the ones who seem, since birth, to shine a little brighter than the rest of us. Doyle wanted so badly to be "golden" that she found a way to cheat to get on the exclusive court, the court that if selected will set you apart from everyone, and will set you up for life. Suffice to say, I know exactly how she feels. For me, some of the most lonely and painful moments from high school happened when those awkward and excruciatingly mean nominating forms were passed out. The forms where everyone in school writes the names of the eight kids who are the most handsome, cool, athletic, charming, or pretty . . . the most golden of us all. Each year I sat there, secretly hoping someone, anyone would see me as worthy enough to be on that list. And yes, each year, I also wrote in my own name. Not because I knew I would win, but because I just wanted someone, anyone—even if it was only the person who read and tallied the votes—to see my name and know that someone thought I was worthy, that I was enough, that I was golden. The irony is that I wrote my name in because I thought I wasn't enough, but I hoped someone else would think I was. Each year, after I wasn't named to homecoming court, I would go through a mental list of what I could do differently, of how I could be different, to get nominated the next year. Maybe if I was a little kinder, a little funnier, a little louder, scored more goals, or broke more records on the track. But each year I was never enough. Thinking back on it now, all I can think of are all the other kids who were forced to go through that torturous exercise and who were feeling exactly what I was feeling but who, like me, kept it all in and never showed it. How many of us were looking at each other thinking the other was golden and we were not? In a world where deep down everyone just wants to fit in, I wish we could realize that it takes true confidence to have enough love for ourselves, a belief that we are enough. But I didn't understand that back then, and instead I put on my armor each day, piece by piece, to create the facade of confidence that would make the loneliness a little more bearable.

My facade of overconfidence was me overcompensating for my insecurities, for the parts of me I felt ashamed of. Overconfidence is usually overcompensation: no one has it all that together really. Pride, in this unhealthy way, is often a side effect of shame, and believe me, I felt a lot of shame about being sensitive. Pride became an armor that I put on every morning and sometimes never even took off at night. I wanted to be the in-control, assertive, confident one, and to protect myself from the man I really was underneath the armor: the sensitive, unsure, insecure one. Because if I had learned anything, I knew that I sure as hell could not be both assertive and sensitive, confident and insecure.

The Script of Confidence

From a young age, boys are told that we should be self-reliant and self-assured, which plays a role not only in how we come to learn not to ask for help but also in our self-confidence, and ironically in our desire to be accepted by the other guys, to feel like we belong. There's an unspoken expectation of confidence that goes hand in hand with our ability to be stoic. For young boys and teenagers, it's a constant practice of pushing our emotions deeper and deeper below the surface until we've mastered the act of playing it cool and keeping our shit together. Even better is to push your feelings so far down that you "forget" that you even have them in the first place.

In my life, assertiveness then became the antidote to my sensitivity. By definition, assertive means "having or showing a confident and forceful personality." Be sure to notice in the definition that it's having *or* showing, meaning you don't actually have to have a confident personality as long as you can have the appearance of one. I have come to learn that a lot of our masculinity system is built not only to distinguish boys from girls, men from women, masculine from feminine, but to disconnect them as well. And in a society such as our own, the male way always has the upper hand as the preferred approach. So the early messages weren't directly about how being a boy meant you needed to be assertive, but rather that being a boy meant you needed not to be sensitive.

I think the "term" sensitive (as it relates to boys and men) is widely misunderstood. Especially when it's used as an insult. I've been on the receiving end of that insult more times than I can count, by both men and women. Being sensitive is defined as "having or displaying a quick and delicate appreciation of others' feelings," which most would think would be a good thing, but unfortunately, it wasn't. So in elementary school, when my heart would rear its brutal tenderness, it was rejected—I was rejected—and the message was clear: I could not be who I naturally was and be accepted. So began my early acting work of putting on different personas to determine which ones were acceptable for me as a boy to have.

Gentle and nurturing? I'm a girl.

Loud and obnoxious? I'm hilarious (unless I'm trying too hard, and then I'm just a loser).

Kind and loving? I'm a mama's boy or the boy they pretend to be friends with so they can get something from me.

Unbothered and unemotional? I'm chill.

That last one was always confusing to me. The less you seemed to care, the fewer emotions you had, the more valued and mysterious you were—to not just girls but to guys as well. The more it seemed like you cared, the more emotions you had, the less valued you were (unless you cloaked that sensitivity in humor and made fun of either yourself or someone else). Value was synonymous with acceptance, and I desperately wanted to be accepted.

If the ultimate goal is to be accepted by your peers—to be part of the proverbial boys' club—then the ultimate downfall is to be perceived as a traitor to the boys and men who already are part of it. With that understanding, gaining acceptance into the boys' club is pretty simple: just do what everyone else does and follow the scripts of masculinity that have been passed down to us for generations. But what they don't tell you is that the price of admission is high, so high that it's going to cost you one of your most basic needs, not just as a man but also as a human: connection.

The Boys' Club

When the "boys' club" comes up in conversation or the media, the term usually refers to the dominant male culture within a business or organization. It's the frat house, the sports bar, the office water cooler, the locker room, and the man cave. But lately, the boys' club has been given a political weight: male-dominated fields, events, activities, and groups are not just things, but also bad things. And this value judgment is experienced by many men as an attack on each of us as individuals, and not as a critique of the culture, so I understand why that hurts.

When those feelings come up, we have to listen and ask ourselves why. The feelings are real, and even if we see things differently, we have to try to see another side of the same coin. A movement to engage and support men that is only championed by women is like a tree falling in the forest and all of us arguing about whether or not it made a sound.

It's one of the reasons I don't use or like the term "toxic masculinity." I don't believe it's constructive to use; it's too politicized, and I don't think masculinity as a whole is toxic. It's sort of like "If I like the behavior, it's 'healthy' masculinity, and if I don't like it, it's 'toxic' masculinity." We cannot continue to lump all men into one group and label it "toxic." In fact, many of us also recognize that we are suffering from the very same problems we helped create, and many times we find ourselves as both the perpetrators and the victims. We have just never had the tools to be able to see it or call it out.

In the boys' club, the dynamics that are taking place in businesses are also taking place on playgrounds and in locker rooms across the country. What I'm calling the "boys' club" is really just the mental landscape of places where we men gather, where the cultural messages of what it means to be a boy and a man in this world are embedded, enacted, enforced, and then passed on. The boys' club is where the social decisions are made, where the bar is set, and where insiders are distinguished from outsiders; it's where you learn and obtain your value as a boy and eventually a man.

Of course, all of these rules, expectations, and scripts are unwritten. No one is waiting at the door of the club, handing out protocol guidelines, and making you sign a contract that binds you to acceptable actions and inactions. It's all learned, through experience and observing the experiences of other guys in the group, through watching other men in your life in social settings, in family settings. It's like Fight Club. You don't talk about it or acknowledge it, and most of the time you don't even realize it exists. And that's what makes it so dangerous.

So what makes a boy valuable to the group? What grants us admission to the boys' club? To bro culture? Regardless of where we land on interests, politics, or social issues, the same dynamics of acceptance exist within varied contexts. When and where I was growing up, you were valuable if you were athletic, tall, big, muscular, super funny, or loud in perceived confidence—in other words, the "alpha," the guy every other guy thought he wanted to be. There was also room for you if you were someone who would always go along with the group and be willing to take risks for the benefit of the group—in other words, the "beta," the guy no one really wants to be but is necessary to validate the power of the alpha, to maintain the group, to keep it legitimate and keep it from slipping into parody or danger. Every leader needs followers, right?

It's power that determines your place and your value. It's the ability to exercise your dominance whether it be physically in athletics or sheer intimidation, or verbally in making others laugh, exerting your position by tearing others down, or just being a follower and an enabler to satisfy the ego of the leaders of the group.

I learned early on that there was a way to talk if I wanted to experience the solidarity of the group. I learned that I sometimes had to talk in a way that I was morally—and physically—opposed to if I wanted to be accepted. The easiest way for me to know when

I felt like something was off? The knot in my stomach. Throughout my life, I've always known right from wrong, but that doesn't mean I've listened. I believe that most men, most humans, know the difference between right and wrong and know when there's a moral gray area that's being crossed. The problem is that we train ourselves and each other to ignore the emotional and physical signs and instead stay silent. When we feel the tension building in the pit of our stomach and screaming at us to say something, but we instead ignore it, we are training ourselves over time to ignore our intuition and numb ourselves to future injustices. In school, when I put someone else down, usually behind their back, or talked about a girl's breast size, ass, or legs, *definitely* behind her back, I gained social currency. But even if I was feeling bad about doing it, the reward I got from the group was more validating than if I had listened to my gut. This pattern continues long after school and follows us into pretty much any male-dominated social group or setting. And when I ignored my internal moral compass at the expense of not just external validation, but potential excommunication from the group for honoring it, I was training myself to ignore injustice for social validation. Those little Pavlovian-esque rewards are dangerous, as they lead us into the swamp of bro culture, where moral ambiguity thrives and is rewarded for allegiance to the whole. So when I was loud, annoying, sexist, and appearing to be confident, when I was rough and aggressive, when I was a boy just "being a boy," and when it was clear that my allegiance was to the bros, I fit in, I added value, I was seen, and as a result, I was more or less accepted.

However, while I was learning that there was a certain way to talk, I was also learning unconsciously that there was a specific way not to talk. As we already previously discussed, you can't talk about your feelings and you definitely can't ask for help, but there's another way you can't talk. You can't call out the words or behavior of another guy, especially if he's higher up the food chain than you because if you've got nothing else going for you, you can still add value to the club by going with the flow, by letting the guys who think they are leading the club do their thing, by minding your own damn business in the name of solidarity. And the way our unspoken club works is that when you pledge your allegiance, you continue this behavior as long as the person you are hurting isn't you. The whole thing is a gigantic fraud. It's not just the emperor who has no clothes—it's every one of us. We're all naked and afraid. It's like that scene in *The Wizard of Oz* when Toto pulls back the curtain to reveal the con artist who is the Wizard himself. "Pay no attention to the man behind the curtain!" is probably one of the most famous lines in movie history. And probably every one of us feels like shouting it—some of us pretty much every single day.

Keep Your Mouth Shut

In high school and college, it was known that I didn't drink, and therefore I got invited to the parties only because I could be a designated driver for my friends (which was my way of still being able to add value to the group and not be completely ostracized for going against the script). I often felt uncomfortable and out of place, but at the same time it was easy to blend in by being a little louder than normal, talking a little slower, and holding a drink that could pass as an alcoholic one even if it was just Sprite and cranberry juice. I wish I had a time machine so I could go back and tell myself that what made me uncool then is what makes me cool now. I can't even tell you how many men I meet who are in recovery and wish they had never started drinking, or young people who have chosen to not drink for a variety of reasons and feel more confident in their choice knowing that I don't drink. Isn't it odd how some of the choices we make in adolescence, the ones that are, at the time, unpopular and get us picked on or bullied, end up becoming some of the very things that make us interesting, unique, and attractive as adults?

I remember one party in particular in high school, where one of my teammates cheated on his girlfriend right in front of me. I considered myself to be good friends with both him and his girlfriend, and I can still remember the moral conflict that bubbled up in my gut, the heaviness and uneasiness with what he was doing. I was pissed off and angry, yet felt powerless. *Do I stop him? Do I say something? Do I pull him aside and remind his dumb ass that he has a girlfriend?* Then the justification began. *What if it's not what it seems? Maybe they broke up and I just don't know it? It's only a kiss, so it's fine, right?* My mind rattled through the possible scenarios and outcomes, and I did what most young men do: I stayed silent. In that moment, in a trail of subconscious and conscious thoughts, I decided, even if I couldn't verbalize it, that it was better to keep my mouth shut than it was to turn my back on my friend and teammate and be seen as a traitor to my own gender.

So I didn't say anything. Because more than I wanted to be a good friend and a decent human, I didn't want to lose what little value to the group I might have had. The next day I saw my buddy and his girlfriend holding hands at school. If I were re-creating this moment in one of my films, it would go like this:

INTERIOR. SOUTH MEDFORD HIGH SCHOOL DAY

CUE GREEN DAY'S "TIME OF YOUR LIFE"

In a sea of students, we find Justin walking alone. Up ahead he spots Parker. They haven't spoken since the party last night. Passing students block the view but we can see Parker laughing. We cut back to Justin as the scene shifts into slow motion.

> We reveal Parker is with Jessica. Smiling and in love, she buries her head into his chest just as he glances up and locks eyes with Justin. As they pass each other their eyes meet. Parker's face says it all. "It never happened." Justin notices Jessica smiling at him as they pass each other; she's completely oblivious to the silent agreement made seconds before. Off Justin, as he stops. Turns back. Will he say something? His head lowers. The bell rings. Resume normal speed. Justin turns away and heads to class. Today isn't the day to be a hero.

Young boys and men know the rules, even if no contract was signed, no rule book was distributed. And no one breaks the rules. We were both boys, both men, and men keep their mouths shut.

In the groundbreaking book *Boys & Sex,* journalist and *New York Times* bestselling author Peggy Orenstein shares a similar story told to her by one of the hundreds of boys and young men she interviewed. During his sophomore year of high school, Cole was on the crew team when he heard one of his senior teammates talking about hooking up with girls behind his supposed girlfriend's back. Cole and another sophomore on the team spoke up and told the guy to "knock it off" and even started to explain why it wasn't appropriate. The senior's response was laughter. The very next day, another senior on the team was making sexist comments about his ex-girlfriend. Cole kept quiet, while his friend who he'd spoken up with the day before spoke up again. The same pattern continued to play out, with Cole's friend speaking up and Cole staying silent. I'm sure you can guess what happened next. Unsurprisingly, Cole said, "You could tell that the guys on the team stopped liking him as much. And they stopped listening to him, too. It's almost as if he spent all his social currency trying to get them to stop making sexist comments. And meanwhile, I was sitting there too afraid to spend any of mine, and I just had buckets left."

These same scenes get played out in hundreds of different ways in offices and boardrooms, on sets and in studios, in school hallways and gym locker rooms across the globe. Every single day. We know we need to interrupt, and we don't. The message we send to the bullies? It's cool. We're okay with it. We won't stand in your way. And the message we send to their targets? You are not worth it. You are not worth me risking my own standing in the group.

We are socialized as boys to believe that our value, our worth, is determined by our solidarity and loyalty to other boys, but in our quest to belong, we end up being allegiant to the man script and not to the man. And the first man that we break loyalty to in the process? Ourselves.

I think that keeping your mouth shut is actually about keeping your heart shut. It's about ignoring that same place of grit in our gut that allows us to be brave and adventurous and take risks. So much of the language I see in traditional masculinity movements is that men need to quiet the noise and trust themselves. We need to follow our gut—and I totally agree with that. But at the same time, we're also told that following our gut applies only when it doesn't put us in conflict with the rules of masculinity, and when it doesn't have to do with calling out behavior we see in our own gender. Which means that to adhere to the "guy code," we are ignoring the pit in our stomach; that weight on our chest; and that strong, confident, albeit quiet voice that tells us something is unjust. When we cut ourselves off from this place, we are cutting ourselves off from a very real, very human, very biological part of us. It's this act—this continual practice of cutting off—that allows the dehumanization of others (the bullying, the objectification, the injustices) to become so normalized.

The minute we start being socialized as young boys to bury

our feelings is the same minute when we begin to lose the capacity to connect with each other meaningfully. It's the same minute when the allure of the boys' club starts to encroach on real social connection, and the level of friendship that we want, that we *need* as humans, becomes possible only at the cost of our masculinity. And in our world, the loudest message is the one that says that our masculinity is worth more than our humanity. It's almost like hundreds of times a day and thousands of times a year, in large and small ways, boys are asked to choose between their masculinity and their humanity. And on the masculinity side there are seemingly all the rewards—the cars, the money, the fame, the admiration, the sex, the appearance of acceptance, belonging, and confidence. And on the other side? Well, we'll get to feel we did the right thing even if we have no friends.

This can't be right.

And there is another barrier to friendship for men. It's not just that if we admit vulnerability or weakness, really open up and share what we are feeling, share that soft, tender, human place in us, we will be knocked down a peg or two in the masculine hierarchy (if we're lucky) or risk being dropped all the way down the social totem pole (if we're not so lucky.) There is something in the idea of the "American" that is about being alone, an idea that a man's gotta do what a man's gotta do, and what he's gotta do is follow the cowboy riding off into the sunset alone, even though you know it is breaking his heart. When we stand triumphant as men, we almost always imagine ourselves standing alone.

The Force of Masculinity

If soft, gentle, and delicate are associated with femininity, then anything hard, firm (insert teen boy laughs here), and forceful becomes associated with masculinity, again as a way for men to be distinctly disconnected and dissociated from women. We see the force of masculinity play out in so many different ways throughout our everyday lives, most of which I, unfortunately, wasn't that aware of until becoming a husband and even more so a father.

For example, as naive and ignorant as it may sound, I had no idea that it was a well-known thing among women that men often sit in a way that has us taking up more than our share of a seat or space, also known as "manspreading." It's when a guy sits with his knees really far apart, taking up more room than he needs. Before we laugh it off or excuse it—consider that it became such an issue among subway riders that when the Metropolitan Transportation Authority of New York created PSAs to encourage subway riders to be more courteous, one of the targeted behaviors was manspreading.

Another example is that by and large, women know that men do not move out of the way on a sidewalk. They know this because they have experienced it enough times—a man is walking toward them on a sidewalk, and they will move to either side to avoid walking into the approaching man, while the man will stay on the same course he was on. There was even an article in *New York* magazine detailing one woman's social experiment on the streets of the Financial District, where she refused to move aside for passersby and found herself getting body-checked by men every single day. After the article was published, the hashtag #manslamming made the rounds on Twitter with women sharing their own experiences with the experiment. While the experiences shared on social media may not qualify as sociological research, it was nonetheless enlightening to see that women are conditioned to move out of the way, whereas men are conditioned to take up space wherever we are, often without any regard for others.

This blew my mind. How many times had I unknowingly or unconsciously taken up too much space and made women move out of my way over the course of my life? It's this reality check that has been such an important growth factor in my life. Now I consider these reality checks to be akin to the relationship I have with a personal trainer. Isn't it interesting that I will gladly pay for the advice of someone to give me instant feedback on ways to make my muscles grow to get in better shape, but as a man, for most of my life, receiving feedback on my actions or the words I use tends to make me inherently uncomfortable and defensive. But there's an upside, as that discomfort is now how I know I need to listen and that it's actually good for me. I learned recently that if I change my relationship to the feedback and don't take it personally—i.e., as an attack on me—and instead think of it as a way to help myself grow to become a better man, friend, human, etc., then I am not only able to hear it better, but I can also reframe it as a challenge and actually implement the feedback. This reframing has perhaps been one of the most important steps in my personal growth.

As men we are not just aggressively taking up space on sidewalks and in subways, but we're also doing it in conversations and in courtrooms. A study from George Washington University found that men interrupt 33 percent more often when they speak with women than when they speak with other men. A separate study by researchers at Northwestern Pritzker School of Law looked at interruptions at the Supreme Court level. In 2015, with three female justices and six male justices on the bench, 65 percent of all the interruptions were directed at the women.

The evidence from the workplace is even more convincing. Pretty much every woman I know has a story about making a suggestion in a meeting, hearing a man echo that suggestion, and then having everyone else refer to it as *his* idea. And workplace studies consistently find that men's confidence—or bravado—enables them to climb the ladder more quickly (and not just because the supervisors and bosses are also men). For example, if you are working in an office and looking at a possible promotion, you might hear that the job you want requires six things. In general, it's been found that a woman will say, "Well, I have five of them, so I have to work on number six." But men will say, "Hey, I have three of them, that's enough," and put themselves forward. Which is kind of another way of saying that women tend to play by the rules, and we men often believe that we can either bend the rules, they don't really apply to us, or that they are meant to be broken. I'm guilty of behavior like this, and oftentimes I am rewarded for it without even realizing it. Confidence—or pretending to be confident—is more often than not rewarded in our society.

It'd be easy for me to brush these findings aside, or to get defensive about what they reveal. In fact, it'd be even easier to be apathetic about it and go on about my day with my life unfazed because it benefits me. But on this journey, something I keep coming back to is the question "Why?" It's part of the why ladder I mentioned earlier, which helps me be aware of the intentions behind my actions. At the same time, that one-word question also invites me to think more critically, and as a man, to take responsibility for what's mine to own and what's mine to change.

Those studies resonate with me because I have been called out over and over again by my wife, Emily, for the ways that I interrupt and don't listen to her. The problem with this behavior is that because we men have been doing it our entire lives, and because we have learned it from other men and boys, we usually don't even realize we are doing it. Being rewarded for speaking out and being loud so that our ideas are heard almost always come at the expense of someone else being talked over and having their ideas not heard.

But because we are so rarely checked on it, the behavior goes unnoticed for the majority of our lives, and when it does come up, it's easy for us to dismiss it as a one-time situation and not as a consistent behavior that we need to change. It wasn't until Emily started sounding like a broken record and calling me out on it aggressively at the very moment I was doing it that it even registered with me. Also, just the fact that she was forced to become more aggressive in the way she brought it up to me, just to get me to hear her in the first place, is something that really isn't okay. And if I behave this way with the woman I love more than anything in this world, then you know I unknowingly behave this way with other women I interact with. Recently I learned firsthand from some of my dearest friends that far too many women experience similar behavior in both their personal and professional relationships with men every day. Why do we need the women in our lives to get angry, aggressive, or explode just for us to notice their frustrations? What's ironic about this is that it's this very reaction to not being heard in the first place that gets women labeled as "emotional," "aggressive," "bitchy," or "angry," and even more so when that reaction comes from a woman of color.

Back to interrupting. Often, Emily and I would be in the middle of a regular conversation and I would get an idea or have an opinion about what she is saying WHILE she is saying it and would just start talking over her as if my opinion, thought, or idea is more important, valid, or timely than hers. This is messed up, and yet it's so completely normalized that it's become something women almost expect versus a rare behavior that women can complain about. Ironically, once Emily got through to me, I started noticing I was doing it EVERYWHERE! It was as if I had been seeing in black and white my whole life, and suddenly I could see in color. It didn't matter where I was—in the office, on a set, in a meeting, or just with friends—I found myself having the urge to interrupt both people I didn't know and people I loved, ALL THE TIME.

As soon as I noticed it, I was able to start to figure out how to correct it, and I began to realize and think about all the people (and mostly women) I have made feel silenced with my louder, more obnoxious voice my entire life. That shame invited me to feel empathy for how I made others feel and helped me become more aware of when I was doing it and even more so when other men do it. Now even though I continue to interrupt at moments, I am much more sensitive when it happens and often will catch it myself and apologize in real time. I also do my best to, as my dear friend Tony Porter says, "call other men in" when I see them behaving in a similar way. I've learned the best way to do it is after the incident, in private, and by using my own struggles with it as an example. Men hate to be called out, especially by other men, but if it's framed as an invitation versus a threat, our defensiveness level goes from a ten to a four. But no matter how much I change my relationship to this feedback and think of it like a challenge to be better, I still fail. Every day I fail. I also fail at manspreading, and I know this because just last week Emily had to push me away from her and remind me there's a whole three feet of space on the couch not being used. (This is a buildup of thousands of instances over the past nine years of me being completely unaware that I'm a fairly large guy with next to zero spatial awareness.) And while sometimes I am smothering her because I want to feel close to her, most of the time it's just because I'm like an adult dog that thinks he is the size of a puppy. But as it relates to interrupting her, or manspreading, or just simply taking up space, if I am doing that in our home, with the person I love and respect the most, then as I said before, I can be damn sure I'm doing it outside the house as well. In fact, when I started posting more publicly online about challenging the behaviors and the system of masculinity in our culture, my wife challenged me: "If you are going to talk about it and be willing to be seen as a role model, then you've also got to be willing to be really honest and talk about how you don't live up to that model."

In some ways I am trying to break the masculinity mold—to be emotionally intelligent, aware of my feelings, and able to verbalize my feelings—but in other ways I'm still painfully unaware and entitled in the way I do it. For example, Emily and I would get into these conversations or have an argument and even though I am sharing my feelings, I am doing so by being assertive and overpowering in the way that I communicate with her. I was—I often *am*—still taking up too much space in our conversation and not leaving her the space she deserves. I do this by interrupting, by listening to her but also not actually listening because while she was talking, I often am already thinking about what I am going to say next. And then, when called out for not listening, I'd just regurgitate word for word what she said to "prove" I heard her, to prove I was right. I say all this not as someone who has figured out a "hack" to overcome it, but because the truth is, I am not on the other side of it.

While I am a considerably better listener than when we got married, I still suck at it. So I am aware that this is a journey and I am a work in progress. But I'm learning (in my midthirties) that hearing someone is different from listening to someone. I would hear her, but I often wouldn't let her words get deep enough in me to hold any real weight unless I knew without a doubt that I was wrong. If there is a fifty-fifty chance that she is wrong, then my hearing goes out the window. So what I've learned is that my objective shouldn't actually be to hear; it should be to listen. Then it goes from a passive behavior to an active action. Listening is being able to take what somebody says, even if it's uncomfortable, even if you disagree, and be able to process it, hold it, and let them know that you heard it with both verbal and physical cues. And if you want the easiest life hack/shortcut to becoming a better listener, here it is. When someone is speaking, look at them, try to make eye contact, and do your best to let them know with your body language that you are listening. Then, when the person is DONE speaking, take a breath and speak. Oh, and if you ever find yourself in an intense conversation about you or your behavior, please, please resist the urge to defend yourself, and once you have listened, acknowledge that you heard them. Sometimes all that someone you love needs to hear is "I hear you." And there you have it. It's easy, fellas (in theory—much harder in practice). Make eye contact, listen, acknowledge, speak. This sequence, if you can practice it, will change your life and, more importantly, the lives of the people you love. Truly listening is one of the greatest gifts we can ever give to the people we care about, and far too often we fall short in fully giving that gift.

Part of the force of masculinity and what so many of us men have been conditioned to think and feel is that any disagreement can potentially be seen as an attack on who we are as men. It's like we've built up this persona as strong, impenetrable, powerful—but we know deep down it's a house of cards, and if even the slightest breeze comes along, it could topple. So we defend it even before it's attacked. Instead of recognizing a disagreement as just another viewpoint, it's much easier to put up our shields and go into autopilot and defend not just our idea but also our manhood. It's seen as a crack in the armor we have put on. And for me, this all relates back to confidence because my insecurity—my lack of self-confidence—is part of the reason I put the armor on in the first place. I needed a way to appear hard and tough because I knew that underneath, my heart was so damn soft, and the messages of masculinity force out softness any chance they can get.

If our heart is too soft, if we are too emotional, we are weak; we are not men.

If our penis is not hard, doesn't stay hard long enough, we are weak; we are not men.

If our confidence is not assertive and overpowering, we are weak; we are not men.

As I take a deeper look at my perceived confidence, as I ask myself why over and over again—why do I interrupt, why do I need to say what I am about to say—I am becoming aware of my own assertiveness and how there is often a fine line between me being assertive and me just being an ass. I find myself on the ass side of assertive when my assertiveness is lacking an awareness of other people. So basically I'm being an ass when my assertiveness lacks sensitivity.

The Strength of Sensitivity

If being sensitive is about having an appreciation for others' feelings, but we are taught as men to have the complete opposite for our own feelings, it's not shocking or surprising that I've often found myself having a hard time knowing how assertiveness and sensitivity can coexist within me. How do I both wear the armor of toughness and embrace the power of my innate tenderness? How can I be a CEO or a leader while also remaining empathetic and compassionate? I've been told my whole life that nice guys finish last and that kindness in men is mistaken for weakness. But that's just one of the messages we have to undefine. So maybe that's the starting point, having an awareness of just how damn powerful sensitivity is, and reframing the messages that have told us that we as men cannot be, or cannot embrace, that form of power. We must reframe the messages that tell us that our power has to be hard, rigid, and immovable, the messages that tell us to "grow a pair" or not be a pussy anytime we soften up.

Let's dissect that one for a minute. "Grow some balls" and "grow a pair" have become idioms to evoke the courage, power, strength, and confidence that (apparently) inherently come with having testicles. It's a phrase that's so accepted in our culture that even women use it when trying to encourage another woman to toughen up. It's the shout-out to the male anatomy equivalent of "don't be a pussy." Don't be sensitive. Don't be weak. Grow some balls. Be tough, be strong, be assertive. Comedian and host of *The Daily Show* Trevor Noah hilariously cut through the bullshit of these phrases when he turned down going out drinking for the second night in a row and his friend hit him with "Don't be a pussy." Noah said of the situation, in what is perhaps my favorite *Daily Show* segment, "Whenever people say that, I go, 'Do you understand how impressive the vagina is? Do you understand how strong it is?' You realize that human beings come out of a vagina. Human beings come out and still it continues to work as intended. Do you understand how impressive that is? A human being comes out of the vagina. And still it continues to operate, it continues to work, after a human has just come out. You're saying it's weak? You just sit on a penis wrong and it breaks. 'Don't be a penis,' that should be the phrase. I wish I was a pussy."

Putting aside the fact that expressions tying our perceived masculinity to our gender exclude the experience of trans or gender nonbinary people, they actually make no sense! Physically, our penises and testicles are incredibly sensitive, and a hit to them is a surefire way to take the biggest, strongest guy down. At the same time—let's be real here, fellas—the sensitivity in our penis, like the actual nerve endings, all four thousand of them, that make it so painful when we get hit, are the same nerve endings that make sex so damn pleasurable. In addition, our testicles, which produce testosterone and sperm, are also ironically the most fragile and delicate part of our entire body. Do you see where I'm going? Without the physical sensitivity, we miss out on the benefits of physical pleasure. And the things that make us men supposedly tough, happen to also be the most sensitive and fragile parts of us. Now in fairness to a woman's body, the clitoris has double the amount of nerve endings as the penis, yet it is far more resilient. That's probably for a different book, but it's worth highlighting that power and sensitivity coexist in our physical bodies all the time, that power *is* sensitivity in our biological nature. The challenge, for us as men, then becomes to reframe the messages that have told us that sensitivity is weakness and allow ourselves to lean into those tender places and let them reveal their true strength.

Nowadays I try to think about sensitivity and assertiveness in terms of overpowering versus empowering. If what I am about to say or do is with an intent to overpower, then there's a good chance I am landing on the "ass" side of assertive, but if my intent is to empower, then there's a good chance that I am being assertive and sensitive. That was the difference between my dad and me when I was younger and resentful of the emotional, sensitive part of him. I had learned to overpower my emotions—to armor up and not feel them—and I thought that's what made me a strong man. Whereas my dad had learned to be empowered by his emotions—to let down the guard and feel them—and in reality, that's one of his greatest strengths as a father, a husband, and a man. Does it mean he inevitably feels pain more? Yes. But he also feels happiness, joy, peace, contentment, love, and gratitude more too. If we give up or suppress or put an armor over our sensitivity, we inevitably lose out on the good things it has for us—the community; the contentment; the liberation; and, maybe most important, the connection with other people, other men, and ourselves.

Male Friendships, Unfiltered

There's plenty of long-standing research on the direct impact of social connection on our well-being. One of those prominent researchers, Dr. Niobe Way, sums up the vast findings by saying, "Neuroscientists, developmental psychologists, evolutionary anthropologists, primatologists and health researchers agree: Humans need and want close relationships, including friendships, and when they don't have them, there are serious physical and mental health consequences."

Instead of giving you a research paper or just summarizing what the experts have concluded to persuade you into having close male friendships, let me just tell you what I think. I think that deep down, whether they be teenagers in high school or businessmen in their sixties, men want close friendships with other men. Of course, the issue is complex, and therefore the solutions will be too, but I don't think we need to be convinced of the physical health benefits to want to have someone to call when shit hits the fan and we need help; we don't need to be convinced of the science behind the consequences of having (or not having) friends that have your back, that you can spend your time with in a way that means something, a way that invites growth, camaraderie, and acceptance. I think if we could get really honest with ourselves and with each other, we would say that of course we want to have close male friendships, that the issue isn't a lack of desire; it's not even the invisible system that's been put in place to prevent it from happening. The issue is that we have no idea how to make and be friends, especially with other men.

Before I go on, let me be clear. Most men have friendships with other men, and while there are always exceptions to the rule, many of those friendships are on either side of an extreme. They are either superficial in nature and rooted solely in common interests, sports, politics, video games, poker, work, their kid's school, or drinking. Or they are super deep and built on the back of service, shared trauma, pain, or loss, like many servicemen who have fought in the trenches and risked their lives for our freedom. In those cases, the situations men have been in together create the very bond that the rest of us so desperately crave. But we shouldn't have to go to war or save someone's life to forge unbreakable trust and deep friendships.

This all comes back to what we are taught it means to be a boy in this society. While I am seeing positive changes in how younger boys are being socialized to be more self-aware and emotionally attuned, in my experience most of my generation and the older ones don't talk about anything outside of common interests such as sports and video games. It's not easy for us to talk about struggles in our relationships, our mental health or anxiety level, or personal challenges we are facing. I mean, it's barely acceptable to be sad that your grandmother died. The "keep your mouth shut" messaging that keeps us silent when another guy crosses a line is the same attitude that keeps us silent when we need help, when we need a friend or a companion.

Dr. Niobe Way's book *Deep Secrets* tells a very interesting story. She finds that young boys have really deep friendships when they're eight or nine or ten. They share everything and talk about things that really matter. But boys lose those friendships by age thirteen or fourteen, and by the time she talks to boys who are seventeen or so, they remember those friendships fondly, but also tell her they just don't have them anymore. Something happens at about the time boys hit puberty, or adolescence. It's not biological, it's because that fear of being seen as weak, needy, and vulnerable makes us start to pose for those guys and makes us start to pretend we don't feel what we do feel. We will even sacrifice our friends in the name of being accepted by guys who are not even close to being our friends for impunity and protection. It's one of the reasons why I found it so much easier to have close friendships with the girls in my life. As complicated as teenage girls may be, I found my friendships with them to be far less complicated than my relationships with the guys. Now I know women have their own version of this, as bullying, policing, and shaming exist in every social sphere, but for me, my friendships with girls were sacred spaces where I was able to show up fully and be honest without risking humiliation and being bullied.

As a sensitive guy, I liked to talk and they enjoyed listening. It also met an essential need in me to be connected to my heart, share what I was going through, and hear what someone else was experiencing as well. I believe that girls and women can have close friendships at no cost to their femininity because the socialization around their femininity includes emotional connectedness. They were literally brought up with social signals validating them and encouraging them to commune together in groups and share their feelings. Boys and men, on the other hand, have to choose between their masculinity—the messages that tell us what it takes to be man enough, the messages that tell us what an ideal man is—and our human need for connection beyond common interests. Too often we are not choosing our need for connection, and I believe it's literally killing us.

In 2018, the most recent year of data available at the time of writing this book, men were more than 3.8 times more likely to die by suicide than women. White males accounted for almost 70 percent of all suicide deaths, and the rate of suicide was highest in middle-aged men, closely followed by men sixty-five years of age or older.

Chances are, you or someone very close to you has been affected firsthand by a man taking his own life. Losing a friend or loved one to suicide is one of the most confusing and painful experiences imaginable. It leaves an unfillable black hole in families and a lifetime's worth of regrets that generally start with "If only I had . . ." When I was twenty-two, my first cousin Scott died by suicide. He was my incredible and loving aunt's only son, and my only male first cousin. His death left a wake of confusion, shock, and guilt throughout our family. Like most people who lose someone to suicide, I went through all the normal reactions of grief, but no matter how many years have gone by, I still wish I had known how much he was suffering. Sure I may have only been in my early twenties, but maybe I could have done something? Reached out more and told him I love him. Let him know he wasn't alone. But I didn't know because Scott, like so many men around the world, didn't know how to ask for help when he was struggling or depressed. Half the time men don't even know they are depressed or possibly struggling with another mental illness.

This was also true for my friend Kevin Hines, who attempted to end his life by jumping off the Golden Gate Bridge in the year 2000. Hines is one of only twenty-nine people to ever survive the four-second, 225-foot fall into the turbulent cold waters of the bay. Today, Kevin says that he finds himself "on a continuous journey of healing and recovery. Once I began to be self-aware and honest about my brain pain, I started to heal. I learned then that a pain shared is a pain halved. Scientific evidence points to the fact that talking about your inner battles with someone who is empathetic and actively listens actually helps relieve the pain. Twenty years later, I am determined to never suck it up again."

I have so much compassion for men who suffer in silence, some of whom would rather die, as these statistics suggest, than tell another man (or anyone) that they are hurting. So many men struggle with very normal things yet feel very abnormal in their experience. Whether we are struggling with an addiction or a relapse, have found out we are infertile, have lost our job, or haven't had sex with our partner in a month, six months, or years—at times the pain of suffering alone can be even worse than the pain itself. I have so much compassion for these men because as a whole we have never been given permission to have these kinds of conversations, and we have never been given the tools to know how to have them.

So of course our friendships, if we have them, lack depth, and of course we continue to suffer in silence. We are doing exactly what we have been taught to do.

But good news is coming. I believe that things are changing. We are reaching the point where the cost has become too high. All over the world we are seeing things change. I am seeing teenagers bold enough to say, "This isn't working anymore." Every time a young man comes up to me and tells me he watched my TED Talk, it makes me want to cry. In fact, as I was writing this chapter, I was going through what I like to call "a momentary bout of doubt" and wondering if anyone, let alone men, would even be open to reading this book and addressing these behaviors. God works in pretty amazing ways, as at just the right time I received a random direct message on social media from arguably one of the most well-known young musicians in the world (whom I didn't know personally) just to say he had watched the TED Talk and been inspired to reach out to many of the women in his life to open a dialogue about ways he can become a better man. He went on to say that in his message to these women, he openly apologized for the unknowingly insensitive and power-hungry moments that he and the men around them have created. And to his surprise, the responses he received expressed resounding gratitude, as the women were all deeply moved by his willingness to be that open and vulnerable. Just the fact that a young guy like him, who has the ability to influence tens, if not hundreds, of millions of young men and boys went out of his way to reach out and let me know that he was implementing a change in his life gave me hope that maybe the next generation of men would be open to this book and these ideas. Most men, despite getting encouragement from the women in our lives and/or our spouses, also need encouragement from and crave connection to other men. That's why over the past few years, the thousands of messages I've received from men and boys who never felt like they had a place in society because they didn't fit the description of what it meant to be a man are the very messages that keep me going. And each time, as in this most recent case, by giving them a sense that they are not alone, it bounces right back to me: they remind me when I struggle that I am not alone. And perhaps the most meaningful messages I receive are from some of my closest friends, the ones who over the past several years have made and continue to make conscious efforts to trade in that desire of social capital for our need of social connection.

Men want meaningful friendships; we just don't know how to have them.

The Cold Plunge of Connection

In the summer of 2017, when I sat down with my friend Dr. Michael Kimmel, a sociologist who specializes in gender studies, for one of our *Man Enough* episodes, he stated the importance of creating the kinds of spaces where men feel safe enough and confident enough to speak up and share. A space they can trust that what they share won't be used against them. So while I'm not going to tell you to ask a guy out for tea, I am going to tell you that if we want to cultivate these kinds of friendships—the kind that are about more than the game or work or the drink, the kind that give us meaning and fulfill a need that literally helps us stay alive—we are going to have to get comfortable with being uncomfortable. We are going to have to take risks, to do things we have never done, and to say things we have never said. It's going to feel awkward, strange, and at times even painful. It will take effort and work, but it will be worth it.

I like to think of it like a cold plunge, or one of the hundreds of shin splint ice baths I took after soccer and track practice in high school. Willingly stepping into freezing cold water sucks. I hate it. It's uncomfortable, it hurts, and if my mind or body feels weak or I'm under stress, it's literally the last thing I want to do. But it's a practice that has helped me tremendously over the past year, and one that has become an integral part of my life. Sometimes it takes me hours to convince myself to do it. But when I get in and sit in that water, confront that pain head-on, allow myself the space to feel it, and breathe through it, on the other end of that fear and pain lies bliss. In feeling my body adjust and my mind overcome the pain, I feel the benefits. And the longer I have kept up the practice, the more comfortable I get with the discomfort because I know the rewards are worth it. But it doesn't make it easy.

In his personal and wildly relatable book *I Used to Be a Miserable F*ck,* my friend John Kim gives insight into his own journey of self-discovery and the tools he learned along the way. He presents these insights as "dos and don'ts for stepping up and into manhood." One of Kim's dos? Go on "man dates." He tells us not to make it weird, to mix activity with real conversations, and to do it often. For me this looks like working out or shooting hoops with a friend or two but leaving enough time to have a conversation about what's really going on in our lives. This becomes increasingly more difficult as you have kids, but like a marriage, our friendships need watering too. Even if it's just talking a bit while we are stretching—yes, fellas, please stretch, because no one likes an injured weekend warrior. It looks like asking a friend to come over and work out with me, but then also asking him how his heart is when he is here. Often it looks like me sharing how my heart is first, because as we talked about before, there is a permission that's given to the other person when we show up and share our own vulnerability, our own struggles and hardships. (You don't have to literally ask how his heart is, even though I do ask my friends that question.)

I've found that the most difficult part of connection is sending that initial text or making that first phone call to try to set up a time to connect. When I am in a place where I need some support or advice, the listening ear of someone who knows me and will challenge me instead of enabling me, or when I just want to spend quality time with a friend, I can come up with a hundred excuses or reasons not to reach out, just like I do when I don't want to get into that icy cold water. There's always a way to justify ourselves out of something we know in the end will be good for us.

But I've paid enough attention to know that if I can just make that effort to reach out, it almost always pays off.

Okay, so you've conquered the hardest part. You've reached out and have a plan to hang out, but now what? How do you approach having an intentional conversation to connect? You dive in. You take the damn cold plunge, and you stay in the water. Even though it sucks and you want to get out, you don't. You use all those qualities that make you a man, and you man the hell up in the best way possible, by sharing your heart and trying to establish a connection with another man. Get comfortable being uncomfortable. You may need to share first about something you're struggling with or questioning, or an argument you just had with your partner. This is where I use shame as my own internal guide. Where am I feeling shame in my life? Where am I feeling less than? Those are the places I need to dive into.

So I might say, "Man, I've been feeling terrible about how busy I have been recently, and I just feel like I am missing out on so many moments with my kids and wife, and I feel it is taking a toll on me. How do you do it?" The conversation may start in a lot of different ways, but I can confidently say that it will always include being intentional about asking questions. I try to model vulnerability with other men to let them know the water is safe, so to speak. Chances are whatever I am sharing has some sort of parallel in their life. Also, there is nothing wrong with talking about sports or the game and using that as an icebreaker, but that can't be the only connection we rely on. If the surface-level conversation becomes the center of the friendship, it becomes extra hard and awkward to share deeper stuff later. Expect some awkwardness and don't judge it. Let there be space for it. Hell, you can even joke about the awkwardness, but keep going. Dr. Kimmel shared with me that for older men like himself, an instant way to invite connection is to ask about their dad. Whatever the questions may be, wherever the conversation leads, begin to do the work to normalize feelings, emotions, and the desire for friendship, remembering that it isn't about perfection, but connection. And if you're anything like me and the friends that I get to do life with, then you know that it's usually our imperfections that cultivate the deepest connections.

Finally, as Kim said about these man dates, "do it often." But these man dates don't *always* have to include deep and intense conversations. In fact, one of my best friends just called me to remind me that in my quest to talk about the hard or uncomfortable stuff, I've started to forget to show up for the fun, lightheartedness of friendship that is still needed. He asked me to remember to call my friends not JUST to check in on them and talk about something deep or meaningful, but also to just talk about nothing in particular. At times I have a tendency to be too focused on growth or solving problems or becoming my best self, and this reminder was so needed because there is also so much gold in the so-called nothingness and simplicity of my male friendships. Friendships, like our bodies, like our cars or houses, or like any machine we use, require maintenance. We need food and movement to fuel our body. We need gas to fuel our cars, and we need to change the oil in our car and service it regularly. We do this kind of maintenance to keep everything running smoothly and effectively. Let's use the same principle to get to work on cultivating and maintaining the kind of friendships that bring happiness, true contentment, and meaning—the friendships that, at the very least and at the very most, help keep us alive.

Everything Is a Muscle

One thing I know for certain is that I love all things working out, sports, and fitness. I love to push myself, and my drive to move my body, to sweat, to tear down muscle and nourish it to grow is sincere to who I am, independent of the social forces that have contributed to my insecurities and negative self-talk surrounding my body. Movement and fitness continue to do wonders for my mental health and have always helped me in my drive to go deeper in other areas of my life. I try to take the same drive to work out and use it to challenge myself to work *in*—to take account of my emotional and mental health as regularly, or at least as consciously, as I have for my physical health. Men are taught to be, or to appear to be, self-confident, but we are not taught how to develop, or know, our own self. Hot take: you can't be self-confident if you don't have a sense of self. Self-confidence without a sense of self, without self-awareness, is fake and performative. I want to find a way by which we can ground that sense of self in something that is real, so the external expression of confidence is about revealing what is inside, rather than a posture to conceal it.

So I began the work of cultivating a sense of self, of asking myself what I was really like, what I really liked, versus what was put on and performative. Unfortunately, this wasn't a six-week online course or a weekend journaling exercise (no shade to either), and it also wasn't something I even consciously made a plan to do, but more so a continuous practice that invites awareness into my thoughts and actions, what makes me tick, and what fuels me. This kind of conscious lifestyle shift doesn't garner results that are visible in before-and-after photos. It's deep, internal, and extremely personal, and the growth is slow to see. That's not easy for someone like me. I'm a sprinter. I'm built on a foundation of fast-twitch muscle fiber. Slow things frustrate me. I like to build muscle fast, and I like to see the change in my body as it happens. I'm built to sprint, not run long distances, and my mindset has always followed that same path.

One of the first things that I came up against as I started going in was this armor of overconfidence and my underlying insecurity of my sensitivity. I can look back, even at my most armored times, and see my sensitivity flexing its muscles. It was my sensitivity that led me to the concept of making a documentary series on people living with terminal illnesses and on people who are experiencing homelessness. It's what led me to dedicate my life and career to bridging the divides among success, service, and faith. It led to the reason why Rafael as a character was so beloved and to why I started the Carnival of Love on Skid Row, and has led (I think) to pretty much all of my social currency and success. My sensitivity has always been there; it just hasn't always been a muscle that I consistently exercised. Joseph Campbell teaches that the thing that makes us different and puts us at risk of acceptance often is our superpower or our bliss. The *Frozen* movies are a perfect example. The very thing that caused Elsa's banishment would become her greatest gift and an asset to her people. And just like Elsa, once I came to embrace my sensitivity, really incredible things began to happen. Magic would happen, and doors would somehow open that would take me deep *into the unknown*. (That dad joke was for all the parents out there trying to get the song out of their heads, and for my kids who might read this book one day. And when that day comes, there's one thing I know for sure: I will *still* have that song stuck in my head.)

Interestingly enough, as I am working on this chapter, I also have a torn quad muscle. I wish I had a cool story to go along with how I tore it, but in reality I think that part of getting older is injuring parts of your body in really simple, mundane ways. I also think I hold a lot of my stress in my body and that my emotional trauma manifests itself in my body via injuries and muscle pulls and tears. The point is, when I have a physical injury such as this one, I do the work I need to do to rehab it. I rest, I walk differently, I wear a brace, and I get painful deep-tissue work done. If I move in a certain way that aggravates it, I pivot and readjust. I can't just pretend that it's not injured or hurting because I physically can't walk without a limp reminding me. Again, I think we can use this same principle beyond our physical bodies. As we get to know ourselves more, we discover these places in us that need rehab, that need our focused attention, that invite adjustments to be made unless we want to continue to limp through life.

What if these traits of confidence, insecurity, assertiveness, sensitivity, and so on are all different muscles within the same body, but we've been trained to exercise only certain ones? It's like having a big chest and still working out your pecs over and over again, with barely any regard for the opposing muscles of your back. Guess what happens? You end up with bad posture and complete instability. Sure, you might have a great chest, but no one can see it because your chest is so tight that everything is being pulled forward. This is why a lot of men also don't work out their legs, because they tend to focus only on the muscles that are visible. And yes, I have been through that phase too. Our muscles are all designed to work together to ensure that our movement is fluid and balanced, but when we overwork one set of muscles, pain and injury are almost inevitable.

I think our human identity operates similarly. Our society has taken all of our human traits, or muscles, and labeled them on a continuum of masculine to feminine. Then, depending on our body's anatomy, or, for 1 percent of the population who are born intersex, what gender we are assigned at birth, we are trained to develop different muscles to be bigger and stronger than others (or at least to *appear* to be), when in reality we find optimal strength when we exercise all of our muscles.

Researchers have studied facial muscles on men and women to measure emotional reactivity because facial muscles are controlled by the brain's emotional circuits. In one study, they placed electrodes on the smiling muscle, the zygomaticus, and on the anger/scowling muscle, the corrugator, and measured the muscles' electrical activity when the participants were shown an emotionally provocative picture. This study found that men were more emotionally reactive than women in the first fifth of a second; in other words, when it was still unconscious. But then as time went on into the range of conscious processing, the men became less emotionally responsive as the women became more so. This blew my mind! Their findings then suggest that men may be equally as sensitive if not even more so than women, but that we have trained ourselves to disguise, disengage, or deflate these muscles. And if these muscles are controlled by our brain's emotional system, then it further demonstrates that we have been trained to numb or disengage from our emotions. But there is a silver lining, because I believe that if we've been trained to do it, we can be trained to undo it.

All of the Above

I tied these concepts of confidence, of friendships, of male loudness and male silence together in one chapter because I truly believe that when we are able to humanize ourselves in a way that allows for our need for social connection (not social currency), our need to express feelings and emotions, only then can we begin to humanize one another. And when we begin to humanize one another, the ways in which we have dehumanized people—talked trash about others, not spoken up when someone else talked trash, objectified women, kept our mouths shut when injustices occurred—become more obvious and create more cognitive dissonance.

In my experience of talking with thousands of men in person and across social media, a lot of us are walking around with this internal injury underneath our armor. Men who I would say are very confident have confided in me about their deep-seated insecurities. Young men I have been honored to speak with on college campuses are feeling disconnected from their hearts and don't know how to reconcile their very real human emotions with the very confining cultural expectations of manhood, especially in fraternities. The expectation is that we have to choose between being confident or insecure, being assertive or being sensitive, being emotional or being a man. But what if these aren't mutually exclusive?

What if we can be confident *and* insecure?

What if we can be assertive *and* sensitive?

What if we can be men *and* be feeling, emotional humans?

What if the answer isn't A, B, or C? What if the answer is D, All of the above? (I'm not proud of it, but the second time I took the SATs I gave up halfway through and selected D, All of the above, on the rest of the test. I got a 980—the same score I got the first time when I actually read every question.)

As I have started trying to appreciate my innate sensitivity, being honest about my insecurities, getting to know myself as a human, and taking account of—and responsibility for—my thoughts and actions, I've found that I feel more authentically confident in who I am. It's no longer in a way where my pride is inflating a false sense of self in an attempt to deflate the shame I feel, but rather it's knowing that the system that creates the shame in the first place is flawed—not my manhood, not my humanity. It's from that place that I feel a sense of responsibility and a sense of challenge to change the system, to reframe and rework the messages that we feel confined and defined by.

I want men to know that we don't have to be loud, overpowering, *ass*ertive, interrupting, and performative to be seen as confident, self-assured men. I want men to continue to learn, to know that we can be empowering, assertive and sensitive, confident and insecure, men who listen and then speak, men who are aware of and honor the feelings of others as well as our own feelings, men who are self-assured and conscious of community; I want men to know that underneath the armor of masculinity, we are human, and that humans are D, All of the above.

True masculine power is full-blooded power-with—power that strengthens both our autonomy and our togetherness, power that is both hard and soft, penetrating and fluid, finely focused and panoramic, power that aligns head, heart, and guts. Such power, whatever its intensity, does not abuse, and protects what needs protecting. It brings out the very best in a man, backing him in taking needed stands, without forgetting his heart. True masculine power is not out to prove anything, but simply to support the living of a deeper life, a life of authenticity, care, passion, integrity, love, and wakefulness.

—*Robert Augustus Masters, PhD*

CHAPTER FIVE

PRIVILEGED ENOUGH

The Reality of My Racism and White, Male Privilege

> *You have to get over the fear of facing the worst in yourself. You should instead fear unexamined racism. Fear the thought that right now, you could be contributing to the oppression of others and you don't know it. But do not fear those who bring that oppression to light. Do not fear the opportunity to do better.*
>
> —*Ijeoma Oluo*

If the title of this chapter or the above quote has already turned you off, I want to say two quick things: I understand, as at one point it would have turned me off too, and also I'm still going to write about it. Look, I get it. I know how politicized and polarizing the word "privilege" has become. But if you find yourself feeling triggered by my use of the word in this chapter, then I hope you will consider using the tools in the past few chapters to push past that feeling and ask yourself why. This isn't about partisan politics (although an argument can be made that everything is inherently political); this is about humanity and my coming to terms with my own worldviews and the behaviors that have hurt people I love and contributed to a world where inequality and injustice run rampant.

In a book largely based on vulnerability and transparency, I would be remiss not to make it known that this chapter was written last, yet it is going in the middle of the book. I had just finished writing more than eighty thousand words, touching on my whiteness here and there, mostly reiterating that my story—this book—was of course written through my lens as a white male. But I never really dove into the systemic racism, and definitely not my personal racism, that's very much at play in my story and in my socialization.

Then on May 25, 2020, George Floyd, a Black American man, was murdered by police officers in Minneapolis. While Mr. Floyd was far from the first Black person to be murdered by police, there was a difference in the collective response of white people to his murder both here in the United States and abroad. It's been said that 2020 was about finally being able to see things clearly, and for many of us white folks, seeing Mr. Floyd murdered by a police officer while others stood by and did nothing was enough to see clearly that perhaps there has been and continues to be a larger problem, and that we are a part of it. I was forced to really look at why I hadn't responded with the same outrage to previous murders, why I wasn't using my voice, and the megaphone given to my voice, for anti-racism in the same way I had used it for anti-sexism. What was it in me that chose to ignore this problem in the same way that many men ignore their socialized masculinity? Why as a Bahá'í who believes in the eradication of all -isms, who holds tightly to the words of Bahá'u'lláh, "Ye are the fruits of one tree and the leaves of one branch," did I not address this in myself, in our world, earlier? Why was I so willing to "get comfortable in the uncomfortable" in regard to my masculinity, but so unwilling to in regard to racism and white privilege?

It is my job, my responsibility, my duty, not only to figure out the answers to these questions, but also to use the resources readily available to me to educate myself and use the unearned power I have been given as a white man to help change the system so it is more equitable for everyone.

Intersectionality Is Integrity

For the first time in more than thirty-five years, I am recognizing that my socialization as a man cannot be separated from my socialization as a white person—and to be able to separate them for as long as I have is a privilege that I have continuously benefited from. In fact, it's part of why I have the platform I have, why I am able to produce and direct movies, act in Hollywood, and write this book. In other words, the system doesn't benefit me just because I am a man; the system also benefits me because I am a white man (not to mention, an able-bodied heterosexual cis white man from a middle-class family). As Nico Juárez, a Mexican American man with Tzotzil ancestry, said when he shared part of his story in Liz Plank's book, *For the Love of Men*, "Race fundamentally changes masculinity. We need to think about masculinity as a deeply racial issue."

It's only been in the past few years that I have learned that the idea that I exist in intersecting areas of privilege, and should then be using those privileges to advocate on behalf of those on the other end of the spectrum, is part of what's called intersectionality, a term that has been used in the fight for equality and equity by activists and organizers for more than three decades.

Kimberlé Crenshaw, a professor of law at UCLA and Columbia Law School, coined the term "intersectionality" in 1989 when she published a paper that focused on legal cases that dealt with issues of both racial and sexual discrimination. Crenshaw describes intersectionality as "a lens through which you can see where power comes and collides, where it interlocks and intersects. It's not simply that there's a race problem here, a gender problem here, and a class or LGBTQ problem there. Many times, that framework erases what happens to people who are subject to all of these things."

In other words, I cannot write a book, live a life of integrity, and openly discuss wrestling with my masculinity without simultaneously wrestling with the racial bias, prejudices, and discrimination that coexist in my socialization within this culture. I cannot learn about how sexism and gender inequality have benefited me at the cost of women, trans, and nonbinary people without also educating myself on how racism and racial inequality has benefited me at the cost of Black people, Indigenous people, and other people of color.

I have a lot to learn. I have a lot to unlearn. This chapter is merely a glimpse into the work that is just beginning in me, and like the rest of this book, it will never be complete, as my learnings will never be complete. And because it's just a glimpse, I am going to focus mostly on the impact my whiteness and racism have on the Black community, as that is what I'm learning about most right now, while also knowing that the impact goes beyond that into Indigenous communities and the communities of all people of color. Each community has a specific intersection with racism and whiteness, and truth be told, I haven't done enough of the private, personal work in regard to Indigenous communities and other communities of color yet to speak from an educated place of integrity. Even in writing about what I have learned in this chapter, I fear that there's a good chance I will look back in a year, five years, or ten years at this chapter (and really this book) and see that I have said something offensive and ignorant. At the same time I would rather face that fear than, as author and speaker Ijeoma Oluo says, fear my own unexamined racism and the thought that right now I could be contributing to the oppression of others, of people I love, of my own family, and not even know it.

I Don't See Color

Kay and I became friends through our shared faith. She is a Black woman who exemplifies 'Abdu'l-Bahá's words when he says, "Thou art like unto the pupil of the eye, which is dark in color, yet is the fount of light and the revealer of the contingent world." Unfortunately, like many Black women experience, Kay's profound impact on my journey with privilege, racism, and racial justice came at a cost to her—a cost she never should have had to pay.

Soon after Emily and I were married, a small group of six of our friends flew from Los Angeles to Nashville, Tennessee, for a wedding. Kay was in that group, and not only was she the only Black woman in the group, she also was the only Black person at the wedding. The wedding was beautiful and fun, and the newly married couple reveled in the joy of being surrounded by their loved ones. After the celebration, our group of six headed out together to go explore the nightlife in Nashville. As we got into the car, Kay began to cry. Something at the wedding had gone completely unnoticed by the rest of us and had deeply hurt her. And the fact that none of us had the awareness to notice she was uncomfortable and hurt made it even worse. When we first arrived at the wedding, each guest was handed a program and a small bag with instructions to toss the contents of the bag in the air toward the married couple as they walked up the aisle. At some weddings this happens with bubbles or rice; others lead the couple out of the reception with sparklers. At this wedding, however, each bag was filled with fresh cotton that we were to pick apart and toss, like confetti, in celebration of their love.

That's right, Kay was being asked to throw in celebration what her ancestors were forced to pick in slavery.

There are some of you who may read that and have your jaw

drop at how painful, triggering, and emotional that must have been for Kay. Perhaps you instantly knew, before you even read it, that the bag was filled with cotton. You will empathize with her, and if you are Black, it will undoubtedly remind you of similar stories in your own life and the lives of your friends and family. There are also some of you who may read that and wonder what the hell the big deal was. Of course, the bride and groom didn't choose cotton for its implications of slavery! You will not only be confused by Kay's reaction, but you will be frustrated by it and feel that it is irrational. I get both reactions, because our initial reaction to our dear friend was the latter, and unfortunately it took us way too damn long to get to the former.

Later that night when Kay shared her raw feelings and her experience at the wedding, and the pain around the cotton, instead of listening, empathizing, and honoring her, as a group we downplayed the whole situation, and in doing so, we downplayed her feelings and really her humanity. We bypassed her pain and came to the defense of the couple, imploring her to know that they were good people and it had nothing to do with race. She felt abandoned and told us that she did not feel seen by us. With the intention of being a "peacemaker" and bringing "unity," I responded to Kay's pain by telling her that when I look at her, I don't see a Black woman, I just see my friend. I don't see color; I see her heart. In other words, I made her exact point.

As a white person, I was taught to say that we don't see color, that we don't see our differences, that we treat everyone equally. While this concept of color blindness initially sounds very nice and idealistic to white people, it not only ignores the socialization and foundation on which the United States was built, it also ignores the very rich, beautiful cultures and humanity of people of color. In fact, the statement "I don't see color" from a white person, regardless of how well-intentioned it is, oftentimes comes across to a person of color just as it did to Kay, as "I choose not to see YOU." Look, it's no secret we all see color, regardless of what color we are. So when a white person tells a Black person they don't see color, what they are actually trying to say is "I'm not racist." But when I said that to Kay, what I was actually telling her was that even though I know she is Black, I have chosen to ignore it and whitewash her into a friendship that meets my preferred boundaries . . . not hers.

What is even crazier to me is that the "I don't see color" narrative also goes against the very teachings in my own faith, and yet somehow, via the way I was socialized as a white person living in America, I changed the narrative and completely misunderstood the teachings. In talking about color and diversity, 'Abdu'l-Bahá tells us to "behold a beautiful garden full of flowers, shrubs, and trees. Each flower has a different charm, a peculiar beauty, its own delicious perfume and beautiful color. The trees too, how varied are they in size, in growth, in foliage—and what different fruits they bear! Yet all these flowers, shrubs and trees spring from the self-same earth, the same sun shines upon them and the same clouds give them rain." And he goes on to say, "If you meet those of different race and color from yourself . . . think of them as different colored roses growing in the beautiful garden of humanity and rejoice to be among them."

How did I miss it? As a group we were oblivious to Kay's pain, and when she held it out in front of us and shared it with us, we closed our eyes—not to mention our minds and our hearts—to her. After we returned home from the trip, Kay emailed the group and in justified anger exclaimed, "That was some fucked up shit." She explained how she expected better of us and how deeply hurt she was by the entire situation. She went on to say, "That night I realized that my dear friends, who aspire to unity in a diverse global society, had no idea what my pain looks like. I was shaking and I was on the same couch as you and you did not see me. You didn't even know to look."

Her email was honest, and it was educational (which she shouldn't have to do—to carry the weight and spend the energy on educating us on why her discomfort, pain, and anger are valid). She finished the email with, "My life as a Black woman has taught me not to react. I'd run the risk of being dismissed as dramatic, volatile or unintelligent . . . or worse, ostracized and completely alone. Airing my deepest emotions in the moment is a privilege I have never had. In a situation where I feel isolated and stepped on, I will bury my reaction and survive."

I wish I could say that her email flipped a switch for us. Looking back on that email now, it's almost unbelievable to me that I didn't get it, that I didn't rush to apologize and then start unpacking all the reasons why I missed it and why I wasn't there for her. Someone I loved bared her soul and showed me her pain right in front of me, and I was too willfully ignorant to see it and too proud and fragile to hold it. I'm profoundly embarrassed by what happened next. Instead of calling her immediately, my wife and I, in our confusion and privilege, flipped the narrative, centered on our own emotions, and in many ways turned our privilege into victimhood, feeling like we were the ones who were irrationally attacked and that she was blowing things out of proportion.

Over the next six years, little by little I would begin learning from—and actually listening to—my Black friends when they shared their experiences that were similar to Kay's. And as I began my journey of self-discovery and dug into my masculinity, little by little I would notice the intersection of these racial justice conversations with the journey I was on. Every so often, I would think about the situation with Kay and I would feel deep remorse about how I handled it, how I mishandled her feelings and her humanity. I would feel that knot in my gut, that weight on my heart, that would tell me I need to apologize to her. But I would inevitably brush it aside, telling myself that we were all friends, and since everyone had moved on, bringing it up again would just open old wounds.

Then George Floyd was killed. It should not have taken his death and the countless other deaths that had come before and would continue to come after. It should not have taken stay-at-home orders during a global pandemic. It should not have taken all that it did for me to pick up the phone and call Kay. It is problematic that it took so much on a societal level, and it is problematic that it cost Kay so much on a personal level for my wife and me to call and apologize, for us to see how wrong we were and how deeply loving and profoundly kind Kay's email had truly been. But, regrettably and embarrassingly, it did.

I have to admit, Emily and I were extremely nervous when we reached out to her and asked to FaceTime. I don't think I had felt that nervous since I took the stage at TED. I'll spare you the details of the conversation, but all in all, what we wanted to convey to her was how deeply sorry we were not only for what happened, but also for how we let her down, as friends and as fellow humans. We let her know that it was thanks to her and her vulnerability and willingness in her pain to educate her white friends that we both had finally chosen to educate ourselves and to begin to unlearn and relearn all we thought we knew. I let her know how problematic my behavior was when I told her "I don't see color" and more than anything how sorry we were it took us as long as it did to wake up. I then promised her that I would do everything I could to educate myself and my family and have those uncomfortable conversations with fellow white people, as the burden shouldn't be on her and other Black folks to educate white people.

Kay responded to our apology in a way that she did not need to, in a way that frankly we did not deserve. She offered us grace from the same deep well of love that she had always lived her life with. She accepted our apology and reconciled with us. She revealed to us what 'Abdu'l-Bahá spoke of—the fount of light within her and the possibility of what our world could look like when we choose to truly see each other. When we see each other, skin color and all, the contingent world, one of justice and equity, will not come at such a high price to Black people, to the phenomenal Black woman that Kay is.

Well-Intentioned White Man

In addition to telling Kay that I don't see color, here are other examples of some of the things I have thought, said, posted, and tweeted that I have only recently come to learn are indicative of the racism that exists in me:

"My first friend was a Black girl."

"He was a great athlete, as are many young Black kids."

"It wasn't about race, man. No need to make a scene."

"Some of my best friends are Black."

"Black Lives Matter, and so do 'blue lives,' and so do 'all lives'—we are one human family."

Unfortunately, the list is much longer, and I'm sure that I will add to it as I continue to learn, unlearn, and relearn what it means to be a man, and specifically what it means to be a white man in this time and in this culture.

Like most white kids who grow up in America, I was taught that racism was the overt, horrific actions of people who believed that Black people shouldn't drink from the same water fountains as white people and needed to sit in the back of the bus, or that Black men deserved to be lynched for being suspected of laying eyes on or speaking to white women. Racism was Black people being enslaved, and after slavery ended, it was Black people not being allowed to vote. Racists are the members of the KKK and the malicious, ignorant, and usually old people who live in the southern United States and continue to use the n-word. In other words, I was taught that after the Civil Rights era, racism was no longer systemic and racists were on the outskirts of society, and if they weren't, then they were old and would likely be dead soon, and then we could all just get along. So basically, I grew up believing, a white, Italian-Jewish guy born almost two decades after the end of the Civil Rights Movement, raised by fairly progressive "woke" parents who believed in unity and the oneness of humankind, couldn't be farther from a racist.

This framework around racism is known as the good/bad binary, and it is what anti-racism educator Robin DiAngelo describes as "perhaps the most effective adaption of racism in recent history." This framework allows good, well-intentioned, nice guys like me not to be racist because I'm not committing these extreme, hateful acts of prejudice and racism. It operates in a way that's similar to the gender binary and the rules and messages around masculinity and femininity. With masculinity there are traits that are acceptable for men to have and ones that are unacceptable for men, and those traits determine where you fall on the "man enough" scale. Within the context of our flawed understanding of racism, there is one side of the binary that's considered racist and the other side isn't. So since I am not out here committing these overt, heinous racist acts, then I don't fall on the racist side of the binary.

DiAngelo explains that while initially this adaption of the good/bad binary seemed like a good thing, what it does in practice is exempt well-intentioned white people from conversations about racism and how we are socialized and conditioned in a society that is deeply divided by race. And here's what I've discovered: when I exempt myself from having racism within me, when I place myself on the "good" side of this binary, then I also exempt myself from the responsibility to change it. Some of those statements that I listed above are subconsciously said to make it clear that I am not a racist. "My first friend was a Black girl." "Some of my best friends are Black." When I stop to critically think about why I make statements like these, it becomes apparent that I am trying to make it clear that I don't fall on the bad side of the binary and I'm defending myself preemptively. Here's the reality, though: not only is the binary false, but also the feedback that DiAngelo received from people of color is that when they hear a white person claim these things, it doesn't make the white person seem woke; in fact, it reveals how unaware the white person is.

Along those same lines, when I make statements like "He was a great athlete, as are many young Black kids," I am committing a microaggression and perpetuating stereotypes that disregard the individuality of each person while expressing the false universality of an entire group of people. The same could be said when people make statements about Asian people being smarter, loving homework, etc. Microaggressions and stereotypes aren't always overtly "negative," and yet their impact adds up. Simply by generalizing and talking about race in that way lumps an entire group of people together based on a false identity; it creates and perpetuates the same problems that we are trying to address in masculinity. Ijeoma Oluo describes microaggressions as bee stings, where "one random bee sting might not be a big deal, a few random bee stings every day of your life will have a definite impact on the quality of your life, and your overall relationship with bees." It's death by a thousand cuts. When I have made a statement like that, even if it's done with the intention to celebrate a kid's athletic ability, it perpetuates a stereotype that all Black people are athletic and therefore disregards the unique talents and gifts of not only the Black people who are not athletic, but even the athletes themselves. It robs people of their individualism. In some ways I think I have done it to make myself feel better for not being as good an athlete as those who were better than I was. In other words, I was propping myself up to incorrectly believe I'm at a disadvantage because I'm white so that getting beaten in a race by a Black kid is more of an expected outcome in a race of genetics versus an outcome in a race of athletics. Going down that rabbit hole, it also creates a false sense of accomplishment if I then beat a Black person in a race and makes me the underdog as a white person because I overcame a disadvantage that doesn't exist genetically.

Now, this isn't something that I think I, or many of my other white friends, are aware of when we make comments like that, but that's also part of the problem. Our unawareness is the very thing that is so damn hurtful. I've learned that it's a common experience for a Black person on a college campus to be assumed to be a member of a sports team and to be at the school on an athletic scholarship. Think about that. The implication of that assumption is that the student was admitted because of their athletic ability, not because of their academic ability or their leadership skills or their volunteer résumé or their personhood.

Another example of a racial microaggression happened when I was with one of my best friends, Jamey (who would later accompany me on that infamous trip to Mexico). Jamey was one of my groomsmen, and we were looking for the shirt I was going to wear on my wedding day. I didn't have much money at the time, but this was the shirt I was going to get married in so we wanted it to be nice. We grabbed Starbucks and walked into an upscale shop in Los Angeles, carrying our drinks. As I walked in, I nodded at the employee and walked right past him with my drink in hand and headed to a nearby rack, while Jamey went to another part of the store and looked at the shirts in that area. Just as I started browsing the overpriced shirts, I noticed an employee go up to Jamey, and rather than saying, "Hello, sir, may I help you?" he said, "You can't be in here with that drink." Hearing this I walked over with my coffee, confused, as people in LA carry their coffees wherever they go all the time, and I'd never been told I couldn't have one in a store. Now, Jamey, having been in this situation thousands of times over the course of his life, knew exactly what was happening. But I was oblivious. The employee was white, it was a fancy store, and Jamey was a Black man dressed very casually. Jamey jokingly replied to the employee, "Okay, do you fear I'm gonna spill it?"

The employee then says, "Well, the shirts here are very expensive." To which Jamey responded, "And you think that I can't afford to purchase them should I tumble and fall and spill my coffee on your very expensive shirts?" Now, I know Jamey well, and he has a magical way of making a point and dropping some serious truth while also disarming you with his humor and tone. It's one of the things I love most about him. So I start smiling, thinking the employee will just go away and let us shop, but he doesn't, so Jamey continues. "I'm looking to spend money in your shop and you're concerned with me holding a closed coffee? Why is he [pointing to me] allowed to hold his coffee and no one is asking him to leave? In fact, he is being helped by your co-worker." I then jumped in and, being the good "peacemaker" (read: problematic white man) that I am, played it down and said to Jamey, "It wasn't about race man. We should go because they don't have the shirts I'm looking for anyway." Jamey then got quiet and walked out of the store. As I caught up to him, he turns to me and asks why I didn't speak up. I said that I didn't think it was a big enough deal to make a scene and it was just a policy of the store. Then Jamey lost his shit. Rightfully so.

"Justin, I love you, but you are choosing not to get it. You mean a policy for ME? No one asked you to leave. No one doubted your ability to pay for the items in the store. No one thought you were going to trip and fall and spill coffee all over their shirts. But not with me! This shit happens to me all the time, Justin!"

My response? I got defensive. I went to the well-intentioned white man in me that doesn't want to be placed on the "bad" side of the racism binary. I started listing the things I did see, the times I had noticed, the ways I stood up for racial equality and tweeted about justice. In other words, I again made the conversation about me and my intentions. I centered myself and my experience, and not his frustration or pain, when in reality the situation called for it to be about Jamey and the impact the action of the employee, and the inaction of me, one of his best friends, had on him.

We then approached another store a few doors down, and Jamey, still heated, walks into this new store and says to the employee (who was a Black man), "Hey man, I got this coffee in my hand. Can I come in the store and browse around?" To which he responded, "If you're thinking about spending money in here, you can bring whatever the hell you want in with you." You see, this new guy didn't see Jamey being Black as a reason to dismiss him. Even then, in my discomfort and ignorance, I just laughed it off, not really getting what had happened. I just wanted everything to be fine and cool and comfortable, and in doing so dismissed my best friend's entire experience while believing race had no part in it.

Jamey has experienced the bee stings almost every day of his life, and so his relationship to bees is different from mine. It was as if he were telling me that he was stung by a bee and hurting, but because I failed to see the bee, I chose to say, "I don't know, man, are you sure? Maybe you weren't stung?" Meanwhile, he has a stinger in his damn arm and his skin is beginning to swell. What matters more in that moment, my intention or the impact of the sting? In relationships, impact must always outweigh intention. But too often, especially when I am being called out, whether it be by Jamey for not seeing a racial injustice, or by my wife for interrupting her, my default has historically been to get defensive and reiterate my good intentions. I also wish I could say that was one of the only times a situation like that happened, but unfortunately Jamey had been trying to tell me about his bee stings for years. In hindsight I have realized that it was simply easier for me to choose ignorance than to make the choice to educate myself. I found it easier to defend the intentions of the white man who "didn't mean anything by it" than to defend my friend.

This is perhaps the most difficult part of getting comfortable in the uncomfortable. This is part of the pause before responding, especially when my initial reaction is to defend myself. Often my defensiveness is a good indicator for me that I need to shut up, listen, and reflect. This is part of taking the risk to peel off the mask I've hidden behind, look critically at myself, and acknowledge that maybe I don't know everything, maybe I have been on the wrong side of history before, maybe I have been ignorant of my privilege and of the full spectrum of racism that very much exists in our society. Maybe I have some work to do.

How ridiculous would it be if we as a society said the same kinds of statements about gender? What if I said, "My first friend was a girl so of course I don't objectify women"? Or "I am married to a woman and have a daughter and my mom is a woman and I have a sister who is a woman, so therefore I can't be sexist"? Or even "I don't see gender; I treat everyone equally"? This entire journey that I am on to undefine my masculinity would not be a thing, this book would not be a book, none of the issues that come out of the conditioning around gender in our culture would be issues. And yet here I am, on this journey, writing this book, unlearning and relearning what it means to be a man, what it means to be a good human.

I need to do the same work with race. Because if I exempt myself from the work, then I place the burden of responsibility on the same people that are being oppressed because of their race. In the same way that if I excused myself from the work around masculinity and gender, then I am inadvertently placing the responsibility of the work on women, trans and gender nonconforming people, when they are the ones who are being disadvantaged because of the systems in place. Additionally, if I exempt myself from the work and the responsibility, then I also miss out on the connection, the healing, and the joy that also come with doing the work. I miss out on the full spectrum of the journey, which isn't always easy but has so far always proved to be meaningful and worth it. After all, more than I want to be a well-intentioned white man, I want to be an impactful partner, father, friend . . . human.

Checking My Privilege

I was not taught to see white privilege, just as I wasn't taught to see male privilege.

Like male privilege, white privilege is an invisible force that gives me advantages that are not given to everyone.

Like male privilege, white privilege is ingrained in us through our socialization within this society and culture.

Like male privilege, white privilege is uncomfortable for me to talk about. In addition, if you are feeling triggered by my saying "male privilege" and "white privilege," then that means one thing: we need to talk about it. So let's take this cold plunge together; the water isn't warm, but I promise you it's good for us.

I can't recall the first time I came up against the concept of my white privilege, but I can absolutely recall the ways I have been deflective and defensive about it. But I found that I have had a misconstrued, misunderstood idea of what white privilege was. When I first started leaning into the idea of male privilege, I felt like I was being told that I didn't work hard, that I didn't actually earn the job or promotion, that my sacrifice and hard work were invisible and I was being told I only got whatever it is I got because I am male. I said things like, "I worked my ass off to get here; nobody gave me anything." And "I earned all that I have." I felt like anytime someone said the word "privilege" or insinuated that I had it, I would become annoyed or angry. It felt like I was being robbed of my individual story and struggle (hmmm, sound familiar?). I felt the same way when white privilege came up. But my defensiveness was a sign of my ignorance.

There are many forms of privilege that honestly deserve their own book. Every day I learn something and have a newfound appreciation not just for where I sit in society but also the privilege that something as simple as being healthy and able-bodied gives me. I mean, how often do I wake up and feel grateful for my health or my arms or my ability to see or walk? It's generally not until our physical abilities are injured or taken away that we actually appreciate the benefits and privileges our bodies give us. As an able-bodied person I can be sure that shops, homes, parks, and neighborhoods are all accessible to me. I can travel and eat out without having to think about how I will navigate public transportation or the security terminal at the airport. But at the same time, when my able-bodied privilege is brought up, I am not defensive or deflective, and it is not uncomfortable for me to talk about. Why? There's part of me that feels like it's because race and gender have become such politicized topics. Maybe it's because of that good/bad binary and not wanting to recognize my white privilege because then I can no longer ignore racial injustices. Or maybe it's something entirely different that I have yet to learn. But I understand that having able-bodied privilege doesn't mean that I did not and don't have struggles or hardships; it simply means that I don't have *those* particular struggles or hardships.

I think of privilege like the 110-meter hurdles in track. First of all, in a very literal sense, I am privileged to even be able to be on the track, running that race, because a person in a wheelchair could not participate in hurdles and has way fewer opportunities to participate in any form of track than I do. So, right off the bat, that's able-bodied privilege. Does that mean that I didn't train my ass off, that I didn't drink enough water and eat enough nutrients (completely hypothetical, as high school was the time I could pound Taco Bell for lunch just hours before a track meet)? No, it simply means that I have an opportunity, an advantage not available to everyone.

Figuratively, I think of privilege like the hurdles in the sense that we are each running our own race, in our own lane, and yet we each have our own sets of hurdles, or barriers, in our lane on the way to the finish line. Oversimplified, white privilege means that the color of my skin will never be a hurdle for me, just like male privilege means that my gender will never be a barrier for me. It doesn't mean that I won't have hurdles—that there isn't struggle, that I am not working hard—it just means that my skin color will never work against me. And in a society built on such a deep racial divide, not having a race hurdle not only doesn't work against me, it often works for me, in the same way that being a male in a patriarchal society works for me.

If I am able to see clearly how my able-bodied privilege is at play, then maybe my white privilege isn't as invisible as I thought.

Maybe once I start looking at it, looking *for* it, it becomes undeniably visible, like male privilege.

Here are some examples of white and/or male privilege:

> Based on the most recent survey in 2018, for every dollar earned by white men, white women earn only seventy-nine cents, Black women earn sixty-two cents, Hispanic or Latino women earn fifty-four cents, and Indigenous women earn fifty-four cents.
>
> I can easily find Band-Aids in "flesh" tones that more or less match my skin tone. (Shout out to Tru-Colour Bandages for blazing the trail in making bandages and kinesiology tape in a wide range of colors to match the wide range of skin tones! #notsponsored)
>
> I feel safe, and for the most part, don't have to think about my safety. One of my close friends recalled a time when she asked her husband, a white male, how often he thinks about his safety. Without hesitation he said that he rarely does, and it's only in extreme situations such as a car accident or maybe if the bank next door to his work is being robbed. He then asked her how often she thinks about it. Her answer? "Every day, multiple times a day. When I'm walking to the car and it's dark out, when a man approaches me in the grocery store, when I go on a run, when I am driving home and notice that the same car has been behind me most of the way, anytime I travel alone and am seated by a male on the plane . . ." After I heard this, I asked Emily the same question, and without hesitation she began telling me all the things she has to think about every day that literally never cross my mind. Like

how, if she is alone and has to walk to her car at night, she keeps her car keys between her fingers like a mini version of Wolverine's claws.

Similarly, anti-sexism educator Jackson Katz has asked men and women the same question for decades in his trainings: what steps do you take daily to prevent sexual assaults? Katz explains that nearly every woman in the room raises her hand when he asks this question and can immediately list countless steps they take—not jogging at night, carrying pepper spray or Mace, locking car doors as soon as they get in the car, parking in well-lit areas, ensuring that a friend or family member knows their location and itinerary, etc. As for the men, what do we say we do daily to prevent sexual assault? Nothing. Not one hand goes up. It's hard to believe the world we live in as men, and especially those of us white men, can look and feel so different just because of the body we are born into. That difference is simply privilege.

Activist Danielle Muscato posed the question on Twitter. "What would you [women] do if all men had a 9:00 p.m. curfew?" The responses poured in by the thousands and were frankly heartbreaking to read. Instead of being wildly adventurous with what they would do, most women said they would do things such as grocery shop, go for a run, listen to music with headphones on, walk to the car without their keys between their fingers ready to be used as a potential weapon, or be able to sleep on the first floor with the windows open. In other words, things that should be very normal for people to do without fear, and quite frankly things that most men like myself feel extremely comfortable doing without thought every single day. It's well worth noting that Muscato's question was sparked by a conversation she had with a friend, where she shared how much her life had changed since coming out as a transgender woman, and how things that she never had even considered before were now part of her daily mental and physical load—a load that weighs heavier on the transgender community, and specifically the Black transgender community, than on anyone else. Similarly, in a conversation with trans-male activist Jevon Martin, he told me that while he was born into a Black female body and experienced the intersection of oppression that came from being a Black woman in the world, once he transitioned to a man, he had to confront another side of racism—as a Black man, he was now seen as a threat.

I have to admit that I knew next to nothing about the unimaginable hardships and struggles of the Black trans community. Recently I got a chance to interview trans activist Devin Michael Lowe, the founder of the Black Trans Travel Fund, which pays for private car rides for Black trans women in New York and New Jersey so they can access self-determined safer transportation options. In a survey conducted by the National Center for Transgender Equality, which included more than twenty-eight thousand respondents (all of whom are transgender), nearly half (47 percent) of all Black respondents reported being denied equal treatment, verbally harassed, and/or physically attacked in the previous year because of being transgender. It was thanks to my conversations with trans male activists that I learned about the ways that even those I have privilege over have their own levels of privilege over more marginalized groups, hence the importance of intersectionality in this conversation.

People who look like me are largely represented in media, entertainment, leadership positions, Congress, the Oval Office, and education. In fact, my entire education was centered around people who looked like me. I didn't have one Black or Indigenous teacher over the course of my education from kindergarten through high school, and it wasn't until I typed those lines that I even stopped to think about it. I can easily find children's books that have characters who look like my children and that have a family structure like ours, but I have to go out of my way to find books that feature diverse characters and stories.

I can also (generally) have a positive relationship with the police. In fact, there was a time in the fall of 2014, after the murder of Michael Brown in Ferguson, Missouri, that I was driving home and saw a Black man being pulled over by police. I decided in that moment to pull over on the opposite side of the street. I didn't know exactly what I was planning on doing other than readying myself to take a video or potentially intervene if things took a turn for the worst, and by the way, who the hell am I to think intervening was even an option for me? That right there is a sure sign of white privilege. See, when that Black man was pulled over, even before he stopped he rolled his window down and he threw his hands out of his window and waved his ID like a peace flag. I had never seen anything like it in person, and seeing it crushed me. Do you know what I think about when I get pulled over? My first thought every time is *I hope I can get out of this.* Meaning I hope I can get myself out of this ticket, even though most times I was guilty and deserved a ticket. In that moment, I realized that while I think about getting out of a traffic stop without a ticket, a Black person is hoping that they can get out of a traffic stop ALIVE. Thankfully, this man did.

That night, my white privilege in regard to my relationship with police became visible. I went home and tweeted about what I saw and how as white people we have a responsibility to the Black Lives Matter movement. I hadn't read any books, nor had I educated myself on white supremacy and the nuanced and complicated history of police, not to mention the complicated history of our country, white saviorism, or white exceptionalism. So when the replies started rolling in about how racist and terrible I was for saying Black Lives Matter, and how blue lives matter and all lives matter, I didn't know what to do. I mean it all made sense, right? The lives of police officers matter, and of course all lives matter, right? I wish I could say that I ignored the replies, or that I had articulated, educated responses, but I can't. Instead, I panicked because people were calling me racist, and I was new to this and instantly felt like I messed up or that I was misunderstood. So I replied that blue lives do matter and of course all lives do matter. But in my ignorance, I didn't understand how those responses were problematic and frankly racist responses to the Black Lives Matter movement.

My phone rang, and it was Jamey. He saw my tweets and said, "I see the good you're doing, and I see where you went wrong." He explained to me how my desire to be a peacemaker wasn't rooted in true peace. Dr. Martin Luther King Jr. said, "True peace is not merely the absence of tension: it is the presence of justice." My idea of peace, as a white man, has often been focused on having an absence of conflict or tension, even in issues outside of race.

Jamey then very lovingly and patiently explained that when there is a fund-raiser or event focused on breast cancer, when sports teams rock pink jerseys for breast cancer awareness, we don't show up with signs and argue that prostate cancer matters too! And when our neighbor's house is on fire and the fire department shows up to help, we don't run from our house that is not on fire and exclaim that we need the resources our neighbor is getting. We need the fire hose! We need the firefighters! No, we don't, because our house is not on fire—theirs is! Regardless of where your political beliefs lie, or what outlet your news originates from, I hope this understanding can bridge the gap between partisan ideologies and fundamental human rights. As I have learned the hard way, when we say that Black lives matter, we are not saying that Black lives matter more than anyone else's; we are not saying that the lives of police officers don't matter or that all lives don't matter. We are simply saying that all lives cannot matter until Black lives finally do.

Whitewashing Hollywood

Early in my acting career I screen-tested for a show called *Greek*, which went on to do several seasons on ABC Family. Screen-testing is one of the later parts of the audition process where you act in front of a live studio audience of generally bored, overworked executives and an enthusiastic director and producer who collectively determine if you're the right one for the part. I remember my agent telling me that I was the favorite and that I just needed to go in there and knock my screen test out of the park. It couldn't have gone any better, and I left feeling confident that this role was mine. My phone rang. It was my agent and manager, and whenever they called me together, it was either really, really good news or really not good news. This time it was definitely the latter. The feedback was that while I was the show creators' first choice for the role, I didn't get the part because "honestly, the network felt your eyebrows were too distracting on camera."

My agent and manager then flat-out asked me if I was willing to trim and pluck my eyebrows because it would help me get these kinds of parts. What exactly were "these kinds of parts"? I couldn't articulate it then, but I am able to now. These were parts that were set up to be played by traditionally white guys. The irony? I am white. But to Hollywood, I wasn't white enough. My features were too ambiguous for the industry's definition of whiteness, and as a result I found myself getting more auditions for characters that were Spanish, Latino, or Middle Eastern.

One of the first roles that I booked was an Iraqi prince on a TV show in the early 2000s called *JAG*. I remember walking into the audition room where there were probably ten other guys there to audition—every one of them Middle Eastern. Guess who got the part? The white guy. When I asked if I should learn an Iraqi accent, the producers told my manager not to worry about it, that I was "Americanized." When it finally came out on TV several months later, guess what had been done? My voice had been dubbed. They took a Middle Eastern man's voice and put it over mine, so it was my face with his voice.

If I can remember, just a few years later, how it felt to be told that my eyebrows were too distracting and how annoying it was that I didn't fit the traditional blond, blue-eyed stereotype that the network had in mind for this role, I can only imagine what it would feel like for the Middle Eastern actors who were finally getting the chance to audition for the role of prince—a welcome break from the usual terrorist or Islamic extremist roles they are pigeonholed into—only to have a very not Middle Eastern man, a white man, come in and take the role. This is an example of whitewashing that has taken place throughout our country's history, and so of course it takes place in Hollywood too.

Our textbooks have sanitized the truth of our country's history and the mass violence that has been committed against Black people, Indigenous people, and other people of color by white colonizers. It's why Columbus Day is still a federally recognized holiday, while Indigenous Peoples' Day is an official holiday in only six states. It's why Juneteenth goes largely unnoticed by anyone outside of the Black community. In fact, it was just recently that I learned that our country's true independence day is June 19, as it represents the emancipation of Black people who had been enslaved. It was just this year, after learning this, that our company finally recognized Juneteenth as a paid holiday for our staff. The consequences of our history, and our repression of its full truth, continue to play out in the present day in everything from how national holidays are and aren't commemorated to how the media portrays white mass murderers in comparison to a Black person who commits a crime of much lesser magnitude (or heck, even to a Black person who hasn't even committed a crime) to how the beauty industry lightens the skin tone of people of color in their advertisements and how the powers that be in Hollywood have long been casting white men to play characters that are not white.

But as I said, I am just beginning to learn this. I didn't have this knowledge and awareness when I was getting rejected for the traditionally white roles and taking the roles of characters who were not white. In fact, I can remember conversations in auditions or on sets with other actors where we would share our experiences, and a Black actor would share about how he was able to book more roles than his girlfriend because even though he knew she was a better actor, he was light-skinned and she had darker skin. In an attempt to connect, which in hindsight I can see how it would do the exact opposite, I would say something like, "Ah, I feel you, man, this town can't figure out my ethnicity and doesn't know where to put me." Now, while that may have been true, my experience is *very* different as a white man, and by overidentifying my experience with the experience of people of color, I am disregarding the structures and systems in place that benefit me and disadvantage people of color.

Fast-forward to ten years later, when I came back from my break from acting and one of the first auditions I got was for Rafael Solano on *Jane the Virgin.* I saw that the character was intended to be Latino, but I didn't give it any thought; after all, I was so used to auditioning for these roles that I often joked that I didn't know I was Latino until I moved to Hollywood. Looking back, it's not nearly as funny as I thought it was, mostly because after spending five years on a show surrounded by Latinx actors, I see the intense barriers that they have all had to overcome to get to where they are, and while, like them, I may have worked my ass off and sacrificed and dedicated years of my life before finally getting a break, I still had an unfair advantage no matter how you slice it. Now, unknown to me at the time, the CW had been looking for Rafael for months and had screen-tested a bunch of guys but hadn't found him, so they ended up opening the role to all ethnicities. That's why, when I showed up for the audition, it was filled with people of all ethnicities, including a few blond, blue-eyed white guys, so again, I didn't think anything of it. The rest is history, as I ended up getting the role, and like I've said, it was the role of a lifetime for me—and potentially one of the reasons you are even reading this book. The role gave me the chance to play an interesting man on a prime-time television show, to find a way to portray authentically the inner life of a confused and beaten-down masculine man who is forced to go on a journey to explore his identity and his masculinity. I didn't think twice, or even once, about if I had taken a role from a Latino actor because there were so many other folks auditioning. Rafael didn't have a backstory, and it eventually was written that he was Italian, but there was a lot of questioning and fair criticism of his character's racial and ethnic ambiguity, considering the Venezuelan roots of the original show.

With the privilege of hindsight and new (to me) information, I can absolutely see how I took a role from a Latino actor. I can see how the systems that are in place—the same ones that gave me the role of an Iraqi prince, the same ones that allowed me to be in a position to write this book and have this platform—play to my advantage. As I have begun to learn these nuances, I can feel my white privilege rearing its head and telling me "but I've worked hard" and "I've been rejected too" and "I deserve roles too." Again, recognizing my white privilege doesn't negate my efforts and worth, nor does it negate my struggle. Just because I am white it does not mean my life is easy and that everything is just given to me. White privilege is not a free pass by any means. At the same time, I can no longer ignore that, overarchingly, white people are not oppressed in the same way that Black people are, we are not judged, pulled over, enslaved, imprisoned, or killed in the same way. I don't have the additional hurdles that have been placed in the lanes of Black people, Indigenous people, and other people of color. And, like in the situation of getting the Iraqi prince role, it means that in some situations, not only do I not have the hurdle, but I also have a head start.

This matters in the entertainment industry because representation matters. It is important for everyone to see people who look like them in characters that resonate with them. It is imperative for people of color to see their stories, gifts, abilities—their humanity—represented in the characters of books, films, ads, careers, and families. In Jordan Flaherty's *No More Heroes,* he takes us back to 1979, when boxing legend Muhammad Ali, one of my personal heroes, invited film critic Roger Ebert to his home to watch

Sylvester Stallone's *Rocky II*. In the film, which I have to admit is also one of my all-time favorites, Stallone's white boxer beats Carl Weathers's Apollo Creed, who was widely thought to be based on Ali. During the commentary, as the credits rolled, Ali went on to say, "For the Black man to come out as superior would be against America's teachings. I have been so great in boxing that they had to create an image like Rocky, a white image on the screen to counteract my image in the ring. America has to have its white images, no matter where it gets them. Jesus, Wonder Woman, Tarzan, and Rocky." That hit me deeply. Of course I loved Rocky. How could I not? He was an Italian American underdog who went on to overcome all odds. He looked like me, and thus it reminded me that I could do it. But I didn't take into account that it wasn't just him that looked like me; the heroes of almost all the underdog stories I loved growing up also looked like me. If I were a young Black boy, what films or TV shows or stories had heroes who looked like me? I mean, as Ali said, even Jesus is white in America. How does that even happen if not by overt racism? Science and history tell us that Jesus was Middle Eastern and had a dark complexion, yet being Black in America today means praying to a white Jesus. Along similar lines, when diverse characters are represented in entertainment, too often the diversity is tokenized as directors and producers cast a Black person, Indigenous person, or other person of color into a role that supports the main white story line so that there is an appearance of diversity. If they aren't supporting the main white story line, the characters still tend to portray inaccurate stereotypes that are rooted in racism, like Latina women who are often cast as cleaning ladies or Native American men as warriors with tomahawks who live in tepees. And as we already know, often these roles can be given to white people to play, further erasing the cultures they are misrepresenting.

In my second film, *Clouds*, which is based on a true story about seventeen-year-old musician Zach Sobiech, who had osteosarcoma and who passed away just before his song "Clouds" hit number one on iTunes, I felt it was important, even though it was a true story, to surround the all-white main cast with people of color throughout the film. Over the course of the five years it took me to get the film made, Zach's family and I had become incredibly dear friends, and while there is nothing wrong with telling a story about a white family, we had to be intentional about making sure the supporting cast and extras were not reflective of just their homogenous community but of the world. I wanted Zach's story to touch people of all races, cultures, and religious backgrounds, but for that to happen, an audience needed to see themselves reflected in the story and on the screen. The simple reality is that Zach and his family are white, they live in a small town in Minnesota that is also arguably one of the whitest places in America, and unfortunately, there was simply no person of color in Zach's life who was integral in how his story played out. But I believe that just like one can take creative license in the retelling of a true story, we can and should do the same with casting Black people, Indigenous people, and other people of color in roles wherever possible, and if it requires it, even going out of our way to do so. We also created a character inspired by two people in his world and cast Lil Rel Howery, a Black actor and arguably one of the funniest people I have ever met. In creating this supporting role we tried to make sure that instead of simply supporting the main character, this person would actually influence and advise him and be one of the contributing voices to the overall hero's journey arc of the film. But even with that choice, I struggled because it didn't feel good enough. I am taking these learnings into my third film, where I am currently advocating and fighting for a diverse cast, starting with at minimum one of the two main leads.

I am learning that there is a distinct difference between appearing diverse and amplifying diversity. Too often, and I am guilty of this, we want to tokenize (which again objectifies and dehumanizes) people of color in an attempt to be seen as not a racist, when in reality the real work of anti-racism is amplifying the voices of Black people, Indigenous people, and other people of color. And while their voices are beginning to be amplified more, they are often being told in stories about race, but their stories are so much fuller than race, and the fullness of their humanity deserves to be normalized, represented, and amplified in media, in our daily lives, in history textbooks, and in Hollywood. There is so much more for me to learn and do as someone who is stepping into a position of power in this industry. I won't always do things perfectly, but I can't allow the fear of mistakes to keep me from growing and learning, as even that, I have learned, is a choice that stems from privilege. The choice to do nothing, while it may feel safer in the moment, is far more harmful to the plight of marginalized communities who are fighting to be seen, heard, and represented.

I Am Responsible for My Response

There is part of me that feels completely overwhelmed at the work that I need to do in myself and that our society needs to do collectively in regard to racial justice. There is part of me that feels ashamed that it has taken me as long as it has to intersect my journey with masculinity and male privilege to white privilege and racism. And then there is part of me that reminds myself that shame is an invitation to lean in, not to run away from or repress. Ijeoma Oluo says, "I know that the issue of racism and racial oppression seems huge—and it is huge. But it is not insurmountable."

I have a lot to learn and a lot to unlearn. I can apply some of the same principles, and use some of the same tools, that I have discovered in my journey to undefine my masculinity to help me on this intersection of the journey as well. I can get comfortable in the uncomfortable, listen more than I speak, pick up some damn books and educate myself, and get brutally honest with myself about what I don't know. And while I'm doing the personal work, I can also be doing the practical, systemic work of supporting businesses and projects of Black people, Indigenous people, and other people of color, and amplifying their voices in all contexts, from social media to donating to organizations that are doing anti-racism work, and voting for leaders who are actively working toward an equitable society.

We aren't taught about masculinity and the social context of it in the same way that I, as a white person, wasn't taught about whiteness and the social context of it. But while I may not have been taught it, I can still learn. I can learn so that I can teach our children, so that they grow up knowing what I didn't because growing up without having discussions about white privilege and racism is a privilege in and of itself.

When author and speaker Layla Saad was about seven years old, her mother talked with her about her lack of white privilege. In Saad's book *Me and White Supremacy*, she details what her mother told her. "She said to me, 'Because you are Black, because you are Muslim, and because you are a girl, you are going to have to work three times as hard as everyone else around you to get ahead. . . .' She was pointing out to me that in a racist and patriarchal society, I would be treated differently. I would not be rewarded the same for the same effort. And she wanted me to know that though this was not fair or right, it was (and still is), sadly, the way things were."

In the same way that Saad has those things working against her, I have my gender and skin color working for me. Since she has to work three times as hard to get ahead in the system, then as a white male from a middle-class family I have three times the responsibility to do the work to dismantle the system. And if I can use a little reverse psychology, I can reframe this as a challenge to myself and ask, am I going to be man enough to handle the responsibility. Am I going to be accountable enough to do the personal work? Am I going to have enough integrity to continue to recognize how my journey with masculinity intersects with my whiteness? Am I going to be brave enough to risk messing up as I continue to learn? Because that's the bad news: I am going to mess up. But I'd like to argue that it's also the good news too. There is no expectation of perfection, and we need to continue to normalize changing opinions with new information, to normalize not knowing it all and even not knowing enough to form an opinion in the first place.

My whiteness affords me the privilege of never being able to fully understand what it is like to have the experiences that people of color do, in the same way that my maleness affords me the privilege of never knowing what it's like to walk through this world as a woman, trans, or gender nonconforming person. But just because I cannot understand something does not mean that I cannot honor it. Just because I do not understand someone's experience does not mean I cannot honor them. As I do the meaningful work of honoring myself, my own humanity, I am also responsible to do the meaningful work to honor others in their full humanity.

And I am late—really fucking late—to be honoring the full humanity of Black people.

I am here now, committed to learning and relearning what it means to be anti-racist, to be a privileged white man in this society, and to be responsible for making our world a more just and equitable place.

CHAPTER SIX

SUCCESSFUL ENOUGH

The Career Ladder and the Power of Service

In my mind, the messages of success and the pressures of providing are tied so intricately with the messages of masculinity that when I start to bump against them, it feels nearly impossible to try to dissect and separate them. At the same time, because it's been so normalized, it can also feel like common sense. I can't imagine a world where men didn't feel the pressures to provide for their families and where, in turn, women weren't socialized to view men who aren't providers or who are unable to provide as weak. Even the men I know who are stay-at-home dads have admitted to wrestling with their worth as men and to being excluded from parenting groups because the groups are predominately run by and for women. This creates an even deeper sense of loneliness for these men, who are already in conflict with society's view on what a man and a father should be. For generations we have been in a place where success is the figurative indicator of the size of a man's penis, the visible scope of his worth as a man. The more successful a man becomes, the more of a man he becomes. Inversely, a lack of success or ability to provide can equate with a lack of manliness, or equally as bad, a lack of direction or purpose, mostly among other men. Even though I believe that most of us are not nearly as successful as we wish we were, I've begun to realize that the burden we are carrying isn't just about supporting our families. It is also about supporting the image, and oftentimes subconsciously comparing ourselves with other men in our circle, our community, or around the world. This comparison creates a sense of shame that often is not talked about, especially among men. It's this shame, exacerbated by the belief that we must figure it out ourselves and the emotional isolation that comes from being told we aren't allowed to feel, that can lead to depression and ultimately suicide.

Often, in Western contemporary culture, success is used synonymously with wealth, status, and/or fame. Americans tend to perceive that if a person has money and social status, they are successful. But because Americans don't have access to other people's bank accounts, we assess using variables like what kind of car a person drives, what size house they live in, the kind of clothes they wear, their job title, and their social media following, as measuring sticks to determine, in our minds, what kind of money and status they must have and therefore how successful they are.

Living in Los Angeles and knowing how expensive it is to survive here, as I drive down the 405 freeway I often find myself asking how the hell all these people are able to drive brand-new seventy- to one-hundred-thousand-dollar cars. It didn't take me long to realize that most of the people I know who have these nice cars (a) don't actually own them and (b) are still living in apartments with roommates and rents comparable to their car payment. It seems that in today's culture, appearing to have money may be even more important than having money. Fake it till you make it, right?

I plead guilty. I remember leasing my first BMW when I was twenty-four. I was running a start-up and felt like I should have a car that matched my job title. Unfortunately, I didn't really make enough to justify owning the car I wanted, so instead I just figured out a way to drive one even though I couldn't afford it. By the way, here is a weird idiosyncrasy I have: I am a Craigslist wizard. There are very few things I am boastful about in my life, but I have no problem crowning myself as the king of Craigslist deals. If there is a deal to be found, I will find it. Sometimes I even take fifteen minutes and search the platform as a weird sort of distraction/meditation for stuff my friends and family need. Cars, apartments, blenders, computers, couches, you name it . . . I've found it! So when it came time to lease a nice BMW, I found a guy who was trying to get out of his lease and who couldn't afford his payment anymore. A guy just like me who got a more expensive car than he could really afford and who realized too late that making a choice between a luxury-car payment and food in the fridge shouldn't be a thing. I took over his monthly payments without having a down payment, as essentially I was doing him a favor (even though we know it was really the other way around). The lease only had eleven months left, but I figured I would rather have almost a year of driving a nice car and projecting an aura of success than not. Plus, if I played my cards right, in my mind I figured a year was all I needed to become truly successful so that I could afford to buy or lease one from an actual dealer and not on Craigslist. Like many young guys my age, I became a rabbit chasing a carrot.

Let me be clear, this is a commentary on lifestyle choices and my particular behavior, not a judgment. I'm not saying there is anything inherently wrong with having a sick car or even one that's slightly more than you can afford. For some, a nice car makes them feel good, and that good feeling then transfers into all areas of their lives and allows them to be more successful. For some, the high payment makes them work harder, so they take it on as a goal; the image then becomes the man. I actually think that's what it has always done for me, but that was also a learned behavior my dad taught me growing up. But if I take my own advice and go down the path of whys, I quickly discover that while driving a nice car might make me feel good, it's also a Band-Aid that is temporarily covering up the larger problem: that my internal self-worth is still tied to the external. And when a material object is filling a void in me, then there is no material object, no high-paying job, no accolades that could ever bring me true happiness. Nice car equals perception of success. Perception of success equals I am worthy. If you take away the car in this formula, chances are that my worth plummets. That's how I know if something is unhealthy behavior for me, even if I try to convince myself otherwise. Subconsciously, or consciously, we compare these *perceptions* of success with the reality of our own, and we use the difference between the two as an indicator of worth. And for men, we use the difference as an indicator of our masculinity.

The Allure and Illusion of Success

Spend five minutes on social media or browsing through any male-focused magazine, and you will see that we are continuously fed with the idea that if we do A, B, and C, then X, Y, and Z automatically happen. It quenches our thirst for logic and control. It's one of the reasons I did not want to write a book that in any way offered that sort of advice, despite knowing that's often what sells in male-based consumer markets. As men we want to "think and grow rich," we want to become "highly successful and influential people," we want to be the best, most successful optimized versions of ourselves—and that's why we consume so much productivity porn and scavenge the world for tips and tricks and idolize men who have done that. But why? What does success really mean? Society tells us that if we make enough money and attain enough social status, we will feel more secure, more confident, more attractive, more capable of providing as a man and as a mate (which also means we will attract a more attractive mate). In other words, if we achieve enough success, we will be happier. But will we be?

What a strange and seductive equation: we want to be happy, and those who are happy seem to be successful, and so being successful is the key to happiness. Even though we've been singing "Money can't buy me love" for generations, it certainly seems that money can buy us love—and a lot of other things too. All around us—in social media, in advertising, and in our celebrity-obsessed culture—we are constantly bombarded with images of people who look happier than we are, who are "better-looking" and in "better shape" than we are, and who have all the "things" we want in life. And we are sold the idea that if we have them, then we will be just as happy as they are. Sure, the truth may be that happy people may in fact have some of those "things," but we end up believing on some weird level that the acquisition of a material object or thing or even a different body will actually make us happier. We reverse cause and effect.

Studies of the superrich actually find that the Beatles were right. The superrich are no happier than the rest of us; in fact, most of the superrich through the twentieth century were unhappy, treated their families terribly, and left a legacy of enormous wealth matched only by an enormous amount of petty squabbling among their heirs. We all suffer, at least a little bit, from "wealth addiction," the belief that our happiness rests solely on how much we have, and if only we had a little more, just a teensy tiny amount, we'd finally be happier. It's a fool's game—and we seem to be down to willingly play the fool with complete abandon.

Ready for a revelation? It turns out that what makes us happiest is not having what we want, but wanting what we have. But you would have had a hard time convincing me of that when I was a kid. The men in my life who were successful during my formative years were the men who seemingly had their shit together. They matched up with the men in commercials, magazines, and movies—you know, the ones with the nice car, the big house, and the beautiful woman; the ones who appeared to be confident and strong, who provided for their families, had agency over their life, power over their emotions, and control over their problems. The alphas. The successful men were looked up to, listened to, respected, and happy. Or at least they seemed to be.

My dad is, in many ways, one of those men to the rest of the world. I watched him intently, subconsciously feeding off of his unspoken messages and mannerisms. I studied his every move and memorized his physicality and how he interacted with the world and how he ran his business. My dad is an entrepreneur who helped revolutionize the film business by being at the forefront of the product-placement industry in the early 1980s. (Product placement is essentially when a brand pays to have its logo or product used in a film or TV show. It's hard to believe that industry is less than forty years old.) I watched as my dad became very successful, but even as I write that, it's crazy to think about how I, as a child, was already using our family's acquisition of things as an indicator of success, despite being raised in a family that often said, "If we are rich in love, then we are rich." Early on, we had all the toys—the nice house, the cool car, and the newest gadgets—and no matter who we were with or what we were doing, my dad, who is charismatic and has a heart of gold, was always the one to pick up the check at dinner or pay for friends and family to go on trips, even when he was in a financial slump and didn't have the money.

As any entrepreneur or businessperson knows, there are seasons of profit and seasons of loss; seasons where business is booming, and seasons where business is tanking. I can look back now and see that there were times when my dad's business dipped and finances took a hard hit, but I can also see how even during those times we still upheld the illusion of success. My dad loves nice things, and even in the minivan period of his life, he rocked the Chrysler Town and Country edition with leather bucket seats. Nice things make him feel good. I also can't remember a time when my dad ever let someone else pay for dinner—that was his thing, often taking the check from another man at the table or from a family member even when we were struggling financially. While I know part of it was that it was his way of being kind and generous, I also think it was far more layered than that. I know now that part of his self-worth was also tied to that image of being the generous one who can afford to foot the bill. So he did. Over the years, we maintained an impression of financial security that behind the scenes we didn't have. Even to this day when I bring it up, my dad tells me that we were doing pretty well back then and that things weren't that bad. It almost feels like if he admitted times were tough, it would mean he failed as a provider or he wasn't a good enough dad, which couldn't be further from the truth. Even so, I remember at a very young age having this feeling of *Wait a second, do we really have money? Or are we just pretending to have money?* I know now as a parent that our kids pick up on far more than we realize.

As I mentioned before, one of the standout moments in my preteen life was the abrupt family move from LA to southern Oregon. It was 1994, and LA had just had three years of back-to-back calamities: the beating of Rodney King, which led to the riots of 1992; the Malibu fires; and then the Northridge earthquake of 1994. For my mom, the earthquake was the straw that broke the camel's back. She wanted us out of the city, and what my mom wanted, my dad figured out how to make happen. I was ten at the time, and I didn't understand why we were moving except for the fact that we had to. Although I knew my mom wanted out of LA, my ten-year-old brain was confused because as a boy I also knew that work and making money were important and that moving would make it harder for my dad to stay successful. I have no doubts that my parents were experiencing some sort of financial instability at the time, as I recall arguments and conversations around money that I was too young to fully process. All in all, toward the end of my fourth-grade year, and with movers in front of us and a minivan loaded, we drove the twelve hours to our new home—a double-wide trailer in the middle of Applegate, Oregon, thirty minutes from the nearest town. To my new classmates I was seen as this "LA boy whose dad was in the movie business," which inevitably, even at that age, brought with it its own impression of success and wealth and in turn, bullying. But little did anyone know that despite the shiny presentation of my life and the name-brand clothes I wore, we weren't as different as we seemed. I didn't have a lot of friends, ironically because I was both overcompensating for my insecurities and was seen as this big-city, rich kid, which honestly couldn't have been further from the truth. If I had friends, they could've come over and seen that the double-wide trailer I went home to after school was far from the mansion that had been created in their minds. The aura of our success in the small town was so big that I even remember getting teased because my dad would show up at all my soccer games and film them, which would make kids on the team spread rumors that he was filming them to send to college scouts because we were rich. I was eleven.

It's those memories, colliding with the societal messages of success, that solidified for me that success wasn't actually about excelling in one thing or another. It wasn't about happiness or contentment. It was about what other people thought of you, how other people perceived your wealth, your social status, and your ability to provide for your family. So I was drawn to the happiness, the confidence, the security that seemed to be by-products of true material success, but when that success is based on illusion and the perception of others, it's a recipe for disaster. And for me, that disaster came fast on some of my first few steps of climbing the career ladder.

All Zeroed Out

When I was twenty-one years old, I got my first big paycheck as an actor after landing a role as a series regular on a beloved TV series called *Everwood*. I will never forget the moment, and the visceral feelings of pride and accomplishment that came with it, when I looked at my bank account and saw six digits for the first time. I was rich!! I had never in my life seen that kind of money, and it would quickly become apparent that I had never in my life seen a budget either. In fact, less than two years later I would have a similar unforgettable moment, except this time I would look at my bank account and again see a bunch of numbers, but this time with a minus sign next to them.

After getting those first consistent paychecks as a working actor, I felt like I could finally start to measure up, and the only way I knew how to do that was to prove that I had money. So I moved into a nice place with expensive rent, and I bought my dream truck, a fully refurbished '76 Bronco. That truck epitomized what was going on in my life at that time. It was the sexiest truck I had ever seen (and not coincidentally, was the same truck two guys to whom I often compared myself in high school drove), and it was probably the least practical truck I could have chosen to drive as a guy who knows nothing about trucks, especially in the stop-and-go traffic of LA. But it represented this ongoing relationship I have with success, with perception versus reality, and with my masculinity. The truck looked good, and it caught the attention of both girls and guys (which was arguably more important), but underneath its shiny exterior and its facade of success, the maintenance was a pain in the ass. If I were being honest with myself back then, I would have admitted that the few minutes a day I got to drive, it was way more work than it was worth.

At the same time *Everwood* was airing, I was doing interviews with magazines and walking an occasional red carpet wearing ridiculous clothes and evidently doing this sort of cool-guy, half-smile pose (I swear I can't find one full-on smiling picture of myself from that time in my life), which makes sense because underneath all of that, I was deteriorating under the pressure of maintaining the illusion of success. At one point shortly after I bought the truck, I was driving down Wilshire Boulevard near Beverly Hills in rush-hour traffic on a picture-perfect, sunny Southern California day. Now when I say this truck was beautiful, what I really mean was that it was sexy. Jet-black convertible with a roll cage, 350 horsepower, 33-inch wheels, and a 6-inch lift. Everywhere I would go, at stoplights and intersections, at clubs and restaurants, people would thumbs-up me, talk to me, and tell me how nice the truck was. It was by all definitions a head turner, and even while driving, guys would pull up next to me and ask me questions about it. If there was a truck that could put a Band-Aid on all my insecurities and make me feel like the king of the world, this was it. And when I was driving it, I was the king. That is, until it broke down. Right in the middle of an intersection in Beverly Hills. At fucking rush hour. Just imagine me at twenty-two, spiky hair, muscles coming out of my too-tight white V-neck T-shirt, ripped-up jeans, wearing some sort of weird necklace and way too many bracelets, trying to push a heavy-ass SUV out of the middle of an intersection while rich people are shopping on Rodeo Drive! Oh, and that was just the first of many times the truck broke down. The best was when it happened at another intersection—not because the engine had an issue, but because it ran out of gas. How embarrassing is that? Who knew the Bronco had *two* fuel tanks and a small switch that told you which one it was using. Turns out there was plenty of gas. All I had to do was switch to the other tank. It makes me wonder how many times as men the easy solution in life is right in front of us, but all this heavy armor we've put on blocks us from being able to see it.

Not all of my purchases were as foolish as that truck, because along with wanting to show off my success, I truly did have a desire to help others. The problem was the feeling I got helping others also became addictive as it started contributing to my own codependency and need to feel needed and powerful. So, following in my dad's footsteps, when I started making money, I started paying for friends' meals, taking the check from my buddies at lunches and dinners, taking the check from my dad at family dinners, paying family members' bills, buying people's flights, paying for outings with groups of people that I wanted to impress, and all the while secretly covering the cost of hospice for Nana Grace, the love of my life. That act of love for Nana and my concern for her were true indicators of who I really was underneath all the bullshit. Even without children of my own, I, at far too young, became the man who could provide in our family. At twenty-one, it was simultaneously an honor and a burden (which has never really gone away, even now, fifteen years later).

On the one hand, I wanted to prove to everyone, but especially my dad, that I could be that man, that I *was* that man. On the other hand, my bank account, along with my self-worth, which was intertwined with it, was dwindling as I continued to overextend myself financially. Then one day, not even ten months after receiving that first big paycheck, I found myself written off the show and unable to book another job. Shortly after, I sold my Bronco and used that money for a down payment on a cool little bungalow (because my girlfriend at the time really liked it and I just wanted to impress her). When I received the first mortgage statement, I realized that I had been a victim of what was called predatory lending and I was part of what eventually led to the collapse of the economy and the great recession. My Neg-Am (negative amortization) loan quickly jumped to a 10 percent interest rate, and everything the loan broker had told me ended up being a lie. I can't blame him, though. Here was a twenty-two-year-old kid who wanted to buy a property for all the wrong reasons and with no financial knowledge. He did what he was trained to do, and I fell for it.

Looking back, every single financial decision I have made from an emotional place, or from a place of lack, has come back to bite me in the ass. When I made decisions from a place of wanting to impress or to fill a void, I always lost. Being reactive for me always comes from a place of fear, and fear is often an indicator of scarcity. But I needed those experiences in my early twenties because I now know that when it comes to success and money in particular, I must make logical decisions from a place of love and abundance. Easy to say, hard to do.

Making decisions rooted in perpetuating the illusion of what I thought success looked like, how I thought success manifested itself in someone's life, was as sustainable as driving an off-road vehicle from the 1970s through the congested streets of one of the wealthiest towns in the country. And while I am still not one to offer financial advice, one thing I can tell you is that I ask for it all the time. Any pride I used to have went away along with the hundreds of thousands I burned through over the course of my twenties. So now, instead of appearing like I know it all, I surround myself with people who know far more than I do, and I humbly ask their opinions and advice. I've made enough mistakes to realize I'd rather have my masculinity and manhood questioned than to make another massive financial mistake because I was too proud to ask for help.

The Success of Connection

At twenty-five I experienced what I would later consider to be one of the most amazing times in my life. I hit rock bottom. I had just gotten dumped by my girlfriend, who had left me for a younger actor, I had to move out of the apartment we were renting together, I couldn't get an acting job to save my life, I was dropped by my acting manager because the same girlfriend broke ties with her and I was a casualty in the end of their relationship, and I had no money to put down for a first and last on my own place. In my heartbreak and desperation, I reached out to two of my best friends, Andy and Adam, and seeing that I was like a lost puppy with literally nowhere to go, they allowed me to move in with them. And by "move in" I mean sleep on their couch. By the way, Andy has since become a well-known musician—you know him as Andy Grammer. These guys, besides being my best friends, were literally my AAs.

At the time, I had what I perceived to be nothing to offer. I was jobless, heartbroken, crashing on their couch, not able to contribute financially to anything, and was experiencing a season of depression as a result. I mean, hell, I didn't want to be around me, so why would anyone else want to—especially other men? And yet those guys, who are two of my best friends to this day, genuinely, sincerely valued me. They saw value *in* me. They encouraged me to stay active, to get off my ass. They loved me and were there for me in such a profound way that it brought me back to life. They affirmed my desire to create and pushed me to take practical steps to hone my skills and bring my ideas to life. They prayed for me and with me, reminding me of a purpose for my life that goes far beyond people's perceptions of my life—far beyond my own perception of my life. The things I had been seeking in the perception of success, I began to find in the reality of relationships, connection, and community—something that I believe is far more important for men than we realize.

Recently, the findings of a groundbreaking study on success in America were released. The 2019 Success Index study consisted of several years of individual interviews and group surveys of more than five thousand people on the topic of success.

Do you want the bad news or the good news first?

Let's rip the Band-Aid off: bad news first.

The study found that 92 percent of respondents thought that others would define success as it relates to money, fame, and power. In other words, everyone is thinking that everyone else is judging each other's success based on financial wealth and social status. This takes me right back to that young man in me who felt the insatiable drive to succeed just to maintain the perception of success.

Okay, but here's the good news. While most everyone *thinks* that other people are basing success off of money and fame, only 10 percent of people surveyed are actually basing their own success on those same criteria. Instead, people are determining the success of their life based on the quality of their relationships, character, and community. Wait, what?!

This is the very reality that sets us free from the prison of perception! Without oversimplifying, so many of us are walking around chasing money, careers, and material success, thinking that those things equate to happiness, all the while actually believing that relationships are an indicator of a successful life. This is so damn liberating. That means that the very guys we think are judging us, and who very well may be, are actually judging their own success by the power of their relationships, as are we. It just goes to show that, once again, it's the messaging that needs to change, not just for men but for all of us. It's society, culture, and mainstream media that are feeding us expired messages that tell us if we make enough money, have enough things, get high enough on the career ladder, then we will be enough, then we will be fulfilled. But the reality is that we know that formula doesn't add up and equate to true happiness, and we are finally starting to push back to discover how to undefine what true success looks like in our individual lives.

The Success of Service

Over the past seventeen years, I have climbed the rungs of the career ladder, taking steps both up and down, and as I mentioned, sometimes falling off of it entirely and landing on my ass. At thirty-six I have directed commercials, music videos, nearly twenty short-form and full-length documentaries, and now two major studio feature films, with a third on the way. I've been the guy carrying a tray in the background of a scene and been the main love interest in a globally successful TV series. I have spoken on the TED stage, and I even host a show with the same title as this book that unpacks and explores masculinity. I have cofounded a production company, founded a nonprofit to help our unhoused neighbors in Los Angeles, and now co-own a film and television financing studio. For all intents and purposes, I have experienced the success that society tells us to chase, I've been mobbed by fans and chased down streets, and I even had to use an alias while traveling—all things I never in my wildest childhood dreams thought I would get to experience. Things I thought would make me feel whole, complete, and enough. They did not. I have climbed "high" on the career ladder, desperately seeking out the top, only to discover there is no top. It just keeps going, feeding off my ego's appetite to be better, to make more, buy more, and all of it feeds off my desire to be man enough.

It's fascinating, really. It feels like an addiction, a thirst that can never be fully quenched, while all around us we see images of people whose thirst does appear to be quenched. Is there something wrong with me? Why can't I be satisfied and happy with what I have? Is it because I don't have this, or that, or . . . more? This is exactly the hallucination that forms the foundation for the ideology of masculinity: it's never enough.

The only way for whatever we have to be enough is to change the story, change the criteria, change the definitions. As I began to look at my relationship with masculinity, I crashed headfirst into my relationship with success. If I wanted to be a man who was strong, confident, and secure, I needed to be successful by society's definition. But as I said, I found myself feeling those things most when I was doing very "unmanly" things. I didn't feel manly when I exerted power over someone on a lower rung of the ladder, and if I did, it was temporary, as soon that feeling of power was replaced with guilt and shame. I felt shame that I hurt someone else or made someone feel less than just to prop myself up. I am grateful for that feeling because it is thanks to my upbringing and trauma as a boy and now as a man that ironically give me the opportunity to have empathy in the first place. My pain has become the very thing that has created my ability to feel someone else's pain. My pain has given me the power of empathy. So no, making someone feel smaller didn't make me feel like a bigger man. Making a bigger paycheck didn't make me feel like a bigger man. And having women want to be with me didn't make me feel like a bigger man. Instead, I felt strong when I had seemingly nothing and still gave myself permission to dream bigger than my current circumstance. I felt confident when I spent time with people who didn't care what kind of car I drove. I felt valued when I was sitting and interviewing friends who had months left to live and was given the bounty of being the custodian of their stories. I felt scared but secure when friends and I would be real with each other about our struggles and encourage each other in our purpose. The same holds true now. I feel most like a man when I put my phone down (which at times can feel like a heavier weight to lift than my one-rep bench press max in college), show up for my family, get on the floor and play with kids, and make memories with my loved ones. I feel most like a man when my wife, kids, and friends know they are loved and that I have their backs. I feel most like a man when I can connect with another human being over our shared human experience, when I can be of service and give my time, presence, and resources to others. When I feel strong enough to cry in front of my wife or in the arms of one of my best friends, and when I show my kids, especially my son, that it's okay, Daddy cries too.

What if the career ladder was never intended to be a ladder? I mean, a ladder keeps going up and up and up. Eventually it's going to fall over—unless it leans on something. But what if it was never supposed to be propped up, inviting us to climb higher and higher, to exhaust ourselves in an attempt to reach its nonexistent peak? What if the measures of success aren't hierarchical in nature? What if the ladder was always meant to be turned on its side?

What if the career ladder was really a bridge?

Society's messages of success—of money and status—lead to nowhere; it's the career ladder with no top. But our personal definitions of success—of relationships, character, and community—serve as a bridge connecting us to what, and who, can truly bring the levels of fulfillment that we are seeking. I know I am an overly optimistic person, but I am not so idealistic to believe that we will ever attain a society where paying bills isn't important and where finances don't play a role. But maybe we can begin to ask ourselves where the practical needs of living and our own individual fulfillment collide. It's an answer that will look different for everyone. Some will find a way for their job to utilize their purpose, and they will feel fulfilled in it. Others will work a job that is, for lack of a better phrase, just a job, and then their time outside of work will be where they find their success. If we are lucky, maybe it's a little bit of both. Or maybe it's neither. The point is that true success will never be attained when it is dependent on the perception of others.

And just because I am on this journey doesn't mean that I still don't struggle with the temptation; the allure of money and fame and comfort is real. I constantly have to check myself and check in with my actions and intentions. I have to catch myself when I am making decisions from a place of fear or scarcity and check in with my family to see how they feel about the choices I am making. I have to come back to my whys and then come back to them again because maybe the first time around I wasn't fully honest with myself. None of this means I have it figured out, but it does mean that, at the bare minimum, I'm aware. I am conscious of the messages that I'm ingesting, I take account of how my actions and thoughts fall in line, or out of line, with my values, with my personal idea of success. Hell, even as I write this, I'm aware that I am not as present with my kids as I want to be. I can hear their beautiful, innocent laughs in the room next to me as Emily gets them ready for bed. And suddenly I find myself questioning if I'm doing this all wrong and if it's all for nothing. So I take that in, honor it, allow myself to feel it, and try to remember why I am writing and why I am making the sacrifice in the first place. I think that's all I can do. It's all any of us can do. I also stop typing and for ten minutes give them my undivided attention as we say prayers and give kisses good night. It's this practice of remembering, of coming back to what I've learned (and am still learning) about success and reminding myself over and over again that for me, success is not about acquiring material possessions and a societal platform, but rather it's about acquiring connections, relationships, meaning. It's about how well my children know me, and I them. How present a partner am I with my wife? How effectively do I serve my community? What do I do with my perceived success and fame? How do I show up for my friends in the biggest and smallest of ways? For me, living a truly successful life will mean that I have acquired far more moments and memories with those I love and have given far more than I have taken. If done right, at the end of my life that amount can never be zeroed out.

Here's a little hack that helps me the most when I am stuck or feeling lost. Imagine you are at the end of your life. You're ninety-five years old, and the doctors have told you that you have days left to live. Who do you want to be surrounded by? When you think back on the season, or the moment of life you are currently in, will you regret the choice you made or be grateful you made it? Did it serve you and the people you love? Did it lead to true happiness, or was it a decision made out of fear or out of pressure? If you feel you are working too much, do you think you will look back at your life and feel like you missed out because you spent your entire life working to pay the bills for your family yet missed out on your family? Are you close with your children and surrounded by their love? Did you say "I love you" enough? Did you show up for the little things? Did they have to compete for your attention with your phone, or were you able to put it down?

These are all just examples of things you can think about as you practice this rather morbid yet important exercise, because at the end of our lives . . . all that matters is not what we took, but what we gave. So let's let our true measure of success not be based on acquiring the things of this world, but in giving ourselves to improve this world.

CHAPTER SEVEN

SEXY ENOUGH

Intimacy, Insecurity, and the Paradox of Porn

Sex. Men want it. Men need it. Anytime. Anywhere.

There's a myth that we think about sex every seven seconds, that we crave it and we're always supposed to be ready for it. After all, we are the more sexual beings, animalistic in ways, always seeking a partner to engage with or to physically conquer. In fact, it's even been said that men give love to get sex, while women give sex to get love. Case in point, we men want, need, and crave sex. All. The. Time.

But do we really?

Confession: this is probably the hardest topic for me to talk about. It's riddled with the most insecurity. The most shame. And the largest confession. I went back and forth on how much I wanted to divulge and why. It gives me the most anxiety and fear of being judged and humiliated. It holds the most pain and remorse.

This topic deserves much more than a chapter to unpack and explore, but my hope is that by opening the door into a larger conversation around a sensitive and oftentimes taboo topic, a process of asking questions and ultimately healing can begin. Not everyone will relate to my story, as it's just that—my story. However, the themes remain the same in that so many of us are walking around with wounds and trauma that, although different in scope, are influencing our decisions, relationships, and overall sense of happiness.

Sex is the thing men are told we must be the most confident about. Yet for many men, this is not true. While the nuances within these messages vary based on factors such as age, race, religion, and culture, each of them effectively creates a box that I felt—and to a degree, still feel—I need to fit within if I want to be a "real man," because being a sexual man is synonymous with being a "real" one.

I always intended to wait until I was married to have sex (intercourse), as I wanted to save that for the person whom I was going to spend my life with. Regardless of whether I was having sex, I still felt the pressure to be ready and equipped to be a king in the bedroom, to have my penis look a certain way and be a certain size, and to somehow inherently know what to do in any situation that came my way, from a make-out session to intercourse, and everything between. When it comes to sex, there is no room for error. At least that's what they want you to believe. But how do we as preteen boys and eventually as men learn about sex and discover our individual sexuality in the first place? Is there some unwritten rule that because we are boys it's prebuilt into our DNA? Are we all supposed to be born with equal knowledge or confidence? One thing I know for sure is that healthy sexual education isn't coming from intimate conversations with our male friends, and it's definitely not coming from our parents or our teachers, especially if we come from conservative or religious households. So if it's not coming from anyone we know, then why the hell does everyone seem so confident and assured sexually? Is it all just talk? Does anyone really feel comfortable and confident in their sexuality as a teenager, or are we all just faking it and taking our cues from porn, movies, and folklore from others who are feigning confidence and experience? All in all, whatever culture we have created and the subsequent bullying and policing that follow have left so many of us men carrying a shame we don't even realize we are carrying half the time. We feel shame because we feel less than, because we feel like everyone else has it figured out, that the other guys just innately get it and in turn fit inside the box of what it means to be enough sexually. But who are we enough for?

I can't think of many places a boy can turn to, to debunk so many of the myths that are passed down generationally as they relate to what makes us man enough sexually. As puberty begins for some, it is delayed for others, and as testosterone fills our body many men just want some sort of affirmations that can reassure us of our "normalcy," or at least paint an accurate humane picture that all is well down south. Sure, there are countless websites and articles informing us of what the average size of an erect penis is, what erectile dysfunction or premature ejaculation is, and teaching us alternative ways we can pleasure our partners—but they exist mostly to sell us something or to "fix" whatever situation we are feeling insecure about. But what other options do we have? Can you imagine being a sixteen-year-old boy and asking one of your friends a super vulnerable question about something sexual you are unsure and insecure about? Hell, no. Because, as we know, even asking a question is a sign that you don't already know the answer, which makes you less of a man and vulnerable to an attack.

Here are a few facts about men, our penises, and sexual trauma.

- Most men believe their penis is smaller than average. In case you're curious, according to one study the average length of an erect penis is 5.16 inches—hardly the length we are led to believe that most men have.

- Mild and moderate erectile dysfunction affect approximately 10 percent of men for every decade of life (30 percent of men in their thirties, 50 percent of men in their fifties, etc.).
- One in five boys will be sexually abused before age ten (and that's based only on what's reported), and statistics show that the perpetrator is often someone they are close to (a family member or friend, a coach, a Boy Scout leader, a priest), which makes it that much more painful and confusing as they develop sexually in their teens. If you're a basketball player, that's at least one of the starting five, or two of the whole team (and, of course, one of them could be you too); if you're a football player, that could be almost ten of your teammates.

That last fact gets me, not just as a human and as a father, but because over the past few years I've learned that some of my closest male friends were molested as children and teenagers. This is not talked about nearly enough, especially as more and more class-action lawsuits are filed and survivors are coming forward against massive organizations like the Boy Scouts of America and the Catholic Church. How many men do we know in our personal lives who have been victims of molestation and sexual abuse yet never told a soul? How many of the men who die by suicide every year were molested as young boys and lived with that shame and trauma until one day they couldn't? How many men were once innocent children who were violated and, with no outlet for their pain and no one to help them, have grown up to repeat the cycle or attempt to numb their pain with substances, medication, or violence? Hurt people hurt people, yet when discussing the issues around masculinity, this topic is rarely tackled. Instead, the messaging we get as men is not about the issues we have around sex; it's how to get more of it, and when we do get it, how to make it great.

On a more elementary level, there's very little mainstream messaging telling us that daily stress, the pressure so many of us are under, and mental anxiety play direct roles in our physical body's readiness and willingness for sex. We're not told that libido varies as much as or more than penis size, that as many as one in five men report a low sex drive, that premature ejaculation, as well as delayed ejaculation, are usually experienced by every man at some point in his life, and that all of these are often directly related to our mental and emotional states. Frequently the only widespread messages that come close to mentioning any of these things are done via jokes and comedy bits about not being able to get hard or stay hard, or humiliating yet often funny stories from comics using vulnerability to elicit laughs. As I was preparing to write this book, the vast amount of research showed that if I wanted to truly reach men, then I needed to disguise all my truths in comedy so men would absorb it. But at some point we have to stop joking about the things that hurt us. It's a defense mechanism, and the more we laugh about it the less seriously we take it. And why do we laugh and gravitate toward comedians who poke fun at their issues and trauma? We laugh because we can relate, because we know there's truth in it, and it's much easier to laugh at someone else's struggle than to laugh at our own. As the adage goes, "Many a true word is spoken in jest." But mostly we laugh because, from a very young age, we have been taught that the only acceptable way to deal with our insecurities, and the insecurities of other guys, is to laugh at them.

So who do we turn to when we need to ask the real vulnerable questions about our sexual health? Google, of course, because everything on the internet must be true. A 2017 *Esquire* article noted that the ten most searched sex questions on Google were as follows:

1. Where is the G-spot?
2. How to make a woman orgasm
3. Can you get rid of herpes?
4. How to get rid of genital warts
5. What is the clap?
6. How to get a bigger penis manually
7. How to measure a penis
8. How old do you have to be to buy condoms?
9. How to insert a male organ into a female organ
10. How long does sex last?

How sad it is that we have built a culture where the only nonhumiliating way for us to ask questions about sex, the very thing that enables life to continue on this burning planet, is a search engine that will then use algorithms to sell us something to "fix" or reinforce the said insecurity we were googling in the first place!

So, like all the other messages in this book, I'm going to talk about it because I have to and because the current messages and the current model aren't working for me and haven't truly ever worked for me in becoming the man I want to be. And throughout this journey, I have found that it's also not working for most of us.

While I'm fortunate that I don't have the level of trauma that one in six boys has, I still carry my own set of baggage from experiences that began as innocent curiosities and then snowballed into shame and addiction. I carry the weight of years of downplaying the effects of what can only be described as "The Sexual Miseducation of Justin Baldoni."

There's lots of pain, shame, and confusion to be dredged up—and also, along the way, some moments of joy, curiosity, and, well, pleasure. Like virtually all the guys I've ever met, we never really got a straight talk about the whole truth, so we made stuff up, cobbled together from fragments of pop science, exaggeration, porn, Google, and an occasional random scientific fact. This homemade sex education was passed off as science, and the results tend to be very long-lasting. Even now we have scars. I know I do. So I carry that anxiety of inadequacy, of fearing I will never measure up to the men who fit inside the box, no matter how many times I tell myself that the box is bullshit, and no matter how many times my wife tells me I am more than enough. And I know I'm not the only one.

The Measure of a Man

I remember the first time that I ever felt like my penis was inadequate. I was eleven years old, and one of my friends—Jake, I'll call him—who was the same age as me, but more physically developed, told me that he had pubic hair and asked if I had any. I didn't. He pulled down his shorts and showed me his penis, and even though by this age I had already seen pornographic images of men's penises, mine hadn't developed yet and I had never seen the penis of someone I knew. Everything seems to register differently when it's your friend, especially in terms of comparison and competition. This was another kid, and yet his penis more closely resembled the images I had seen in magazines and on the internet than mine did, and I, with my prepubescent kid penis, was left feeling like I was somehow lacking, backward, abnormal.

I believe that many men have had close friendships in their preteen years that they don't talk about as adults or have subsequently blocked out of their memories. Those friendships are generally the friendships that allow "experimenting" to take place. Not necessarily on each other, although I have discovered that I know men—both gay and straight—who did experiment in that way when they were younger. I'm referring to experimenting as it relates to pushing the boundaries of our sexual curiosity as young boys and, as our bodies change, discovering why we have a penis in the first place.

My friend, actor and activist Matt McGorry, in a moment of pure courage and vulnerability, told us on an episode of *Man Enough* that he experimented with other boys who were his friends. He said, "It's so common and no one talks about it. It wasn't based on attraction per se, in the sense that I am straight and not sexually attracted to people of the same gender. But I did still experiment sexually with other boys as a part of exploring and learning about my own sexuality and body." For years Matt felt so much shame about it until he decided to share his experience and as a result found out how common it is for young boys to experiment in the same way. "If you keep it [shame] in the dark, it gets wet and moldy, and it festers. When you let it out there, not only are you giving other people the strength to live their truest lives, but you actually get people to see you authentically."

My friendship with Jake was an important one for me, even at age eleven. We were on the soccer team together. His father was a truck driver and therefore was never home. His mom worked full-time, and Jake had an older brother who was two years ahead of us. Because the boys were always left unsupervised, especially during the summer months, they would always have various porn magazines or videos as they discovered their father's "secret stash" in the garage. The older brother and his friends were constantly talking about sex, girls they were hooking up with or wanted to, and the size of their dicks. I even remember them pulling out their pubes and hazing us younger guys by trying to sneak them in our food or put them on someone's face when they were sleeping. It was a nightmare. As a young boy just learning about all of this, I often found myself wanting to fit in yet feeling super insecure that they would discover I hadn't even really started puberty yet.

One summer day, Jake and I went to the local lake for the afternoon with his older brother and their friends. The lake had two-seater paddleboats that you could rent, and my friend and I took one out. The plan was to go out in the paddleboat, bring his backpack, and once we were out in the middle to pull out his dad's porn magazines and look at them with no one else around. As we paddled out to the middle of the lake, I was really enjoying the fact that we were in this strange combination of a boat and a bicycle. I probably would have been content just paddling around all day.

I wish that was what happened. When we reached the center of the lake, far enough away from other paddleboats and swimmers, he grabbed one of the magazines. I thought we were just going to look at it and make jokes, but he pulled out his dick and said he was going to jack off and told me I could as well. Clearly he didn't know that I had never done it before and that I didn't know how, because of course I had never told him. He opened the magazine and started touching himself, which I would later learn was masturbating. I turned my back to him and pretended to do the same. A few minutes later he asked, "Did you finish yet?" and while I would later learn what that meant, I didn't know at the time because my body wasn't where his was. So there we were, in the middle of this lake, he with white stuff on him, me confused as fuck and needing a way out of the situation. I told him I needed to pee so I asked if we could paddle to the shore and I would "finish" there.

Once we made it to a nearby rock formation that was jutting out of the water, I stepped out, climbed behind it, and peed. When I got back into the boat, I made a joke about how good that felt, and we headed back to shore. I would have never guessed that such a perfect summer day would turn into a day I would remember for the rest of my life. The day started out as innocent fun but was now burned into my memory with feelings of shame and insecurity. My penis couldn't do what his did, it didn't look like his did, and I didn't know the things that he knew about it. Was there something wrong with me? Would I ever learn these things? Was I going to be behind forever?

I'd seen penises before. My dad and I had had a few conversations about the male body, and his own body wasn't something he ever hid or made me feel ashamed about, but something changed in my brain when I was being compared to another guy close to my age. I was used to Jake and his older brother joking about their penis size, sex, and girls, which made me uncomfortable, but now I know it was a discomfort with myself. I felt shame around feeling uncomfortable and out of place, I felt shame that I didn't have the penises they did, that I didn't know how to talk about girls in the way they did, and that I didn't know how to talk about my body in the way they did.

So how did I process this? Easy. I started acting. First, I found someone else like me. His name was Lee. Lee and I were the same age, but he hadn't yet been exposed to what I had and was even a little behind me in his physical development. As a kid who was now "experienced," as I knew all about porn, sex, and masturbation, I got the chance to make up for my insecurities by exposing his. By playing Jake, and getting Lee to play me, I perpetuated the same shame and cycle I had experienced in an effort to make myself feel better. Sound familiar? That's because it is. It's the same behavior repeating itself that we have seen in every other chapter, but this is the one I hold the most shame around.

I often think about Lee, the innocent kid I exposed to pornography before he was ready—hell, even before I was ready. I can only hope it didn't affect him in the way it affected me then and still affects me today. These preteen memories were foundational in beginning to form the idea that my manhood was measured by the size of my penis, which as an eleven-year-old, meant that I did not measure up.

By the way, have you ever thought about the word "manhood"? It's actually used to describe our dicks, while at the same time used in a general sense to describe an experience. The language and the problem are baked into each other before we even realize it. Now let's fast-forward a few years to the testosterone-filled locker rooms of middle school and high school, where this message would be cemented. The experience of being naked in a locker room with other guys, all with various body types and all in various stages of development, is a prime example of a shared experience that we never talk about. Sure, there are a few guys that are cool being naked, and yes, we are used to seeing pro athletes with ripped bodies walking around naked and in towels being interviewed, but for the most part, regardless of body type and penis size, the majority of us were terrified of being looked at, of being seen, measured up against, because the majority of us feel like we don't measure up.

Interestingly enough, more than fifty years before I was showering in the middle school locker room, brands such as Cannon Towels and Ivory Soap used pictures of naked male athletes or soldiers, all showering together, in their advertisements. These pictures embodied the epitome of American manliness, as well as the ideals of same gender bonding that defined that time period. In maybe one of the strangest advertisements of all time (and definitely one that would not fly today), Bradley Group Showers used posters of topless boys happily soaping up together as a way to market their water-saving column showers. And to top it off the poster read, "Why did we put our heads together? TO SAVE MONEY" ("heads," of course, in reference to all the shower heads being on one column . . . but one can only assume that the pun was intended).

Even though most of my generation never saw these ads and never experienced the mandatory showers after the PE class era, I can still look at those images, and despite the smiling faces on the models, be instantly taken back to the fake smiles and superficial craziness that played out in the boys' locker rooms of my youth. I can look back now and sense the collective nervousness and self-consciousness that comes along with undressing in front of each other, knowing we were exposing our bodies, and opening ourselves up to the policing and bullying of our own gender regardless of how much we did or didn't measure up. I mean, even today I can feel the nerves when my buddies and I go on trips and change in front of each other. Even in our thirties we are strangely resistant when we strip down on a guys' trip or in the gym. And let's be honest, most guys just feel more comfortable wrapping the towel around their waist and then taking off their underwear than they do just letting it all hang out there in the open. It doesn't mean we don't strip down in front of our friends, but it also doesn't mean we don't feel that resistance. Everyone is self-conscious in their own way, and while I am learning to have more compassion for myself, my heart breaks for the boys who were overweight and had to deal with a level of bullying I was exempt from. Those kids, along with the ones who were skinnier than I was, who had a disability, or who were super "late" bloomers all had it far worse than I ever did.

As you can see by Google's search queries, men tend to be both pretty obsessed and also fucked up about our dicks. That's as plain as I can say it. I mean, we even give names to our penises as if they were separate beings with personalities all their own. And while not all of us name our dicks, we've all heard the names: Willie, John Thomas, Peter. Or we name them after fast food: Whopper, Big

Mac. Or we think of them like machines: a tool, a rod, a hammer, a drill. And beyond being uncomfortable in public showers, some men experience what's called, affectionately, a "shy bladder" and can't pee in public urinals (but have no trouble in a private stall). Did you know that at one point all urinals were just trenches that we peed in without any issues? Then over time, many men became more self-conscious and found themselves unable to pee in front of other men, and thus urinals were invented. If we get performance anxiety just taking a leak, do we really think we don't have it in the bedroom?

At the most extreme end, there's even a surgical procedure for guys who think their penis is too small. Penile enhancement surgery involves lengthening the penis, and every year about fifteen thousand men undergo this expensive and often painful procedure. Now, I'm no mathematician, but I would wager that if fifteen thousand men actually end up going through with this procedure, then it's probably equal to about 1 percent of all the men who search it on Google. Why? Well, you might think it's just because men want to be better lovers, or to please women more. In some cases that may be true, but the data suggests that most of the men have what urological surgeons call "locker room syndrome"—the fear of being judged inadequate by other men.

But even the guy with the big dick, that kid who started puberty before everyone else and grew that hideous mustache in seventh grade, was at some point ridiculed because of it. Because that's the policing thing we do to each other as boys and as men when another man makes us feel less than. I can still almost feel the visceral reaction my body had to the moments that led up to group showers after practice. Strangely it feels strikingly similar to what my body experiences today before I force myself to sit in a cold plunge. The nervousness. The anticipation. The mental gymnastics I have to do just to get myself to get in the water knowing that no matter what I do it's going to suck. At least now I don't have to deal with homophobic jabs like "Balboner, don't drop the soap!" The sad part is that those teasing jabs, the eyeing, observing, the bullying, were such a normal part of being a guy that even if the jokes weren't targeted at me, I was so uncomfortable in my own skin I never did anything to stop it.

These types of memories were catalysts for the inferiority complex that plagued me through most of my adolescence and into my twenties, and one that I still battle with today. The irony is that if any of the guys from middle school or high school find themselves reading this book, I wouldn't be surprised if they called bullshit on these stories. There's a very good chance that the teen Justin they remember was one of the ones doing the teasing, making the other guys feel less than, and that reading this will feel in some way like revisionist history. But that's the point. How we feel and how we act as men oftentimes couldn't be more different. And these memories and the insecurity that they bred were some of many things that led me to feeling lonely. And unfortunately, when I felt lonely, I could always find a friend in pornography.

Curiosity, Shame, and Addiction

When I was young and we still lived in LA, every day on my walk home from school, my friends and I would pass newsstands on almost every corner of our route. They were filled with newspapers, tabloids, maps, magazines, candy, and cigarettes. Just to the side of the fitness, fashion, and news magazines sat *Playboy* and *Penthouse*, strategically placed to be mostly covered up. Depending on which stand it was, we were often able to reach the magazine and purposefully shift it in a way that would allow us to see what was being hidden. At that age it was more about the curiosity of what's being hidden from us than any sexual desire to see a naked body. I was always the kid who wanted to push boundaries, who wanted to know why something was off-limits, and to a child, when things are off-limits, they automatically have an implied moral value of being "bad" or "wrong." So even from those early experiences of innocently and curiously peeking at *Playboy* covers (and nervously giggling with the other boys when we saw boobs on the front of it), there was already a dueling sense of both excitement and shame that began being associated with seeing a woman's naked body.

We moved to Oregon at about the same time that dial-up internet was becoming more popular and accessible. If you're under twenty-five years old, it's nearly impossible to imagine that to get on the internet you had to wait at least two and a half minutes while your computer screeched with sounds like "urrrrr eeeeeeee urrrr nnnggggg eeeee cccrrrrrrrr ngg eeeee grrrr urrrrr ng ng ng." (If you don't know what I'm talking about, just google "AOL dial-up sounds.") Apparently I had a lot more patience then.

I was ten years old when I was first introduced to porn on the internet. I was spending the night at my friends' house, who like me came from a loving, religious family that had become close with mine. The boys, Scott and Elijah, who were twins, were my age and told me that once their parents fell asleep, they wanted to show me something. I remember waiting in eager anticipation for whatever was off-limits when the grown-ups were awake.

We sneaked out of their bedroom and into the living room, where they had a family computer. They turned it on, opened AOL, and shockingly the obnoxious sounds of dial-up didn't wake their parents. Once connected, they typed in a search and a modest sixty seconds later, the photo finally loaded. A full-length picture of a naked woman, laying in a provocative pose, long before I knew what the word "provocative" meant.

Since that night I have probably looked at hundreds of thousands of similar images, and as dial-up turned to blazing fast Wi-Fi, those images became videos, but still, that first one seemed to have cut the deepest impression in my brain as it opened a Pandora's box, so to speak. Each time I would stay over at their house, we would wait until their parents were asleep, sneak through the darkened hallway, and with only the light of the computer, porn would teach us about sex. Over the next year or so, I would sporadically look at porn when I was at friends' houses, but then my family got a computer at about the same time I started middle school and eventually puberty. Before I knew it, I was sneaking out of my room at night to log on to our computer. Later I even got a tiny TV with a VHS player for my room, where I would watch movies that had actresses I had huge crushes on (generally ones with large breasts) in scenes that showed their cleavage, or if I could get away with renting an R movie I'd watch sex scenes or topless scenes behind my closed door. (By the way, some of the weirdest moments of my life have happened in the past few years as my teenage fantasies have merged with my midthirties professional life, and some of these women have become friends.)

Anyway, I didn't know it then, but this continual, repetitive use of porn was forming pathways in my brain that paved the way for what would become an addiction of sorts and led to a distorted view of not only sex, but also of my body, how it performed, women's bodies, and how they performed. This all started as a curious and innocent exploration at a time when schools were teaching very brief, abstinence-based sex education—if they were teaching it at all—and parents didn't have the sex ed resources we have now. For me—and a lot of guys—pornography was "sex education."

There was literally nowhere else to turn to where it was safe to ask questions, and often it wasn't even about fantasies; it was about understanding what sex looked like and how to have it. As I got older, especially in high school, porn was something I could turn to, something I could "trust," when I needed an emotional escape. When I felt lonely, insecure, anxious, or even bored, I would turn to porn to masturbate until it became so habitual and reflexive that it was just something I did to help me fall asleep. Pornography was what I sought when I wanted an escape from my own feelings of inadequacy, and yet the very message that porn encoded into my brain as it was forming in those middle and high school years was that I was inadequate—inadequate because I didn't have enough of a penis, because penises were meant not just to give pleasure to women but to be so big it caused them pain. Inadequate because penises were meant to make women have multiple orgasms and scream in pleasure over and over again for hours at a time. And inadequate because I didn't have any actual experience with sex, because I wasn't getting with enough (or any) girls, because I obviously wasn't enough of a man.

The First Time

In high school, when other kids were starting to have sex, I wanted to abide by my spiritual beliefs, so I was not having sex. What's funny is that I say that now as if I actually had an opportunity to have sex. Those first few years, I did not. A lot of my friends were Christians who reiterated the mainstream message that sex is only intercourse, so anything else was fair game, even anal sex, which didn't make much sense to me.

I was probably sixteen or so the first time I was ever in a situation with a girl that was anything close to what the other guys were doing, or let's be honest, what they *claimed* they were doing, as we all know that most of the guy talk at that age was a combination of lying and exaggerating. I remember feeling scared and nervous that I was going to be judged by her, that I was going to finish way too soon, that I wasn't going to be enough. We were riding in the back seat of a car her friends were driving, and she was two years older than I was. I didn't even know why she liked me, but she was hot and older, and I wasn't about to mess that up. We were on our way back from some party, and I remember her asking me if I wanted her to go down on me, to which I whispered back to her, "Umm . . . now!? Our friends are like two feet away!" Combine all of that with the reality that while I had seen a lot of sexual images and videos of what that meant, the only physical relationship I had until then was with my own hand. So yeah, I was awkward and terrified and yet strangely also feeling like a badass because I knew if I let her do it, I would have a real story to be able to tell the other guys that could make me look like a legend.

So I did what I had learned to do when I felt insecure and nervous: I overcompensated. I played it cool and began playing a role, acting out what I had seen on TV and in porn, projecting confidence when really I felt wildly insecure. I said okay, she threw a sweatshirt over me, and started. Thirty seconds later, it was over. I was feeling like a king, and also like a little boy who was totally out of his comfort zone. I was ashamed at how quickly I had come and worried that she would think I was a loser because I was a younger guy who couldn't control himself. Yet when telling the story to my guy friends, you better believe that I absolutely left out the latter.

I continued playing that role for the rest of high school and into my first relationship in college, while simultaneously pushing down any confusion, anxiety, and insecurity that I had around sex. Now, while I could fill this book with stories about my confusing relationship with sex and my oftentimes embarrassing and painful experiences in high school, what I've learned unpacking this chapter is that I actually have a fair amount of undealt with trauma around sex that I honestly didn't even realize I had. As a man, I have been socialized to not give myself permission to feel any feelings or have emotions around sex. All I was allowed to feel around it was that I wanted it and that my social status and worth as a man depended in some part on whether I was having it.

Flash forward to freshman year of college. I was nineteen years old, and my girlfriend—let's call her Sofia—and I were in a committed, albeit dysfunctional, relationship. She knew what I believed in terms of not wanting to have intercourse, but during one instance when we were doing what is colloquially called "everything but," she put her hand around my penis and inserted it into her. I immediately pushed her aside and asked her what the hell she was doing. I hadn't said it was okay, we hadn't talked about being ready for it, and in fact we had previously talked about how I wasn't ready for it. There was a brief moment of pause before she brushed it aside while climbing back on top of me, saying, "Come on, we were basically doing it already. It's not a big deal."

To that extent she had a point. In the eyes of God, in my faith . . . it was sex, but that didn't necessarily make going further okay. Despite feeling an instant emotional reaction inside, the voice in my head quickly dismissed those emotions with the message and expectation that real men always want sex, and I should feel grateful that I'm even getting to finally have it. So I pushed that shit down too because who was I ever going to be able to talk to about it? I mean, what was I going to tell my college roommate, who was a typical bro? "Hey man, so my girlfriend put me inside of her and I wasn't ready to have sex and I'm feeling really weird about it." He, along with all the other guys on the track team and in the dorm, would have made fun of me for months! I couldn't talk to Sofia about it, as despite being someone I thought I was in love with, somehow she actually found a way to make me feel guilty and even more less than in that moment. She reminded me how patient she had been in waiting (six months), and again hit home the point that we had been so close anyway that it really wasn't a big deal. She essentially told me what other guys had been telling me my whole life, to "man up" and quit being a pussy. I'm also fairly certain she used those exact words to me at various points in the relationship. What I later learned was that she would use this moment and tactic to manipulate me in similar ways that men manipulate women into staying with them in abusive relationships. Once I gave her my virginity—willingly or unwillingly—Sofia knew I would do anything she wanted, that I was a sensitive guy, a pushover, and I'd stay with her even after I found out she had been cheating on me. Which I did. Twice.

This is an uncomfortable story for me to share, but I know I'm not alone, and that gives me some strength to share it. In 2017, NYU sociologist Jessie Ford published a study in which she interviewed college men on their experiences of unwanted sex. She saw that scholars were giving greater attention to sexual assault against women, while not taking into account that men were reporting unwanted sex as well, so she set out to research their experiences. During interviews men revealed that the gender expectations of how men were expected to act, what men were expected to want, and what actions might make them lose face with their partner or others were the reasons they had unwanted sex. One student said, "I think it's an undercurrent to my thought-making that guys are supposed to enjoy sexual intercourse under any circumstance." Another student echoed that there "is a social pressure that men like sex a lot and women can choose yes or no . . . so it makes you unmanly if you don't want to have sex."

In her book *Boys and Sex,* Peggy Orenstein details an interview with Dylan, a college sophomore, where he reveals that when he was fourteen years old, he attended his first high school party and a seventeen-year-old girl led him into a bedroom and performed oral sex on him when he didn't want her to. Another interviewee, Leo, a high school senior, shared that in one encounter a girl was performing oral sex on him when suddenly she straddled him and "put my dick inside her." Both Dylan and Leo experienced depression and aggression as a result of these encounters. Leo said, "I knew it was linked to what had happened, but I didn't want to admit it to myself."

Like these young men, as well as the ones in Ford's study, I wanted to fulfill gender expectations of manliness. I wanted to prove myself to be man enough, even when the cost was incredibly high—that cost being a connection to myself and my feelings. It was so profound that it shook my emerging sexuality, my faith, and whatever sense of self I had developed and left a scar, similar to the one I had after tearing my hamstring that would follow me through the remainder of my twenties and even into my thirties. The strangest part about it is that it wasn't until I wrote this book that I even realized I had an injury in the first place. I never told anyone that story until now. I think I had buried it so deep that I actually forgot it happened. I guess you can't heal something if you don't even know it's broken.

The Anxiety of Inadequacy

Over the remainder of my relationship with Sofia I became more insecure, and playing the role I had been playing in an attempt to prove my manhood was becoming more and more difficult as my insecurity seemed to get closer and closer to the surface, despite my best efforts to push it farther down. After the initial unwanted experience, we kept having sex, but I was not able to last for more than a minute or two every time, as deep down I was living in internal conflict. Regardless of what I said, how I acted, and even my own desire for it, I still wasn't emotionally ready to have sex, especially with her. I carried the crippling weight of anxiety that comes with learning about what sex should look like through the distorted lens of pornography, the countless memories of all the times I felt like I didn't measure up, and the subconscious trauma of my first time technically being unwanted. It all makes complete sense to me, now, that I had so much anxiety around it, constantly wondering what was going through her mind, while feeling unable to control how my body reacted, and internalizing her very open disappointment when I couldn't last longer.

All of this was compounded later when I found out she was cheating on me with other guys. The message was clear: I am not enough. My girlfriend isn't satisfied by me, and she had to find someone who was more of a man—someone with more experience who was able to give her everything I couldn't. And of course I told myself she needed to find someone with an even bigger penis, because that's the thing with these messages—it doesn't matter if you're average, above average, or even big. It doesn't even matter if your partner is actually happy and content with your size. It doesn't matter how much money you make, how broad your shoulders are, or what kind of car you drive. There is always a guy out there whose car is newer, whose shoulders are wider, whose bank account has one more zero . . . whose penis is bigger. There will always be someone to compare yourself to. And comparison always, always leads to suffering.

Flash forward two years. I've fallen into acting, I've had success, money, minor fame, and I'm in phenomenal shape. Oh, and I also drive a sick Bronco. Enter Jessica.

Jessica would be my girlfriend for four years and would eventually leave me for another man she met while making a low-budget horror movie. We were living together at the time, and while I intuitively knew that it was a terrible relationship, I wasn't strong enough to end it myself. So she did. I'll never forget lying in our bed, sobbing, holding our shared dog, and watching this guy tweet photos of them at church together, out with his family, going to dinners, etc., while we were technically still together. The wave of depression came like a tsunami as I buckled under the anxiety of inadequacy, inferiority, and insecurity. I was not enough.

Even when I instinctively knew it wasn't the right relationship for either of us, I wasn't man enough to leave. The end of that relationship was one of my first invitations to the slow, painful, empowering, courageous, fulfilling journey I am on now—a journey that will last the remainder of my life—one of discovering and embodying my genuine, authentic self, of trusting my intuition and knowing my worth, and of honoring both the good and the painful experiences in my life as they come, instead of burying them so deep that I forget they ever happened in the first place.

If I were going to make a film inspired by my life story, I could take the route where my heartbreak takes me on a spiritual journey into myself, I go through a ton of challenges, date a lot of people that I just don't click with, suffer some sort of terrible loss, and come out the other side to find my one true soul mate waiting for me, someone who was probably there and in front of me all along. I could make it sound that easy, or at least that attractive, but it would be inauthentic and bullshit, like so many of the films and messages depicting love and romance are. While yes, I did do a deep dive into my spirituality, and yes, I began to cultivate meaningful friendships with other guys as well as a meaningful relationship with myself, none of it was easy. In fact, it was far from it. And even when I eventually met the woman who would one day become my wife, our love story wasn't easy either. You will read more about that in the next chapter, but for now I want to share what did begin to happen when I was able to slowly start sharing my insecurities, when there was room in a partnership—and in my own perception of myself—to be more than *just* a sexual man, but also to be an emotional, intellectual, thinking, feeling, living human being. I want to share what happens when we as men begin to learn how to measure ourselves by more than the size of our penis and instead focus on the size of our heart.

The Dopamine Fix

Sex is complicated. It usually involves two people, both with their own histories, experiences, likes, dislikes, and emotional trauma, coming together to connect in an emotionally raw and vulnerable way. I believe sex should create connection and, in an ideal situation, even help facilitate, not just a physical experience, but an emotional and spiritual one as well. It can be healing, joyful, hilarious, serious, and even angry, but at the end of the day it's important to note that there are all kinds of sex, and even more kinds of reasons people have it, so no one will ever be able to sum up or capture the full experience of sex for us humans in a way that makes everyone happy. Sex is both a basic human need and for some a means to an end. It's why sex is perhaps one of the most personal and vulnerable experience one can have, and why it's been used for thousands of years as a way to manipulate, repress, and exploit entire groups of people. But while sex may be extremely complicated, it seems that porn is simple. At least, that's what we are told to think.

Porn offers every one of us a smorgasbord of options to fulfill fantasies, release stress, self-medicate, and orgasm without the use of another complicated human being. But is it actually good for us? This is a debate I have no interest in participating in because depending on how it's used, the poison can become the remedy, and vice versa. I'm not here to call out everyone who works in porn or say that sex workers should be judged or shamed. Everyone has their reasons and stories. I'm not calling out pornography as a whole, but I am calling out my own relationship with it. While there may be individuals who can have a healthy relationship to porn, a lot of people simply cannot. I am one of those people. That's why I can only speak from my own experience and the research that validates what I am struggling with, and the very personal opinion that it's not good for me or for the tens if not hundreds of millions of men who are secretly battling an unhealthy relationship and addiction to it. This addiction is contributing not only to a rise in depression but also to sexual dysfunction, loneliness, infidelity, sexual violence, abuse, and human trafficking. But there are other books that can tackle those facts. This one is personal.

In my experience, I don't know many people who truly like how they feel after they use mainstream porn. Sure, there's a high that comes from being sexually aroused and a release that comes from orgasm, but the feeling I'm talking about is what follows those things. It's the low that follows the high. And for the most part, I don't like how I feel when I am looking at porn, let alone after, so it makes my pull and craving to use it that much more confusing and also concerning to me.

I want to be clear that I am intentionally writing the word "use" when describing the watching of porn because I believe that is what I'm doing when I watch it. I am using. There is a reason that porn websites and pornographers are often using tricks and tactics, like random reward theory, to encourage people to stay on their websites for hours on end. And why they are creating websites and porn that appeal to younger and younger groups of men and boys. Exposure of porn to kids under thirteen went from 14 percent in 2008 to 49 percent in 2011, and those numbers are just rising the more we put cell phones and tablets in the hands of younger and younger kids. It's similar to what we've seen the tobacco industry do time and time again with cigarettes and now with vaping. The younger they can acquire a user, the more long-term gains they create. Like with tobacco, alcohol, drugs, gambling, and even video games, porn use triggers a dopamine hit in the brain and carves out neuropathways.

Here is my understanding of how it works. Basically, our brains are like supercomputers that are constantly processing information at light speed. The brain has this thing called a "reward center," which is a complex system that releases chemicals that make you feel good or bad depending on what you are experiencing. It's like giving you a cookie or a treat when you do something awesome. Dogs have them too, which is why the easiest way to train dogs is by giving them a treat when they do something good. It's how Pavlov trained his dogs to salivate when they hear a bell; it's called a "conditioned response." Our brains do this too, but for us the treat is a chemical called dopamine. Dopamine is awesome, as it gives you a quick high that makes you want to repeat whatever it is you are doing, just like a dog treat but for your brain. The real reason we have this is to help us survive and make positive choices, ideally so that the human race can continue on, which is why sex can be such a powerful trigger for our reward center in the brain.

A commonly used analogy to describe the relationship between dopamine and our neuropathways is a hiking trail in the woods. Before your brain rewards you for something, there is no trail there, so you can't hike. But once you give your brain a taste of something it likes, it rewards you with dopamine, which makes you want to experience said thing again. Dopamine is kind of like your brain using a machete to chop through the bush so you can experience more of the good things it likes. It wants to make it easier for you to experience pleasure, so it incentivizes you to keep hiking. But scientists have found that not all dopamine hits are the same in the reward centers of the brain: some rewards are bigger than others. What gives your brain one of the biggest dopamine hits? Sex.

So think of the hiking trail in the forest as being a neuropathway. Research has shown that the pathways we form around sex are less like someone clearing a path in the forest with a machete, and more like someone driving through the forest with a massive tractor knocking over everything in its path. To the brain, the larger the pathway, the more you want to walk down it and explore, and the harder it becomes to stop exploring. It's also why sexual trauma can be so debilitating and hard to overcome. For someone who experienced sexual trauma, violence, or abuse, that large hiking trail is now associated with pain, anger, and shame, and the larger the trail, the harder and more time it takes for nature to heal and grow back.

In an article titled "How Porn Affects the Brain Like a Drug," Nora Volkow, director of the National Institute on Drug Abuse, explains that "Dopamine cells stop firing after repeated consumption of a 'natural reward' (e.g. food or sex), but addictive drugs go right on increasing dopamine levels without giving the brain a break. The more hits drug users take, the more dopamine floods their brain, and the stronger their urges are to keep using. That's why drug addicts find it so hard to stop once they take the first hit. One hit may turn into many hits, or even a lost weekend."

So basically, the more you watch porn, the more you take that bulldozer through the neuropathways in your brain and flood your brain with dopamine, and therefore the harder it becomes to stop. But this is where it gets really tricky. The more dopamine your brain produces, the more it gets used to it, needs it, and craves it. It becomes a new normal for the brain, and men who suffer from an addiction to porn find that they can't feel normal anymore without that dopamine hit, so they keep using and watching more and more. It's at this point that men report sex becomes less pleasurable, friendships and relationships are less fulfilling, and they develop an overall sense of apathy, and for many, this is when depression really sets in. It's also where all these cravings and urges come into play, and why in our hypersexualized society, everything can become a trigger for brains that are addicted to porn.

So where do I fit into all this? Since being introduced to porn at ten years old, and with my fairly constant use of it during middle school and high school, which were also some of the loneliest and painful times of my life, I trained my brain to associate sexual images with feelings of loneliness, sadness, anger, pain, and anxiety. As my body changed and developed, my use of porn, while it may have started out innocently and with curiosity, became something I used more to escape reality. In doing so, my brain formed new pathways that connected those dopamine hits with all those feelings of being less than. As I got older, I noticed that my porn consumption either shrank or grew based on how I was feeling. There were seasons I would have no desire to look at porn and even found myself disgusted by it, and seasons where I would look at it every day. When I was in an extreme season emotionally, it seemed like my porn use followed suit. In essence, porn became my medication.

As a single guy in my twenties, I'd use it to curb my sexual appetite to help make sure I didn't sleep with any of the girls I was dating. Like Andy Grammer sings in his song "Holding Out," I often found myself (as hypocritical as it may be) using "a little bit of prayer and a little bit of porn" to keep myself from having sex.

Throughout my twenties I found myself in what I've come to

see as an internal war. I felt like there was a war between good and evil going on inside me, all taking place under the surface where no one could ever see it, where, filled with shame and confusion, I would put on my armor, go into battle, and find myself losing. I desperately wanted to stop looking at porn, but because I wasn't using it every day, or even every week, and what I was consuming wasn't progressing into more intense or extreme things, I found myself justifying my intake and attributing it to being a normal guy in his twenties with a strong sex drive. At one point after a breakup, I made the decision to stop looking at porn, as I just didn't like the way I felt and I wanted to win that internal battle I was having.

This would continue even after I met Emily and fell madly in love. It also didn't matter how spiritually deepened I got, how many prayers I said, or what acts of service I performed. It didn't matter what I learned about porn and how destructive it is and can be—my pull to it wasn't rational. So instead of fighting my pull to it, I started trying to understand it. And this is where I am today.

If you are a man reading this, I want you to know that if you struggle with porn, you are not alone. In fact, many researchers believe that because porn use and addiction are so secretive and many men are too ashamed to talk about it with anyone (including their own therapists), the numbers are far larger than we realize. I can't even tell you how many messages I've received privately from boys and men on social media asking me for help and for resources. Even though I can't read all of my DMs, when I do come across someone who shares this, I am in awe of the bravery and trust they put in me to reach out and ask for help. I've also received quite a number of messages from women asking for advice or help for the men in their lives who struggle with porn. All that to say, to the boys and men out there, not only are you not alone, I would argue that you are in the majority. Let that sink in. You don't have to suffer in silence anymore. You don't have to hate yourself or think you have something wrong with you because you don't know how to stop. You don't have to believe that God hates you or that you're a bad Christian, Muslim, Jew, Bahá'í, monk, etc. You are a human who was exposed to something his brain doesn't know how to handle because our brains were not built or wired for instant, on-demand, twenty-four-hour-a-day access to dopamine hits. This is a new problem created by the advent of technology that we need new solutions to fix. We do not have to struggle alone. We are in this together, and I believe there is hope.

If you are a woman reading this who has ever struggled with self-worth because you have a man in your life who struggled with porn, if you've ever had a man choose porn over you, or continue using it while in a relationship with you, I want you to know that you are not broken or less than. And while I can imagine it would be hard not to compare yourself to whatever images he is consuming, I want to offer that there is a high chance that your partner, if he uses porn and if he is anything like me, is not using it because he is unsatisfied in your relationship. He is not using it because you are not enough or because he doesn't find you beautiful or sexy. He is not using it because he feels unfulfilled in his sexual desires. I say this because Emily is everything I have ever wanted in a partner, yet that didn't stop my cravings for porn, especially during emotional or turbulent times of my life. While every case and every man is different, chances are he, like me, is using it because his brain tells him he needs to in order to feel safe, seen, wanted, or even loved. Long before a partner ever existed in his life, he had a relationship to porn and sex, and those pathways were formed.

In an interview with Truthaboutporn.org, John D. Foubert, PhD, mentioned a recent study that scanned men's brains as they watched porn to see what parts of the brain lit up as they watched.

As it turns out, the part of the brain that lights up when watching porn is the part of the brain that deals with objects . . . not people. So it's not about your love and relationship; it's about what porn is doing in our brains. I would be remiss not to mention that it is this aspect of porn—the very fact that the images register in the object part of our brain—that dehumanizes people, creating a solid link between porn and rape culture. The more we dehumanize someone or an entire gender, the more possible it is to commit violence against them.

The key now, for both men and women—for both the person struggling with porn and the person who is also impacted by that struggle—is being able to talk openly about it without judgment, recognize there is an issue, and start to do the hard and heart work to reverse some of those deep emotional connections to porn and the shame that is associated with it, and to heal what is underneath it all. To be clear, I am not claiming that all porn is bad or that all people can or even should work through their partner's porn addiction, as every situation is different and some are far worse than others. My hope is that this can become something we learn about as a society and that couples talk about openly, asking each other direct questions about insecurities, secret struggles, and addictions. But no matter what your gender is, if you or your partner is struggling with using porn, I hope that this information and perspective can help begin to create a safe space for loving, and above all radically honest, conversations about how you feel, the impact porn may be having on your relationship, and what boundaries are important to you. This is where love, communication, patience, self-acceptance, and kindness come in.

For me, this is also where therapy comes in. As I keep learning about and struggling with my use of porn, it's helpful for me to have the resource and accountability of a therapist. Every man who has shared his story with me has a different relationship to porn and to the damage it does in his life. Some men will need to go to Sex Addicts Anonymous (SAA) meetings in addition to therapy. Some may have to check themselves into rehab, and some may be able to use online tools like JoinFortify.com to beat it. The key is just being willing to recognize that you have an issue in the first place and that you need assistance. Regardless of the issue, I don't believe there is anything more "masculine" than a man who is willing to stare his shame in the face and seek out and receive help.

The Arousal of Intimacy

Prior to meeting Emily (the second time), and after a yearlong spiritual journey that led me back to my faith, I was several months into an intentional weekly gathering that my friends and I called the Spiritual Talk. We would get together every Sunday evening to talk about real stuff—how we were hurting, what was happening in our lives, how we were grieving and finding joy, and how we could serve. The evening was rooted in the Bahá'í teachings and the idea that no matter who you were or what you believed in, you were welcome and your thoughts and feelings mattered. We wanted, and craved, the substance that we felt was missing from our relationships in the Hollywood community and in the world. Because we were so vulnerable about our struggles and our stories, these gatherings were profound in opening me up to doing the work to know my conditioning, while introducing me to the power of relational connection and intimacy that was not in a sexual setting. Before I knew how to name all of that, the one thing I knew was that those gatherings made me feel like I was not alone. That is the power of faith and human connection. And that for me is foundational to healing and growing, and it's a big part of why this book is so important to me. I want people to know, especially men, that they are not alone.

So how do we as men come to have deep and fulfilling relationships when we have been conditioned to cut ourselves off from our hearts and told that we are only capable of thinking with one head at a time? The answer will be different for all of us, but I continue to offer my story as an invitation to your own. The first thing, and the thing I come back to over and over again, is that realization that we are not alone in our thoughts, experiences, conditioning, or shame. We were not the only middle-school boy who felt insecure in his prepubescent body. We are not the only man who feels inadequate in his postpubescent body. We are not the only one to get our sex education from pornography, and then to take that education and use it to objectify and hurt others, ourselves included.

I truly believe that if we were to become aware of our sexual stories, and the experiences and messages that shaped those stories, if we had the tools to be honest with ourselves, to know our conditioning and our wounds, we would find that we all carry our baggage into bed with us.

With the help of our weekly gatherings, I began to cultivate honesty and gut-level transparency in my personal friendships, and as a result I began to experience the freedom that comes with vulnerability and intimacy. I began to learn how to lean into my shame, knowing that it would be lessened if I broke my silence around it. I began to learn practices of communication, accountability, listening, and openness. By learning how to keep it real in these friendships and experiencing the power of connection that comes with it, I gained valuable experience for when I would be in a relationship again. In fact, I even remember feeling a bit of naive pride around it, thinking that I was much more ready for a relationship than I had ever been. While I was aware enough to know that there would always be room to grow, I still felt like I had accomplished significant growth and could now be freed from the pain I experienced in my childhood and from my adolescent insecurities. (I can hear you laughing . . .)

Of course, when I met Emily and fell madly in love with her, the freedom I thought I found was in fact not final at all, as it all came roaring back, but this time it might as well have been a billboard with neon lights demanding me to keep looking at it, keep working at it, keep acknowledging it. Its lights were so bright that it didn't take long at all for Emily to notice them. In fact, the first time we were beginning to be physically intimate, she suddenly stopped and before I could even pause to ask her what she was feeling, my mind was inundated with all of its old messaging. My brain hit "play" on the old loop: She didn't like what she saw or felt. I'm not enough. She needs someone bigger, more successful, more confident. She needs someone smarter, sexier. She needs someone who is more of a man than I am. It's over.

The truth was, it was none of those things. Emily stopped because she knew my heart and my beliefs. She was honoring me, and it was completely opposite to what I had experienced with my first girlfriend. We had previously had intimate conversations about sex and faith, and while she didn't fully understand it, she knew I wanted to try to wait to have intercourse until marriage. Emily stopped because she respected me, my body, and my heart—the story is of course slightly more complex, but that is maybe for a future book or for Emily to share one day if she chooses. Until that moment, these things had been the epicenter of my insecurity, and in previous relationships they were used as weapons against me, my masculinity, and ultimately my value as a partner and as a man. But Emily used them as a means to get to know me more, to respect me, and ultimately to love me for the man I was and aspired to be. For the man I am.

Her love helped create an environment where I felt safer to expose parts of myself that I had previously pushed down in an attempt to keep them hidden. It took four years of marriage before I felt comfortable enough to tell Emily that when I was stressed, insecure, or down, I at times sought refuge in porn and that I was ashamed I had never talked to her about it. I told her I felt it was preventing me, and, in turn, us, from taking our intimacy to the next level and going even deeper, and that I badly wanted to show up as my full, open, broken, and vulnerable self. I was really worried about how she would respond and worried that she would internalize my struggle as a message about her worth—that she would feel not good enough, or less than, because when I felt the worst about myself, and strangely even the best, I felt a pull to look at porn. I was so nervous about how she would react, knowing that so much of my work in the world was as an ally to women. I mean, how can I accept this label as a feminist when I secretly struggle with a compulsory relationship to something that I believe hurts and exploits so many women?

But by this point in our relationship, I also knew that we had years of practicing open and honest communication, not to mention countless proactive individual and couples' therapy sessions. When I finally sat down with her and told her I had something I needed to share that had been weighing on my heart, she listened intensely and responded with how deeply she loved me, how difficult it must have been for me to talk to her about it, and how proud she was of me for sharing it with her. And let me tell you, nothing is sexier than having a partner who will look at you and hold you when you are your most vulnerable, hurting, human self, when you feel the most worthless and less than. This is why Emily and I often say to each other, "I love the shit out of you." Because that's what love is. And if we allow it to, that's what love does.

That is the arousal of intimacy, of partnership, vulnerability, and connection. And in case you might be thinking that I am the only man who desires emotional intimacy as well as physical intimacy, let me assure you that so do the thousands of men I've spoken to across the country and world. Even high-school boys—the ones who are quick to be misrepresented as walking erections—desire emotional intimacy. They reported to Andrew Smiler, a psychologist who specializes in adolescent male behavior, that their greatest motivator for pursuing sex was not physical but emotional. I had always feared that if I softened my armor—the hard exterior of protection I wore across my chest—I would also be softening my penis, my performance, my manhood. But I can firmly say (pun intended) that almost nine years into our relationship, Emily and I are communicating more effectively and openly, and as a direct result we are closer than we have ever been, both physically and emotionally. But that doesn't mean it's been easy.

The Inclusivity of Connection

It is from that place of intimacy that I have come to discover the inclusivity of connection and how liberating and exciting it is to expand our society's narrow definition of sex at the same time that I am working to expand the narrow definition of masculinity. When we see sex as merely intercourse, we are discounting the myriad other reasons that intercourse might not be an option (think medical conditions, disabilities, birth, not to mention the very normal seasons of life that cause fluctuations in how we are able to be physically intimate with each other).

In addition to making the conversations more inclusive, I've found that it's more fulfilling when I expand the definition of sex to make the goal connection, rather than intercourse and orgasm.

In fact, I use the same principle as the why ladder that I mentioned earlier in the book to help me continually reframe my thought patterns around sex, but instead of asking myself why, I ask myself, *How can I connect with my wife today?* It doesn't mean it always works, or that I will remember to do it, and it doesn't mean she will always notice, but the question remains important.

Connection is so important because so much of my sexual identity formed around disconnection. I've used pornography to disconnect from whatever pain or uncomfortable feeling I was feeling, and I've used orgasming to temporarily relieve the building pressure of everything I was holding down below the surface. So this question is also an invitation to pause and be intentional in the ways that we weave intimacy throughout our day. Maybe it's holding her hand, having her coffee ready for her when she gets up, making eye contact with her across the living room that's covered in our children's toys, telling her I see her and naming something I appreciate about who she is and all she does, hugging her for a few seconds longer, brushing my hand against her butt to let her know I think she is sexy, a little kiss on the back of her neck when she doesn't expect it, or a stroke of her arm when we pass each other in the middle of the night as we tag-team trying to get our kids back to sleep. These gestures are all part of sex because they are all part of connection, and when the focus is on connection, there is room for more than just our erect penises. There's also room for our full bodies; our full hearts; our full manhood; but more importantly, there's room for our full humanity.

CHAPTER EIGHT

LOVED ENOUGH

The Real Work of Relationships

Love.

Where do we begin?

What are men taught about love growing up?

Where do we learn how to love? From our parents? From our friends? From the movies?

Do we fall into it, or do we choose it?

When it comes to love, I am one of the lucky ones. My grandparents on both sides were married for more than fifty years. My parents have been married for thirty-six. And these aren't just marriage partners who stay married for the sake of it. These are overall happy, communicative, and healthy examples of marriage. How do I know that? Because I also got to see, especially when it came to my parents, how hard and at times uncomfortable a long-lasting and loving marriage can be. It was through witnessing the seasons of love, the ups and downs, the struggles and the communication failures of my parents, combined with the *Notebook*-esque romance of my grandparents, that I learned how to love. To this day, I've never seen a man so deeply committed, so madly in love as when my grandpa Danny was with my grandma Blanche. Even in death, she held on just long enough for me to literally carry him to her bedside, so he could sit and read prayers for her soul from the Torah, hold her hand, and tell her how much he loved her. I'll never forget leaving that hospital with him and seeing a massive double rainbow right over the home they lived in for fifty years. Before my mom even called me, I knew she had passed the second he left that room. She had waited for him so he could say goodbye, and then she said goodbye with that rainbow. He never stopped loving her, and more importantly, he never stopped respecting her. I think that's what made his passing a little easier for me; he kept saying that he wanted to go home, and that his beautiful bride, my grandma Blanche, was his home.

Unfortunately, with the third highest divorce rate in the world, this simply isn't the case for many Americans. That's why, instead of writing about what love looks like for most men, I can only write about what it looks like for me in hopes that a glimpse into my relationship and marriage with my wife can prove helpful when combined with what I learned from my family and what the world was socializing me to believe love is. So regardless of your gender or sexual orientation, I hope that we can unpack love and, as Rumi says, "all the barriers within yourself that you have built against it."

When you have a concept as massive and universal as love, it really helps me to break it down and think of it in smaller ways. In my faith, we are told that for every spiritual law God gave us, there is a physical counterpart to help us make sense of it. So when it comes to love, which every religion in the history of the world has built their faith on and which is so important in our scripture that we're told that "love revealeth with unfailing and limitless power the mysteries latent in the universe," it's helpful to think of it in tangible, everyday language because we can't just walk around with logos on our clothes telling us to love without actually understanding what it means.

Let me simplify. While I believe there are infinite ways and kinds of love, this chapter is about love as it relates to romantic relationships and, even more specifically, in a marriage. I like to think of a marriage as a house (but you can also apply this to any relationship). And like any house, it has to be built brick by brick, beam by beam. But a house can't be built unless you build the foundation first. A house without a foundation isn't a house. It just looks like a house. And the first storm or gust of wind will blow it over like the sets that we work on in film and TV. Production departments are incredible and can build full-scale homes in days that look just as good as homes that can take years. But when you go inside them, and lean on the wrong wall, you discover that it can't hold your weight because it was only designed to look good on camera. TV and film sets are all about appearance, not functionality. The houses on sets have no foundation, which takes contractors in the real-world weeks, and sometimes months, to lay. They have no internal wiring, and nothing is built to code. The walls are movable so you can get a camera in and out in different positions, and nothing is built to withstand the test of time. They are built to be used, then taken down as quickly as possible, and then reused for different sets or productions.

This is how I think of the current dating landscape. With swipe culture and our collective "on demand" and "I want the shortcut to happiness" attitudes, we are literally building millions of relationships that have no foundation. We are starting with what looks good on the outside, and as long as that meets our needs, we are using these structures to build the foundation. Now again, this is an overgeneralization, as amazing things have come from on-demand dating and apps such as Tinder and Bumble. In fact, my sister-in-law found her husband on Tinder after a painful divorce and they couldn't be happier. But they are also two adults in their forties, both had gone through difficult separations, and both knew exactly what they were looking for and put in the work and made an effort to build a solid foundation. There are always exceptions to the rule, as every person on this planet deserves love, but one of the effects swipe culture has on love is that we are being trained, and oftentimes encouraged, to build multiple houses at once. As it stands now, it's currently easier and more widely accepted to be emotionally and physically intimate with multiple people at the same time. We have to understand that each of these movements or institutions comes with its own set of societal messages and pressures, and ultimately we need to decide what is best for us. But my personal belief is that we each have only so much energy and time in a given day, and what we choose to water, grows. What we choose to build, gets built. Ever hired a contractor who is building four or five different houses? I have. It sucks because their attention to yours slowly starts to diminish with every other home that they are building. It always starts out great. The employees show up on time and crush it for a few weeks, and then little by little, as they add other houses to the schedule, it becomes increasingly harder to get them to show up on time or sometimes even at all. The quality goes down, and it often takes twice as long and ends up costing twice as much. But again, at the end of the day, we all have different homes, and the way we choose to build them is up to us. I just want to see a lot more houses standing strong and able to weather storms in the future.

I have a radical idea. What if instead of building relationships from the outside in, we built them from the inside out and spent our time "investigating character"—while really getting to know what a person is made of?

There aren't a lot of conversations happening, at least for men, that help us learn about the reality of what investigating someone's character even looks like. From the time we are born, the old Disney films, and pretty much every male-centric box-office hit ever, have reinforced the idea that to find love as men, we must first save a damsel in distress. By contrast, at least until recently, most rom-com films teach women that they actually have to heal and "save" their deviant but adorable man so that he can finally, fully, become himself. It's a recipe for disaster: two saviors looking for someone to save without ever knowing themselves. This is problematic for a lot of reasons, and while there have been countless books and talks about how this hurts women, I think it's also important to point out how this hurts men.

There are libraries filled with research on the different ways in which women and men experience and understand love. But few of them really help us understand what love is. It seems like we understand love only through the media images of it that we've consumed. And we define love using the terms set out by and for women. It's almost as if "love" itself is feminine. And we know that there are absolutely "his" and "her" ways of loving.

In the 1980s, sociologist Cathy Greenblat asked college women and men who were involved in serious relationships (but not married), "How do you know you love this person?" and "How do you know that this person loves you?" Prior to marriage, the answers differed. The men "knew" they loved their girlfriends because they were willing to do so much for them, willing to sacrifice, willing to go out of their way to make her happy, willing, as one guy said, "to drop everything in the middle of the night and drive three hours in a snowstorm because she was afraid of a spider in the bathroom." And women "knew" that they loved their boyfriends because they "wanted to take care" of them.

It gets better. The men "knew" that their girlfriends loved them because they felt cared for and that they could express their feelings. And the women "knew" their boyfriends loved them because their men were willing to make such heroic sacrifices for them. Perfect symmetry: the women knew they were loved in exactly the ways that men knew they loved—and vice versa.

Fast-forward. The researcher then asked twenty-five couples who had been married for at least ten years the same questions, but added one: "Do you ever wonder whether your husband/wife loves you, or if you love them?" Now the answers diverged in a really interesting way. The women had no doubt that they loved their husbands, but they weren't so sure their husbands still loved them. And the men were sure that their wives still loved them, but they were also not so sure that they still loved their wives.

Amazing—and kind of scary. Why was this? Well, let's think about marriage for a second. Marriage in many ways "domesticates" love; it brings it inside and makes it more "pragmatic." It takes the thrill of the chase out of it, plus it's pretty hard to wake up and drive three hours in a snowstorm to make your partner feel better when you are sleeping right next to them. So in a hetero marriage like mine, marriage and domesticity tend to enhance "her" way of loving and reduce "his" way of loving. How often have relationships and marriages fallen apart because the "passion" disappeared? Because the sex got boring and eventually was nonexistent, or because the couple felt more like roommates instead of lovers? Being married for seven years now I can tell you without a doubt that of course there are moments when I miss the thrill of the chase, when I miss the distance and the longing I had for my wife when we were just dating and not fully committed. I miss the feeling I got when she texted or called me or when I knew I was going to get to take her on a date. How I ached for her when we were apart or when she was too busy to see me. I remember the endorphin rush of new love, and the way the chemicals in my body and brain reacted to her smell and her touch when our love was so new. It is easy to focus on the loss of some of those things as opposed to what I've gained by marrying her. It's easy to get distracted and focus on everything we don't have. So with millions of social media accounts showing us images and videos of people who seem to have it all figured out, who are happier than we are, having more sex than we are, and living the life we wish we were living, it's no wonder that marriages are more vulnerable now than ever. Just think back to those first six months of the pandemic quarantine. How many couples in your life or in the public eye broke up? It seemed like every week a new beloved couple ended things. The weaker the foundation, the easier it is for the winds of life to blow over our house.

Clearly we have to change some things around. Maybe we have to make love less a matter of the operatic performance and more about the inner experience of connection and intimacy, revealed less in the heroic sacrifice and more in the everyday things, the practicalities of everyday life. That's what we should romanticize. After all, the little things really are the big things, right? The problem is, we men are constantly bombarded with images that trick us into thinking we want something that we really don't. There is no foundation on that house built in a week for the movies.

The current environment provides an illusion—the illusion of a luxury of choice, endless possibilities, and perpetual happiness. I am honestly so happy that I missed the global rise of online dating, though I can imagine there could have been a lot of short-lived and empty fun to be had by the gamified dating apps that play on our dopamine triggers using random reward theory (sound familiar?). Basically, apps such as Tinder use science to get us hooked in a very similar way to gambling and porn. It's actually the same science casinos use to keep people pulling on the slot-machine levers all day and night, hoping for a triple seven. It's also the same tech used to get us to waste hours of our lives mindlessly scrolling Facebook, Instagram, and TikTok. With dating apps, you can be with someone while seeking out other options in the palm of your hand, which makes it feel that much easier to run—to end the relationship—when the butterflies go away and shit gets hard. I know way too many people who have told me stories like this. I've even heard how normal it now is to go to the bathroom on a first date just to scroll for other options. Even worse, a psychologist friend of mine recently told me that in her practice they were finding that clients were experiencing a new phenomenon—mind swiping—when meeting someone for the first time or even seeing someone on the street. The finger-to-brain connection created such a strong link that people are now swiping left or right in their minds when they meet someone! Separately, there have been many studies on what we now know as the paralysis of choice and what happens when a human is given too many options to choose from. As soon as someone is presented with too many options, the odds are that upon making a decision the person will more often than not question that decision and feel remorse or even regret for choosing it. They will never be satisfied with their choice because in the back of their mind they will always wonder if they could have made a better one.

But I believe there is hope, because there's one relationship that's impossible to escape, one relationship every one of us has the opportunity to choose without regret or remorse, one we can't swipe our way out of: the one you have with yourself. That's the starting point, and like the foundation of a home you want to be able to withstand the test of time, it's the part of the house that you rarely pay attention to, that is hidden from plain view, that supports the relationship you will have with your partner.

Laying the Groundwork

In 2008, I was cast in a super cheesy, almost comical, horror film in which my character, his girlfriend, and their group of friends found themselves shipwrecked on an island where we were, of course, savagely eaten one by one by cannibalistic half-human, half-ape humanoid creatures. It was an epic failure. As the story goes, the producer presold the film to a studio (off the trailer), and when they finally got to see the finished film, they backed out, essentially saying the film was garbage and that the acting was terrible (can't disagree there). That same producer, instead of fixing the film or doing reshoots, then decided to scrap the entire thing and remake it. Same premise. Almost identical story line.

So the time comes around to remake the film with a new director, new crew, some new cast members, and a new title, and rumor has it that a beautiful young Swedish actress has landed the lead, which just so happens to be the role of my character's girlfriend. That actress was Emily Foxler, my future wife. Serendipity? Fate?

Neither. I had turned down the offer to be in the remake after I was told that I would need to get paid under the table, that I couldn't tell the Screen Actors Guild, and that we would be shooting on a drug lord's beach in Panama. However, Emily and I would briefly meet at an event held by the producer of our two award-worthy films. While it was nothing more than an introduction of her and her boyfriend at the time (who also happened to be cast in the role that I played), the moment we met is still burned into my mind like it was yesterday. But as fate would—eventually—have it, we would get another few chances to meet, and something good would actually come out of those two terrible films.

In August 2011, I was a mess. I had just been dumped, was sleeping on my friend's couch, and was having a full-blown quarter-life crisis. That week I had been called to audition for a JCPenney Christmas commercial. I rarely ever went to commercial auditions because I hated the cattle call aspect of sitting in a room with fifty other guys who look just like me. It never made me feel good, and I also rarely booked commercials. But I went to this one because what's better when you are feeling shitty about yourself than seeing a bunch of other guys who could be cast in various versions of your own life story? So I go to this audition, (super late, mind you, because I secretly wanted to miss it) and there she was—the beautiful woman I had seen around town the past few years and whom I had met at that producer's party. Was it destiny that we would meet again now? Would sparks fly this time?

No and nope. It was more of a "Hey, how are you?" "Oh hey, I'm okay, how are you?" "Yeah, I'm okay. Great, wish you the best of luck." "Yeah, you too." I'd come to find out later that Emily's relationship had ended the week prior, just as mine did, and neither of us was in a good head or heart space that day. So after being called into the audition together, where I put on my best happy face, we went our separate ways. I didn't get the job. She did. And we wouldn't run into each other again for another year. Almost to the day.

For the next year, between when I saw Emily at the commercial audition and when I would see her again, I was pretty much a walking contradiction. On one hand, I would spend the year taking a deep dive into my faith and beliefs and would experience these incredibly spiritual moments as I began to connect with God in ways I hadn't before. And on the other hand, I would dive almost as deeply into the scripts of masculinity and try on all these different roles of men to see if any of them fit. I was lost and I was trying to find myself. I was hosting these awesome spiritual gatherings, while hooking up with women and then numbing myself with porn. That year, which ended up being the most profoundly spiritual year of my life, began with a very apparent cognitive dissonance between who I was at my core, who I was coming to be in my faith, and who I was trying to pretend to be as a man.

In fact, the best way to summarize this time in my life is to share a bit about a backpacking trip through Europe with one of my best friends, Travis. About six months after the breakup, I had decided that I was done trying to be the "good guy" and wanted to be like every other guy my age (or at least who I told myself every other guy my age was). I wanted to do what they were doing—having casual sex, drinking, smoking weed, dating multiple people at once, and just all around not giving a damn. The problem was that many of those things made me uncomfortable. I have never been able to date multiple people at once, and I had never been drunk or high. But here I was, twenty-six years old and ready to throw caution to the wind.

That summer Travis was filming a little horror movie of his own in Tbilisi, Georgia (the country, not the state). Travis was one of those guys I so badly wanted to emulate. Blond, handsome, ripped, and carefree. Seriously, google him—his last name is Van Winkle—you'll see what I mean. He did whatever he wanted, whenever he wanted, and women loved him for it. So, who better to go on an adventure with? We decided that I'd meet him over there, we'd backpack and travel all over Europe, and we'd just let loose. One day before he took off for Tbilisi, we were looking at the map, deciding our tentative route, and I got this super inspired idea. I said, "Hey man, Tbilisi is really close to Israel, and I've always wanted to go visit the Bahá'í Shrine in Haifa, so how about we start there and then take off to Greece and make our way up to Europe?" See, Travis was also reading a lot of the scripture with me and was on his own journey with spirituality at the time and yearning for a deeper connection with God. What better way to kick off a boys' trip, right? I mean, the spiritual center of my faith sounded like the perfect place to start a journey where we're going to go do everything that is, very arguably, not spiritual.

Prior to booking our trip, we made an important agreement, because we were both young actors essentially working paycheck to paycheck. That agreement was that the only thing that could ever stop this four-week excursion from happening was if one of us got an acting job. But it couldn't be just any acting job; it had to pay more than ten thousand dollars, which was much more than the trip would cost each of us. The chances of us booking a job like that were slim to none because, well, as actors you only book one out of a hundred auditions anyway, and the only auditions would have to be done on tape from the trip and callbacks weren't an option. So we shake on that agreement, knowing it's very unlikely that a job like that would happen, and we solidify our plans, beginning with meeting up in Israel.

The Bahá'í Shrine in Haifa, Israel, is arguably one of the most beautiful places on the planet. Aside from some considering it the eighth wonder of the world, it's also one of Israel's top tourist destinations. With its nineteen terraces cascading down Mount Carmel and overlooking the ocean, it feels otherworldly, sacred, peaceful, as if God constructed it to be a calm in the storm, a light in the darkness. Growing up a Bahá'í, I had always dreamed of going there. But perhaps even more special to me was to have the chance to visit the resting place of Bahá'u'lláh (the prophet founder of the faith), which was located twenty minutes away in Akka. For years I had heard stories describing the power and the spiritual effect it had on so many of those who visited it. I was also nervous because I was starting to realize this may not have been the best place to start this trip.

When we got to Akka, Travis was tired and decided to take a nap while I visited the shrine. I remember being annoyed at first, as for me that would be like a Christian visiting Jerusalem and choosing to sleep through the tour. But my frustration soon paved the way to gratitude as I realized that I had a chance to be alone in such a holy and magical place, and soon I would experience, for the first time in my life, what it felt like to purely and sincerely ask God to touch my life.

I was sitting on a bench facing east. The sun was hot, and the smell of roses was all around me. A small group of German tourists were just finishing up their tour and taking the last few photos of the gardens. As I closed my eyes, I felt this urge, this prompting to ask God to use me in whatever way she/he/it wanted so that I could be of service. I prayed for God to make me an instrument. I prayed for guidance, for clarity, and to be used in whatever way could be useful and beneficial to humanity. It was perhaps the sincerest prayer of my life, and I've often thought back to that moment and wondered what had taken me so long to pray like that. As I sat in meditation, I felt the nudge to make the five-hundred-foot journey down the path to enter the shrine of Bahá'u'lláh, which for Bahá'ís is the most sacred place on earth, the place we directionally face and think about as we pray each day.

For years I had heard about the energy and power that surrounded the shrine. For years I had heard how often those who enter the threshold break down in tears even when they think they won't. My mom had told me that when she was in the shrine as a young woman, she had a vision through prayer that she would soon meet my father (which she did just a few years later). As I walked toward the modest, house-like structure, I felt nervous. I was suddenly filled with doubt, like I wasn't enough or that maybe I wasn't pure enough to enter. *What am I supposed to do or say? What if I don't have a big experience? Does that mean I'm not spiritual enough?* As I took off my shoes and entered the structure, I felt this weird, almost distinct change in the physical quality of the air. It felt like it was thicker or something. The only way I can explain it would be to compare the difference between what it feels like to be surrounded by air, versus what it feels like to be surrounded by water. It felt like the air enveloped me, air that normally I'm not even aware of as I move through the world. In this room, it felt thick, like it was holding me. Like it was loving me. Like it was reminding me that all I am is not just enough, but more than enough. At that moment, almost as if it had been scripted, just as my lungs took in that extra-thick air and filled every cell in my body with that knowing that I was loved, I broke down in tears. My legs got weak, and it took all I had to not collapse and just break down sobbing. I got on my hands and knees and prayed. I thanked the unfathomable entity that God is for my life, for my strengths, my weaknesses, my challenges, for bringing me into existence, for never leaving me alone, and most importantly for loving me. For loving the darkest, ugliest parts of me that I can't love. For loving all that I am. I would never be the same again.

After that, no matter how hard I tried to rebel, my heart was made new. That doesn't mean I would become perfect, or suddenly have superhuman patience and kindness and grace, or not say stupid stuff and act out, or stop using porn, or be overcome with my ego and my trauma. Rather it means that my soul and even my body would, from that moment on, instinctively know when I was living in my lower nature instead of my higher nature, when my actions were not in line with who deep down I knew I was. In short, this idea that I am more than who society tells me I am, more than my body, more than my career, more than who I even think I am, is now kind of tattooed on my heart in a way that helps me come back faster when I get stuck in the swamp of superficiality. I say all this as a preface of sorts because while I know that I had a profound experience, I have often avoided talking about it because I have heard so many people talk about their own "spiritual awakenings" only to see said people living a life that seems to be anything but spiritual. But now I realize that all a spiritual awakening or enlightening moment does is give you a glimpse into the realization that you are more than you thought you were. That you are part of something beautiful and bigger than yourself. That you are enough. It doesn't mean you're going to act or be different every hour of the day, just like we know certain foods aren't the best for our bodies, yet we still eat them. But it allows you the perspective to know that when you do eat them, you know you won't feel your best, and at the end of our lives, we are only responsible for what we know.

I tend to think of that moment on my knees in prayer as one of the pivotal moments of surrender in my life. It was as if the core of who I am was exhausted from trying to be who I wasn't, from trying to be who I perceived the world wanted me to be. It was the deepest, most authentic part of me asking for help, *begging* for help, because despite what masculinity had taught me, I knew I couldn't do this alone. Looking back, I think it was perhaps the first moment where I subconsciously surrendered my desire to be man enough with a desire to simply be enough (which would later lead to the realization that maybe I already *am* enough).

The tension never really goes away, but my perspective on it did. The only difference between being "man enough" and "enough" is, of course, that one word, "man." Maybe if I could challenge that, the path to the other would be revealed to me? I believe that we all have two natures, our higher nature and our lower nature, and I believe that the goal of our time here on Earth is to win more battles than we lose between the two, and that's where spirituality comes in.

After three days in Haifa, and not even a week into the trip, I got a phone call and a job offer for a little Hallmark movie they later called *Bulletproof Bride*. It turns out that a self-tape I had made as an audition on the train ride to Haifa, surrounded by teenagers in camouflage holding automatic weapons, would actually land me a job for almost the exact amount of money that Travis and I had agreed would be the deal breaker in our trip together. *This* was the kind of fate I needed. It just wasn't the fate I wanted.

I flew back to the States and vicariously lived through Travis's experience, which had enough fun for the both of us. I filmed that TV movie for three weeks and soon after began the Spiritual Talk that laid the groundwork in me for this journey that I will be on for the rest of my life—the journey of undefining what it means for me to be a man in this world, and making room for me to be a human, for me to be, as French philosopher Pierre Teilhard de Chardin says, "a spiritual being having a human experience." I'd also like to say that Travis has been right by my side all these years. He has dived into faith as well and is on his own path in undefining aspects of his masculinity. Little did I know that the guy I wanted to be like was suffering just as much as I was; we just didn't know it because we were both too man enough to share.

Exactly one year after Emily and I exchanged hellos through our heartbreak at the JCPenney Christmas commercial audition, I get a random call to audition for another commercial. I had gone to two or three commercial auditions that entire year, but I was in a great place and so I thought *Why not?* Turns out it was, of course, JCPenney's annual Christmas commercial. This time, for some unknown reason, I go four hours early instead of being late, and as fate would *finally* have it, who is the first person I see there? The most radiant being in that entire place, the woman who would a year and a half later become my wife, Emily Foxler. So here we are, at the same audition, exactly one year later to the week. As I'm sitting down filling out my casting paperwork, I feel this almost gravitational pull to look up. And there she is. She doesn't see me at first but boy, do I see her. I gently call her name to get her attention. She looks over and we catch eyes. She smiles. I smile. Time slows down and then quickly speeds up again. We begin to talk. She tells me that she's been on quite the journey this year. She shares with me some thoughts she's been having, something about a mentor that she's had, and mentions that she's been on a pretty deep spiritual journey. My heart drops. I hang on her every word and feel what I can only describe as a knowing, that there is more to this chance meeting than meets the eye, a knowing that this bright light and powerhouse of a woman could be my person, and I could be hers. Before we head our separate ways into the audition, I invite her to the Spiritual Talk. She comes to the very next one, and that begins the beautiful and uncomfortable journey of our love story.

Now, if this was a story made for the movies, it would effectively end there, leading the viewer to believe that we had those near-miss meetings because we needed to go on our own self-discovery journeys before we could reconnect, fall in love, and go on to live happily ever after. The reality? We would find our happiness in the work. In the discomfort. In the struggle. A happiness that doesn't just happen, a happiness that is earned and must be chosen each and every day.

The Dating Years

From the outside looking in, our relationship was magnetic, sparks were flying, and it was often said how perfect we were for each other. From the inside looking out, it was true—the sparks were flying because our individual stories of insecurity, trauma, and conditioning were like two rocks constantly colliding with one another. As individuals we were being set ablaze by the real work of being in relationship, by the contradictions between our true selves and our conditioned selves.

Early on in our dating relationship, like *very* early on, when I saw her at that commercial audition, I had this deep knowing that Emily was my person, that she was the one I wanted to marry and build a life with. I can't quite explain how I knew it, but I did. It was different from any other feeling I had ever had before, and she was different than anyone I had ever dated, in many ways because she was the opposite of me but also because she challenged me and triggered me in ways I had never been triggered. It's kind of like when you find a new exercise to hit a muscle at the gym. The sorer you are the next day, the more you know that movement worked. That's how I felt about Emily. No matter how hard it was at the beginning, or how much I was challenged, it still felt right. It felt like growth, and even though it was uncomfortable, I believe that growth is always, *always* good. I really don't think I could name one thing in my life I love, or one experience I have had, that didn't come with some form of discomfort or growth. The two are inextricably linked in the best way, and nowhere is it more present than in our relationship. In many ways it was our challenges that confirmed my initial knowing that she was my person. The problem was that we are two distinctly different people, and my experience wasn't hers. Longer story shorter, she didn't feel the same way about me. At least not at first. Emily was cautious and tentative, and didn't always know what to make of me and the figurative "us" despite what the outside world was telling us. In fact, our date and subsequently our first kiss are perfect examples of how those first several months of dating went for each of us. On our first date I had taken her hiking in search of waterfalls. Our intention was to find one, but we were both on board with simply getting lost together. I was nervous but excited. I wanted to make her laugh, but that morning I just didn't feel funny. I was intimidated by her self-assuredness and graceful power. I wanted to act like I was comfortable hiking and in nature, but deep down I knew I was a city boy, and I knew she could sniff out any trace of inauthenticity or insecurity I was feeling. I remember wanting to be so much more than I was, because I thought that she needed so much more than I was, and yet trying to convince myself in real time that who I am was enough for her. The sun was shining when we started the hike, but eventually the rain came. To me the rain was a get-out-of-jail-free card from the heavens. I think it relaxed us both. At one point we sat down on a log near a creek. There was awkward silence. I had been thinking about how I could overcome my nerves and kiss her. *Should I ask her or just find the moment and do it? Do I need consent? Is she someone who wants me to just man up and take charge, or would she respect my asking her permission?* All of these thoughts were attacking me like a swarm of angry bees, and finally I just did what my soul felt was right and asked her. She looked at me, hesitated for a second, and then with a small smile said yes. *What was that moment of hesitation? Was she judging me? Did she think I was weak? Shit, I should have just done it and risked rejection. Was she just being nice because we had been hiking for an hour and it would have been super awkward if she said no? Fuck! Shut up, Justin! Do it!* So I leaned in, kissed her, and she kissed me back. It was magic. Or was it? I could have sworn I felt this electricity between us. Sure, it wasn't perfect, but it was sweet, and I for sure felt something magical. I would later find out that she felt absolutely nothing.

As I said earlier, in my faith we are encouraged to investigate character when we are dating, not to rely solely on a wild, passionate physical relationship, as we know that the chemicals in our brain can often cause confusion between what we are feeling at the moment and what we know to be a lasting truth. With Emily, what was so odd was that despite how "attractive" the outside world thought we were, both individually and as a couple, our physical connection was almost nonexistent. We struggled in that department. Big time. Call it a polarity issue, or as men in the hypermasculine workshops I started attending in my desperation would call it, an imbalance of our feminine and masculine energies. I read every book I could get my hands on and went through the obligatory David Deida men's group workshops to try to find that inner masculine warrior. Nothing seemed to work. Regardless, just to be very candid, Emily simply struggled with her attraction to me. Now, as I write that, part of me wants to put it in all caps and say something like . . . TO ME? SERIOUSLY? SHE SHOULD BE SO LUCKY! But that's my ego talking and masking what is really an insecurity triggered by a powerful woman. The truth is that the issue wasn't just about physical attraction, it was rooted in something deeper, something I was doing, an energy I was giving off that, when mixed with Emily's wounds and triggers—ones that many women share—created a massive polarity problem. It wasn't as simple as the masculine/feminine dynamic; it wasn't going to be fixed with books and workshops and tapping into my inner alpha. I tried it all. I did it all. It was something deeper. So, yeah, fellas, it's true—my girlfriend, the woman I thought and knew was the one, wasn't physically attracted to me.

Okay, so the fact that I even wrote that last paragraph makes me immediately want to go back and delete it, to tell the fairy-tale story, not the real one. But I can't, because leaving this part of the story out would do a disservice not only to the people I hope read this book, but also to myself. It's part of our story, and I shouldn't be ashamed of it, and neither should she. The fact is we are here now. We have overcome and conquered so many of these issues that it would be a shame not to talk about them for the benefit of other couples who could be, and more than likely are, experiencing similar things.

I'm a passionate person, if you couldn't tell already. When I see something I am drawn to, I become fixated on it. Whether it's a gadget, a piece of workout equipment, or even an idea, I learn everything I can about it, I try to become an expert on it, so much so that it can even come off as obsessive (and oftentimes it is obsessive). It's one of my greatest weaknesses and also one of my greatest strengths, as it's one of the reasons I've been able to find success in multiple creative fields and businesses. (I also recently found out that I'm an Aquarius with a moon in Scorpio, which evidently explains all of it, even though I have no idea what that actually means.) But that passion can also come across as overbearing intensity when it's transferred from a thing or a hobby and onto a person. Here's a small example that contributed to our polarity issues. Early on, if Emily and I were at a party, I would have almost no interest in hanging out with anyone else at the party; the only person I wanted to be around was Emily. I was completely smitten, and regardless of who I was talking to, I'd always look around to see where she was and then find my way over to her. Our relationship was new and exciting, and I couldn't get enough of her. Little did I know that many women experience that as smothering and needy behavior. Two things that do not go over well, especially when you are dating a strong, independent woman who is not used to dating a sensitive and emotional man.

So while I thought I was being charming and making her feel secure in my attraction and desire for her, I later learned it was actually having the opposite effect. Emily often refers to me as a little puppy during that time of our relationship. It was as if I couldn't be alone, and if she left my sight, she could feel me searching for her in the crowd, and it made her want to hide from me. And while puppies are cute, they are also annoying. I was so confused. My excitement and passion for her and the new relationship made me want her and at times even need her, which in turn made her feel claustrophobic and confused. This then pushed her away from me, which triggered my insecurities of not being enough and turned into a full-fledged trauma and insecurity crisis.

The more I dug into this later, the more I realized there were two things happening for me. For one, I always thought that as an emotionally available man, I should make sure—especially at a party—that the woman I was with felt my attraction to her and that she would want me to publicly demonstrate it. I had been in relationships where the opposite happened, and I was yelled at by my previous two girlfriends for not paying enough attention to them, or for being more interested in other people at the party (there was definitely truth in that). This is something that I know a lot of other men get confused about. One woman may want us to behave or interact one way while it may turn another woman off. Both are completely valid, and in the same way we can't clump all men together, we also can't clump all women together. This is why it's important for us men not to play roles and put on different masks, but instead to be true to ourselves and listen to our intuitions and at the same time listen to the people in our lives while getting feedback in real time. If we don't, we end up with no foundation, and the second a strong woman sniffs us out she will run in the opposite direction because she knows we aren't acting out of love but out of fear—fear that our instincts, that we as men, aren't enough. As it relates to my behavior at those parties, if I really think about it, in addition to doing what I assumed all women wanted, some of that behavior was also stemming from insecurity. I wanted, as a man, to "claim" her publicly, as on some level I knew it would make me feel more like a man. I mean, she was a ten in my eyes, and what man doesn't want a ten wrapped around his arm? As a man, I wanted to make sure that all the other men in the room always knew she was with me. I also didn't want to give in to the bad-boy bullshit and feign emotional distance or pretend I didn't want to be near her and put on an act to give her space to want me. I read all those dating books too, and while some of it may work, none of it creates fertile soil for a long-lasting and healthy relationship. This was my person, not a fling and not someone I was trying to conquer. If she was going to reject me, I wanted her to reject ME, not whatever guy I was pretending to be. So I took a shot, threw caution to the wind, and just went for it. But I definitely didn't do it perfectly, as no matter how hard I tried to show up as my authentic, vulnerable, passionate self, I was still finding myself plagued with feelings of inadequacy, fear, and doubt. None of which acts as good fertilizer.

And just as a warning, the opposite scenario is also possible and happens all the time. Men go to parties and ignore their partners and talk to others to show they are independent and free. While that in some ways might manipulate a woman to temporarily want a man more, it's just that, manipulative, and eventually that wears off and the relationship is again left with no foundation to build on. Nothing good comes from intentionally manipulating anything or anyone.

Another thing that I did that many of my friends have done is this: we take what didn't go right in our previous relationships (which, for us, weren't the right relationships to begin with) and we apply what we think we learned to the new relationship with who we hope is the right person. But what we forget is that every relationship, like every person, is completely unique. The only common variable is you, and the odds are that you will make the same mistakes over and over again no matter how many times you tell yourself you won't. This is because you are a human being and you, like me, regardless of your gender, are living out your childhood stories (traumas and all) in your relationships. In this case for me, something that seemed as simple as going out of my way to be near my new girlfriend at a party and make sure she knew I was proud to be her man, ended up being one of many ingredients that over time mixed together to create a recipe for a loss of physical attraction.

Physical attraction aside, our spiritual connection and faith were the glue that kept us together. We had moments of bliss where our chemistry was undeniable and moments that, from the outside looking in, would have been signs that it was time to end it. But as with any close, intimate relationship, there were so many wounds, so many narratives in our heads from previous experiences and past traumas, that kept rising to the surface. These kept causing a disconnect from that free and deeper connection. While we were dating, both of us felt like we were continually triggering each other's insecurities to the point where we even had some people in our close circle of friends tell us that dating wasn't supposed to be this hard, that we should still be in the honeymoon phase. In fact, both her closest friends and a few of mine, at multiple points in our relationship, told us that we would probably be better off as friends and that it wasn't going to work.

I want to talk briefly about this mythological expectation our culture likes to call the "honeymoon phase." First of all, I believe this is a modern idea; after all, arranged marriages were pretty much the rule for most of human history. Also, the goal of marriage for much of history was not love, but babies—reproduction for the sake of having a child or children to pass your property and assets on to. So for a couple who had never had sex, suddenly to be married and told they had to produce babies, the "honeymoon phase" was supposed to be a time of passion, but with a goal in sight.

Have you ever noticed how we portray relationships in TV and film? As a filmmaker I can tell you that there's a time-tested formula to ensure success. It starts out with a "meet cute," where two opposites fall in love against the odds. The sex is amazing, the friends who are all single are jealous, and the married friends all wish to be transported back in time to when their relationship was fresh and sexy. Then a shoe drops. Something goes wrong. A secret is revealed, one person sabotages something. Trauma and pain come out, and the two split up. One person realizes the mistake the other made and how their past led to this mess and tries to get the other back. It's generally too late. It's not until they are gone that they realize what they lost. Cue the sad music and emotional montage. But it's not over. All good things are worth fighting for. The other person is also miserable. Maybe one is in a relationship with a new person, but they aren't happy. Everything reminds them of the one they lost. They are both thinking of each other. Was their relationship worth saving? Breakups aren't ever easy, as a heart doesn't break evenly. Finally, in a thrilling heroic act of love, one person puts it all on the line for the other and they end up happily ever after. But do they? Or is that just where the movie ends?

The whole idea of the honeymoon phase as a theory is actually meant to be the opposite of the way we interpret it. It is supposed to teach people that even though relationships start out exciting, passionate, and sexy, eventually the real work will begin, and much of that excitement and passion will fade away. So in reality the honeymoon-phase idea is to point out the illusion rather than suggest that it is supposed to start off with rainbows and butterflies. I would argue that the problem is most of us now have somehow been socialized to think of the honeymoon phase as something that is normal, expected. Therefore, if the relationship doesn't start off amazing, then there must be something wrong. That's why, regardless of the intention, I think the idea is actually doing far more harm than good. It might be far better if we flipped it and stood it on its head. What if the expectation of the start of a relationship was the opposite? What if it was expected to suck? That the start was supposed to be messy and uncomfortable? What if sex was replaced with conversations? What if instead of going out and drinking we got to know each other's wounds and past trauma? What if a great date was actually a deep therapy session where both parties discovered an underlying trigger that kept them stuck in the same cycle as their parents? What if uncomfortable conversations about raising children, religion, political beliefs, and finances replaced Netflix and chill?

One of my favorite quotes about dating and marriage comes from 'Abdu'l-Bahá, when responding to a question from a man about whether he should marry a certain woman. 'Abdu'l-Bahá responded with something so simple and yet so profound that I believe it applies to everyone, regardless of gender or sexual preference. He said, "Before choosing a wife, a man must think soberly." Soberly. Think about that. In many ways during the dating phase in modern society we become drunk on love. Drunk on the chemicals and endorphins. Addicted to the person we are with. It's one of the reasons breakups are so hard and often go so poorly. We don't know how to live without that person, as we have made that person our world. Instead of us being whole and finding a partner to complement us, we look for partners to complete us. We are actively dating to fill holes and voids in our life with other imperfect people looking to do the same. We aren't thinking soberly at all, but the opposite. Then a few years into the marriage—and often even sooner—we sober up, and that's when it all seems to fall apart. But what if we could date soberly? What would that look like? Sure, maybe it doesn't have to be as extreme as turning dating into therapy, but I do think there's something about vulnerability, transparency, and honesty that feels synonymous with sobriety as it relates to dating and the investigation of character of the person you want to make a life partner.

I say this because eventually everything I listed above will have to happen at one point or another in a marriage or any long-term relationship. All of those uncomfortable conversations will need to happen. The sex will slow down. Bodies will change. Both people will age, unless you are Paul Rudd, because Paul Rudd doesn't age. Loss or financial hardship will eventually happen, and the relationship will be tested. If all we have is a house that is made to look good on TV, when the real shit hits the fan and difficult conversations begin, there's not much that's going to keep the house from blowing over. Think of it like the big, bad wolf huffing and puffing those first two houses down with ease. He didn't meet his match until he came to the house made of brick. We need to be conscious of what we are using to build our relationships—our houses—out of, especially in this on-demand swipe culture where the illusion of happiness and the grass-is-greener mentality are simply a few clicks away.

So while Emily and I may not have had the stereotypical honeymoon phase, I'm now eternally grateful for it because we were able to build a foundation that has carried us through nine years of being together, seven and a half years of marriage (at the time of writing this book), and into parenting two children together. Speaking of houses, a few years ago Emily and I bought our first home together and completely remodeled it. We gutted it and stripped it down to its foundation. We left some of the frame and the roofline and then reinforced the existing foundation and built it up from there. Looking back, I can see how our dating relationship was a lot like the beginning of remodeling our home. It was looking at the walls that were in place and figuring out which ones needed to come down to create the room we needed. It was digging in and doing the hard labor to tear them down and, when we hit problems, working together to find a solution. It was going through every detail of the design and figuring out where it could be more open. If we needed something we weren't thinking about or needed to maximize the space, it was digging into and under the foundation and calling in experts to help us fill the cracks. And it was constantly and continually reaffirming that our home had good bones, that it was going to be beautiful—that it *was* beautiful—even before we touched it, when it was covered in shitty wallpaper and had nonworking toilets, even when there was nothing left except the beams. (In fact when we got to the point where all the beams were exposed, we had some of our closest friends and family write prayers and affirmations on them so their words would live forever inside the foundation of our home.) Oh, and if you want to really test your marriage, then buy a fixer-upper and do what we did. You'll find that at many points in the remodel process, your marriage will start to resemble your home. But if you hang in there, the result, just like the house, will be beautiful. That's also where the work begins. You never stop working on your home, and you never stop working on your marriage.

When we can get beyond our conditioning, our egos, our learned behaviors that cause us to react from a place of wounding, what we had and have is really fucking beautiful. Sure, it may not have been all fireworks and fairy tales all the time, but what marriage is? Our marriage continues to be grounding, connecting, and calm; it has sweat equity. It was and continues to be hard, but boy, is it worth it. Our dating life gave us so many opportunities to practice choosing our core selves over our conditioned selves, and even when we failed, there was room to come back to that choice. And by exercising that muscle of choice—by realizing that we had the power to choose love and not just be in love—we continually learned how to choose each other as well. I say this with the understanding that we are only seven years into our marriage and far from being experts and knowing how to do this. We definitely haven't arrived; we aren't perfect, and our way is just one way. Love and marriage are infinitely deep, as unique as the two souls who are in it together, and impossible to fathom, but little by little and day by day, we work on it knowing that it's truly about the journey, not the destination.

Fuck the Fairy Tale

Don't get me wrong. I love a good fairy tale. I am a romantic at heart, and if over-the-top gestures could be a love language, it would definitely be one of mine. There is a very innocent, pure place in me that loves making the people I love, especially Emily, feel special. There is also a conditioned place in me that knows I'm really good at creating magical experiences for people and that I have to be careful not to use it to my advantage or rely on it when I'm feeling insecure and need a win. I know how to be Prince Charming because Prince Charming is one of the roles society told me I needed to play. And while I may not know exactly how to sweep a woman off her feet and into my arms in a ballroom dance (although I have faked it plenty of times on TV), I could most definitely put on a choreographed parade for her without the help of a magical genie.

Fairy tales, like masculinity, like gender construct as a whole, taught us that love looks and feels a certain way. As I highlighted earlier, older Disney films, all based on folklore, taught us that there is a damsel in distress, a woman who needs saving, and that there is a knight in shining armor, a man who comes to save her. All that to say, I have probably seen both *Frozen* movies at least five hundred times, thanks to our kids, and I'm very happy they broke from the formula. Also, can we talk about why every children's movie ever starts with the death of the parents? I get that it's about finding our way and healing the wounds of our lost parents, but enough already. Give me some living parents, please. Opinionated, messy, living parents! Those relationships can at times feel even harder to heal, but when you start to heal them it's the greatest feeling in the world.

Most of the time in fairy tales, the man usually has his shit together and the woman is usually losing hers—that is, of course, until the calm, cool, collected man swoops in to rescue her from whatever evil witch is trying to take advantage of her virgin beauty and innocence. The result? Wedded bliss and happily ever after! Or it's exactly the opposite: the guy only SEEMS to have it all together, but inside he's a mess, and the woman, through her patient devotion, never giving up on him, can finally heal his pain and transform him into the man she always knew he could be. For many women, in the fairy tale, she saves him, and he just THINKS he's saving her.

We know this is bullshit, that this isn't how it goes, that movies and rom-coms are not real life. But they do inspire real life, and art often imitates life. So what happens when we bump against the reality of relationships in marriage? Before Emily, I think I wanted to be married because I was in love with the idea of being married. I was in love with the scripts of marriages that I had seen played out on TV shows, in movies, and even in my life. I wanted what my parents and grandparents had without realizing the work that actually went into it. But these scripts only made room for certain emotions, specific story lines, and conditioned characters. When you're living for happily ever after, there is no room for you to be human, let alone for your partner to be human. It's this very conflict that led me to propose to Emily in the way that I did. (I realize how unromantic it sounds to use a conflict as an inspiration for a proposal, but bear with me.)

Because I love big gestures, when we felt that we were ready to get married, I wanted to do something over the top and extravagant. But if I'm being real with myself, it didn't all necessarily come from a pure place. Yes, I wanted to show and prove how much I loved her, but I think a part of me also wanted to show her, and everyone we knew, how much love I had inside to give. That's the part that's important to recognize and to honor. I believe we all have this dual purpose when it comes to grand gestures and big events in general. I mean, look at weddings: they tend to be these massive, expensive days that couples can spend years planning. Millions of couples delay diving into marriage just to experience that one day. Girls oftentimes grow up dreaming more about the day they get married than the man they get married to. It becomes a fantasy waiting to be fulfilled. We take out loans and spend more than we have, often to make our bride, our groom, or our parents happy. But weddings in reality are never for the couple; they are a show for the people who come and attend. Many people have said they barely even remember their weddings because there is so much pressure leading up to creating the perfect day, that they forget to actually enjoy it. Hot take, pure and simple: love doesn't need a show. It doesn't need two hundred people in an audience. It doesn't need catered food or the perfect backdrop for pictures, and it doesn't need the stress of a wedding planner yelling at everyone to make sure the flowers are color-coordinated with the napkins. Love doesn't need any of that, but sometimes we do. And that's also okay. It doesn't make us bad people, and it doesn't mean our love isn't real, but knowing ourselves and why we want things is an important step in understanding ourselves. I actually believe that future generations are going to look at our current cultural wedding traditions and find it kind of ridiculous. I don't think our kids will need a day that costs tens (and in some cases, hundreds) of thousands of dollars to start their lives together. Instead, they will use that money to actually start their lives together and just celebrate with their friends in a way that feels true to them and their unique love story. Now please know, I am not knocking all weddings, but I think the more and more divorces we see over time, the more we will realize that we may just have to rethink not just how we marry, but how we date, and why. And while it may be uncomfortable to admit, it's important to, at the very least, think about and reconcile in each of us why we want or need the things we want or need. It's that need, or lack of it, to "show" or not show our love that is one of the reasons I am, to this day, madly in love with my wife.

Emily has never needed public declarations of love. She is the kind of person who would have been okay eloping or being proposed to in private with no cameras and no one knowing about it and never having video evidence of it. She doesn't need to post something on social media to prove that it happened and is content having her inner experience validated with no need for the outer. She just happened to marry someone who has, for years, operated from the outside in, constantly seeking validation from the outer world without knowing how to find validation from the inner. At about month three of dating, I decided to go all out and let all our friends know I was madly in love with Emily. So like a true romanticist, I spent days creating the perfect, way-too-serious spoken word poem for her. I surprised her and read it at an event with a few hundred people attending. I had never written or performed poetry before, so I thought I was putting myself out there and being vulnerable and risking humiliation, but that the risks of sucking would far outweigh the joy of seeing her melt with my words of love.

That didn't happen. In fact, it created the opposite reaction.

While many of the other women in the audience "melted" and told Emily how "lucky" she was (something that to this day she hates hearing, as it completely takes her agency out of the work she did leading up to meeting me and negates the fact that I am also who SHE chose to be with), Emily picked up on the need underneath the need. She saw that I was trying to win her over with a public proclamation, and she was *not* having it. That's why nearly a year and a half later, when it came to my grand gesture for her, I knew that while I wanted to do something "big" to propose, it would have to be honest and tailored to her, because all she ever really wanted was me. Not my public performative version of what I thought I should be for her. Me.

At the time, viral proposals were becoming a thing. People were making these wild and crazy proposals with flash mobs and fake movie trailers and were recording them with hidden cameras. As a music video director, this was for sure my lane and my area of expertise. But while I had tons of ideas, not one of them was for her; they were all for me. She didn't care about excessive gestures or how many people were involved or what anyone would think of her proposal. She didn't need, or want, a parade from me to prove I loved her enough, as that would have actually been me just trying to prove to myself that I was enough. But necessity is the mother of invention, and I believe that the reason our twenty-seven-minute proposal experience has been so well received and gone viral so many times over is because it was just that: unique. It wasn't just like everyone else's proposal because it was ours. Our story—our struggles, our pain, our inside jokes, and our experiences all wrapped into one massive, super cheesy, love explosion.

At the end of the day, I honored that part in me that wanted to express my love in a big way, making friends with where it was coming from and why, and making sure it wasn't at her expense.

So what did I do? I simply molded some of what you have read in this chapter into an interactive experience that would touch her heart while also satisfying that part of me that longed for this moment since I was a boy. Basically, along with tons of help from our friends (and specifically one of my best friends, brothers, and business partner, Ahmed Musiol), I gave her all the cookie cutter, viral proposal experiences I had thought of for years before meeting her and made sure I failed at each of them. The idea was to take her on a journey through my heart. I showed myself wanting so badly to give her the "perfect proposal" and failing each time because I wasn't thinking about the way that SHE would want me to propose as I was stuck in the way I thought I SHOULD propose: from a failed radio interview that malfunctioned just as I was asking her to marry me, to slightly homoerotic boy-band videos, to a flash mob turned action-movie trailer that ended with her sister reminding me who Emily was and what she really wanted. And what would she want? She would want to be at our favorite café, the place where we had our first unofficial date, the place we first talked for hours about love and loss, about her dad who had passed away, about God and the universe. The place we would continue to go for years to come on special days and normal days. And she would want it to be just us and, if possible, our families. So the movie of my failing attempts all led to me walking in the door of Blu Jam Cafe, in real time, to her seated at our usual table. I took her hand, asked my family to come in to witness, and surprised her by flying her mom in from Sweden so she could be there as well.

To end it, I showed her a video I had taken in Sweden at her father's gravesite. It was important to me that he be part of this too because I knew that deep down he was a huge part of our marriage, that Emily was on a journey in many ways thanks to him. She was healing, and our love was providing that cocoon to heal, both from her experience with him, and now her experience with me. I often told Emily I wished I would have had the chance to meet him, to bring him into a big bear hug and thank him. To show him that I loved his daughter more than I had ever loved anyone in my life and that I would spend the rest of my life respecting her and doing everything I could to make her happy. That I would honor him and her by not repeating the patterns and the suffering he experienced that caused her so much pain growing up. I also wish I could have thanked him in person, because despite the pain he may have caused as he navigated his own unhealed trauma, he also did so much good. The strong, creative, powerful, sensitive, and healing woman I love is a by-product of all of his light and darkness. As a man and as a father, while he struggled with his own version of masculinity, he loved her deeply until the day he passed away. And it was through the fire of that struggle, through the joy and pain that comes with experiencing all the seasons of life, that he helped mold her into the beautiful dynamic human she is today. And that's why there was no way I could ever ask her to marry me without first asking him and thanking him in the process. THIS was the proposal my soon-to-be wife would want. And while I of course had my friends ducked behind plants in the corners of the room filming, I think it summarizes the best of what I learned dating Emily: know yourself, know your love language, but don't love your partner the way you want to be loved; love them the way they want to be loved.

The proposal represented so much more than what met the eye. It represented this journey we had begun to take with ourselves and with one another, to choose to see and love the person for who they were, to let ourselves be seen for who we really were, not who the world told us to be. It represented letting our relationship be what it was, and not what the scripts of fairy tales told us it should be. Wedded bliss leaves out the fact that life gets really hard, marriage gets hard, having children gets hard, parenting children gets harder, and if we never see the real stuff get played out, then we bail as soon as we lose the proverbial butterflies.

Of course, there are still moments when Emily takes my breath away and I can barely speak, but they aren't the moments I expected them to be. It's not when she steps out of her horse-drawn carriage and I'm waiting in my tux at the top of the stairs to walk beside her into the castle. It's not when we are getting ready to go to a movie premiere or some swanky industry event and she's dressed to the nines. No, it's when she lets her guard down, lays her heart and her wounds open before me, allowing me to see them—to see her—and know her more. It's when she has a breakthrough in therapy and comes out of the bedroom with tears in her eyes, feeling like she is carrying a thousand pounds on her shoulders yet still finds the energy and will to play some silly game with our children. It's when she wakes up in the morning and slurs her words because she has her Invisalign in. It's when she's frustrated with all the technology in our house because nothing works for her and she starts to swear, which always makes me laugh because that's when her Swedish accent comes out. It's when she's covered in sweat, blood, and literal shit (sorry, babe), calling on God for assistance to help her birth our children. It's when she's mothering and gives herself a time-out when she temporarily dislikes our children. And it's when she comes back from that time-out with apologies and more grace and patience than I could ever have.

There is no room in the scripts of fairy tales for the reality of being human together, and as much as I love a good movie, there're just not that many big commercial hits that come close to doing true love justice. I guess that's why I make movies that try. Before I got married, one of my best friends, Noelle, told me that marriage is taking all of your shit, dumping it in the front yard, and then having your partner take all of their shit and dump it there too. So now you have a big pile of shit, and by committing to marriage, you're committing to digging through the shit, mixing it, and letting it become the fertilizer that helps beautiful things grow.

So fuck the fairy tale. Give me *that* movie script.

Again, it's why Emily and I use the phrase "I love the shit out of you" so much. We even put it in our wedding vows. Because that's what we do for one another: we love the shit right out of each other. But don't get it twisted; it's hard work. And the first step is recognizing you have shit to begin with and then being willing to let that shit come out, and then loving that person when they're covered in shit—theirs and your own. You're probably saying, that's a lot of shit. You are right; it is. And it's not pretty—there's nothing fairy tale about it—but it's real, and I will take real over fabricated and filtered any day.

Buyer's Remorse

Similar to the concept of paralysis of choice is a term that has been used for years, "buyer's remorse." The concept is simple. The bigger the financial decision, the more one questions and researches whether it was a good decision. The catch is that this generally happens AFTER the item has already been purchased. Many people experience this feeling when purchasing a home or a new car. You suddenly see a better deal somewhere else, and that's when the onslaughts of guilt and remorse set in. You feel like you made a massive mistake and that you will never recover. You begin to question the process by which you make decisions and wonder if your instincts that told you to buy it were wrong. The strange thing is that even with purchases that have been mulled over and planned out and that you love . . . you are still apt to experience some form of buyer's remorse at some point in your life. But nowhere is this more apparent than when it comes to men and marriage. The difference is that for men it also happens BEFORE a man finally proposes or between when he proposes and the wedding date. This is called COLD FEET. Have you ever seen a movie or a TV show where the bride is left standing at the altar, humiliated in front of all her friends and family? Art imitates life, and it happens far more often than we realize.

For me it came like an earthquake in the middle of the night. It surprised me, and I had no idea where it was coming from or why. About a month before we were set to get married, I booked a decent-size commercial campaign as a director. At the time we were pretty broke and hadn't combined finances yet, and this job felt like a divine gift. I had been living off pennies making documentaries and a few commercials a year, and this job was not just going to pay for our wedding but also our honeymoon and would help get us through the first six months of marriage. The catch: I had to go to New York to shoot and would get back the week before our wedding. I ended up taking the job, as we needed it, and Emily agreed to take on the majority of the wedding planning. We had both decided after the proposal to have a very short engagement—three months—because we had already done the work. We knew we had found our person, and honestly, why wait? We didn't need a massive, fancy wedding, and we were ready to dive in, move in together, and start our lives. On top of that, neither of our parents were in a place to help us pay, so we decided to bootstrap our wedding together, gave ourselves a limited budget, and got creative. Then a little less than a month before the big day, I took off for New York.

Have you ever been to New York in the early summer, just when it starts getting hot and muggy and people are wearing as little as possible since they have been bundled up in massive coats for the past six months? Well, it's pretty spectacular to witness and also easy to see why it feels like everyone in the city is single. All it takes is a morning walk to a coffee shop to be reminded of all the reasons why a guy who isn't even thirty yet should keep himself on the open market. I mean, it's madness. I felt like I was living in some sort of alternate reality or like I was being Punk'd. Everywhere I went, it felt like literally everyone was hot, and no one was wearing clothes! Not only was I about to get married to a woman I had been fighting for over the past year and a half, but I also had been trying to be abstinent while in a straight-up war with my lower-nature pull toward porn. This was a deadly combination.

The more we were apart those few weeks, the more stressful it got. I was stressed trying to make this commercial come to life so we could afford our wedding, and she was stressed dealing with the remainder of the wedding plans (thank God we had a community of friends helping us put it on). The last few weeks as single people, while in theory magical and joyous, are generally quite terrible for soon-to-be newlyweds. The pressure and stress of putting on an event take their toll on you, and the mushy conversations quickly become about planning and details and all the shit you don't want to talk about . . . especially when your job is about planning and details. All that to say Emily and I would have no idea that this situation would end up a foreshadow to what marriage would actually look like one day when we eventually had kids.

When I finally got home, exhausted from the shoot, my mind was racing. Every question imaginable was going through my mind, and I felt like I was alone on an island with no one to talk to. Who could I confide in? Half of my friends had witnessed my near-obsession over Emily this past year. Everyone was in love with her, and I'm pretty sure my closest friends honestly loved her more than they did me. I couldn't sleep, and it occupied my mind 24/7.

Was I making the right decision? Was she the right woman for me? Were those single friends right . . . should things have been easier this whole time? Will we get bored with each other sexually? Am I *enough* for her? Is she enough for me? Will I still be attracted to her in ten years? Am I even ready to commit? I'm still so young! You name it, the question crossed my mind, and for someone who was as sure as I had been for the past eighteen months, this was really, really freaking me out. I thought it would never happen to me. I thought I was immune to the messages of masculinity that told me that the single life was the best life. I thought I was different. I wasn't. I was getting cold feet.

But why? I wasn't someone who got cold feet. I was sure of my decisions, especially when it came to love. But now, at the end of the fourth-quarter, with the ball on the one-yard line, I was questioning myself. Little did I know that despite my emotional maturity, I was not exempt from the socialization many of us men experience when it comes to marriage. Think of how we think of marriages, how the movies portray them. When a couple announces they are getting married, for women it's like VICTORY! She wins! She is happy, she's going to be taken care of, and her friends throw her a bridal shower filled with sexy anticipation of all the fun she's going to have. She tamed the beast! And the man? He loses. He's trapped. It's the old ball and chain analogy. The jokes about how life ends with marriage, or for a man, sex ends with marriage. He and his friends get together to mourn the last night of his "freedom." They joke that men aren't designed for monogamy. That we're built to plant our seed in as many women as possible. That we will always think about sex, and if we don't marry the right person, we will cheat. And how do they celebrate their last night of "freedom"? By going to a strip club, of course, just so he can see all the ass he is never going to get again. It felt so out of the blue that all of this subconscious programming was coming back with a vengeance—programming that I didn't even realize I had been exposed to. This is where some deep, intense heart work began. But this is also where my willingness to be vulnerable and expose my heart to my close friends saved not just me but my marriage as well.

I remember exactly what I was doing and where I was. Emily had wanted to visit her acting manager at a dinner party the week before the wedding. I had just gotten back from New York and was definitely acting distant, as I was feeling everything I just described. Emily knew something was wrong but was giving me space, as she always does, somehow a step ahead of me with her magical intuition. I stepped out into the driveway in the hot summer sun and called my friend Rainn. You may know him as Dwight from *The Office*. Yep, in my most dire situation, my phone-a-friend is none other than Dwight. But the man I know is far from his character on the show. A recovered alcoholic, spiritual gangster, guru, friend, and fellow Bahá'í, Rainn is someone I know I can call and spill my guts to because he will tell me the truth. He had always been open about his challenges and in many ways had been a mentor to me. When I told Rainn what I was experiencing and all the thoughts running through my head, he listened and then validated my feelings. "Ah man, yeah, that sucks."

Normally he would make some wiseass, uncomfortable joke as an ice breaker, but he could tell I was really struggling, and he reminded me of a quote from Bahá'u'lláh that essentially talked about our lower nature as a concept called the "insistent self," which is really just our ego telling us we need to be "better than" or "apart from" others. He went on to explain that Bahá'u'lláh called the ego "the evil whispering one" that "whispered in men's breasts." He validated the feeling that my ego and lower nature were attacking me, and while he on one hand had compassion for what I was going through, he also didn't hold back from telling me the full truth, which was exactly what I needed to hear. He told me how awesome Emily was and reminded me how rare it was to find someone like her. Then he helped me see how I was overthinking and doubting myself and what I knew to be true. I thanked him and told him I would see him at the wedding. And that was it. He got through to me. It was totally my lower nature, my ego attacking me. My subconscious understood that in some way my getting married was going to be the first step in the death of a version of my masculinity. Even though at some point most men get married, it's almost like the system has been rigged against us and we are set up to fail. I was fortunate to have supportive friends who reminded me of my spiritual purpose and were willing to tell me the truth. Other men, without such support systems, often find themselves in situations they feel the need to escape from, whether it be escaping literally and backing out of engagements or escaping with drugs, alcohol, porn, or even sex outside of marriage.

As men, we've had this idea beaten into us for years telling us we have to go at life alone; it's the greatest myth of masculinity. So when it comes to marriage and committing to one person for the rest of our lives, even if it's someone we are madly in love with, it's important to remember that none of us is immune from the societal subconscious pressures that have been programmed into us since we were kids. It's okay if those feelings come up. It's okay if we get scared and fear enters our minds and hearts. It doesn't mean we are with the wrong person; we may actually be with the right person. And the only real way to ensure the fear doesn't win is to take away its power, and the only way we can do that is to talk about it. That's why after I spoke to Rainn, and later a few other close friends and even my own father, I found the courage to talk about it with Emily. If she was going to marry me and become my partner, I thought she should know why she may have been feeling me pull back a little. She deserved to know the truth.

One night I asked her to sit down with me and told her I was having second thoughts, but also that I was working through them. I told her that I would get through it and that I was doing the work in understanding where my doubts came from. I assured her that none of it had anything to do with her, that it was about me and my journey as a man, and that I just needed to work through it. I apologized for being distant because I knew she could feel it, and I promised her that nothing had changed. I was still madly in love with her, but there was a dragon I had to slay. And how did she handle it? The same way she handled that thirty-six-hour labor a few years later. And the same way she would eventually handle my confession that I was in a secret twenty-year-long battle with porn. Like a fucking Jedi master. She looked at me with so much love, compassion, and empathy and reminded me how much she loved me and thanked me for being willing to share that with her. She let me know that she was here for me and gave me the space to work it out without any pressure or shaming. She didn't make herself a victim or make me feel bad. She held it. And when she did that, it was all I needed. Fuck this idea of the ball and chain. But if that's the way it's going to be and she is the ball, then sign me up for the chain. I'm all in.

The Mirror of Marriage

Being married to Emily is like constantly having a mirror held up in front of me because she is always reflecting me back to me, while I am simultaneously doing the same for her. In our marriage there are no Instagram filters or Photoshop apps to diminish any of our blemishes. In my best moments, when I'm feeling connected and happy, when we are in a rhythm and life is going smooth, I don't mind looking at that reflection, my reflection. But the mirror becomes much harder to look at when it requires me to see how I react when I am stressed, how my insecurity can lead to me being closed off or getting lost in my work, how my desire to be of service to the world can be confused with my desire to provide financially for our family, and why my drive and focus to build my career can also keep me from being as present in our home and with our kids as much as I want to be. This list could go on, but if I want the reward of partnership, of doing life with someone, then I have to be willing to look in the mirror; I have to be willing to do the hard work of self-work, not from a place of selfishness, but from a place of true humility, of wanting to show up more fully for myself so I have more capacity and awareness to show up more fully for someone else, for Emily.

My faith tells us that marriage is "a fortress of well-being and salvation," and yet too often the societal messages around relationships focus on the well-being part. I love the idea of marriage being a fortress. A fortress is often associated with war or with protection from calamities or extreme situations. A fortress is what you would build to hide out or to protect yourself from an oncoming attack, so in some ways it's kind of fitting that it's used to describe a marriage. So when I think about a fortress, I think about how it needs to be built from the inside out, with your partner, hand in hand, to protect you both from yourselves and from the outside world. Because in our world, which is so focused on the exterior and the material, marriages are literally under attack—not in an overt or intentional way, but in a way that puts the emphasis on the presentation of marriage and not the reality of it. Some of the best advice my dad gave me when I was struggling in year two or three of marriage was to remind me that love is a verb. It's a choice that one has to make every single day. He told me that there were times in his marriage to my mom where he had to literally choose to love her, especially when he didn't feel like it. It was that choice, that act of watering their marriage, that has allowed them to stay married and in love. And knowing my mom, I guarantee she had to do the same thing with my dad. It goes both ways, and like all seasons in life, it is cyclical in nature. It's not some mix of chemicals or pheromones. It's not sex. It's not even connection. It's the choice, and in that choice lies the work.

As men we are taught to be brave, strong, and tough; we're taught not to give up but to be mission-oriented explorers relentlessly searching for truth. As men we are taught "No pain, no gain," and we willingly tear down our muscles to build them up. What if we could take those messages that we have been taught and apply them to our relationships, our marriages, our own emotions? What if we could take those attributes that have been instilled in us and use them to go inward, to search for the truth of who we are? What if we looked at relationships the exact same way we look at the gym, in the sense that when we go to the gym, we are working out *with* the weights, we are seeking the discomfort, knowing that it's good for our physical growth and health? We have to make a choice to go to the gym, and no matter what new pill or shortcut workout device they try to sell us, nothing will get us the bodies we want faster than the choice to do the good, old-fashioned work. The exact same thing is true for marriage and relationships in general. What you water, grows. It's that simple.

When I began to make that shift to approach my emotional and relational growth with the same ferociousness and tenacity that I approached my physical growth, it changed everything. Instead of getting defensive about Emily's actions and reactions, I began to use those triggers to figure out why I reacted with defensiveness. While I screw up all the time and I am far from perfect in this area,

I am practicing using triggers as invitations to look in the mirror, as opportunities to grow, to build the fortress. A fortress doesn't just last forever on its own; it needs to be constantly maintained and, yes, even rebuilt. Sometimes the winds and war from the outside world are going to test it and tear it to its bones. But as long as it's standing, that fortress can be rebuilt. In our marriage, Emily and I are both continually making the choice to build the fortress. She is looking in the mirror that I hold up to her, and she's also doing the hard work of self-work, which is honestly one of the sexiest things ever. Screw just having a hot wife who takes care of her body; abs will last only so long. Nothing is sexier than the emotional maturity to know that your heart and mind need the same attention as—if not more than—your body. As a result, together we plan on continually building and rebuilding our fortress to protect us, not just from the outside world, but also from ourselves. And thanks to those shiny mirrors we reflect on each other, we are both committed to growing and weathering the tests, trials, and storms that life will undoubtedly bring us.

CHAPTER NINE

DAD ENOUGH

Raising Children When I'm Still Growing Up

In 1982, my grandpa Loui, my dad's dad, passed away suddenly of a heart attack at seventy-seven years old. A few years later, on the anniversary of Nana Grace and Grandpa Loui's wedding, I was born. I think that being born on that day is one of the reasons I became so close to my nana, who, despite having passed away years ago, will forever remain one of the most important people of my life. When I was born, my dad didn't have a father to help guide him through the process of fatherhood, and honestly it wasn't until just now, as I'm writing these words, that I realize how lonely and terrifying that must have been for him, and for every man who walks into the role of fatherhood without having the privilege of a healthy blueprint, or even a presence, from their own father or father figure to help guide them.

One of the most memorable moments of my life was when we surprised my family with the news that Emily was pregnant. Seeing the look on my dad's face when I told him he was going to be a grandpa and that his boy was having a child of his own is something that will forever be seared into my mind and heart. Shortly after, when I confessed to him that I was terrified and didn't feel ready to be a dad, he told me he remembered feeling the same way when he found out that he and my mom were pregnant with me. Wait—so he didn't know what he was doing either?

Nope.

He even told me he wished someone had given him a how-to manual for fatherhood. I kind of laughed it off, but the more I thought about it, the more I respected his honesty, and it made me feel a lot better about how nervous I was to become a dad. I wasn't alone if my own father had felt the same way.

Just like masculinity and manhood, there isn't a one-size-fits-all approach to fatherhood. There isn't one book that can prepare you for all the ways your life is about to change. There are thousands of books, blog posts, TED Talks, and podcasts, and they are all from different perspectives. No matter how many books you read or YouTube videos or documentaries you watch, there is no way to truly understand what happens inside a man when he becomes a father until it actually happens.

What happens to each of us who identify as fathers can be shockingly different. I know men who don't change at all and continue going about their lives almost exactly as they had before, and I know men who dive headfirst into fatherhood and seem to do everything they can to prepare. There are men who don't want their lives to change and never see themselves being a dad. There are men who are unhappy in their marriage or partnership who think having a child will "fix" things, only to realize very quickly that is not how it works. There are men who become fathers of other men's children and show up for them in ways the others couldn't, raising them as if they were their own. And then of course there are men who thought they wanted to be fathers who soon realize, as their child is coming into this world, that they actually aren't ready, that they are terrified. This last example is far more common than we realize, which says something about what it actually means to be "ready" to be a father. Unfortunately, the method by which we measure fatherhood readiness is the exact method by which we measure masculinity. Have we done enough? Have we made enough money? Are we secure enough? Are we able to provide enough? Are we man enough? In fact, this is a conversation I had just a few weeks ago with a dear friend who despite his wife being ready and asking for a child, at forty years old still doesn't feel he is ready because his career is so up in the air, they don't own a home, and they have no financial cushion. As men we've been socialized to believe that if we can't provide for our families, then are we even men? Just the possibility of financial hardship and not being able to provide for our partners and children is enough to put most men into a state of paralysis and choose not to have kids. But as we have discussed, these false external measures don't necessarily hold the answers.

The Positive Pregnancy Test

It was October 24, 2014. I had always wanted to be a dad, but having just turned thirty, I was much more focused on getting my career to a stable place than bringing a new life into this world. Emily and I had only been married for about a year and were settling into each other and this whole new world of what it meant to be married. We had just rented a little place near the beach to inject more carefree fun into our days, and I had just fallen back into acting and thanks to *Jane the Virgin* was on the verge of becoming a ten-year "overnight success." We were filming episode six of *Jane*, and I had no idea that the show was about to become a global phenomenon and would provide us employment and a steady income for the next five years. I was taking it day by day, trying to figure out how to build something bigger, as my time in the entertainment business had shown me just how quickly success can come and go. But I was now a husband and not only wanted to make my mark on the world as a man, but also felt that pressure to provide and build a nest egg for when the day finally came, the day we would decide together to grow up and have kids, the day I would become a father. So yeah, parenthood was definitely in the plan, but we thought it was down the road . . . way, way, way down the road.

Apparently, my wife and I have no idea how a child is made because along came the positive pregnancy test that rocked our worlds. I'll never forget the way she told me. I have seen so many cute pregnancy reveal videos since then, where the woman tells her man she's pregnant and they both cry and celebrate. That is not what happened.

I had just gotten home from a long day on set and earlier in the day had been asked, for the first time, to appear on *Entertainment Tonight* as a guest. It felt like a milestone for my career. I eagerly walked into our little apartment. Emily was sitting on the couch. I sat down and kissed her. We started small talk, and I was so distracted about my big news that I didn't even realize that she wasn't being herself. I excitedly told her that *ET* had called and wanted me on the show. I thought this would be a bit of a celebratory moment for us, but when I looked at her, I noticed she wasn't even looking at me. Something was off. Then without warning, as I was in midsentence, she just looked at me and blurted, "I have to tell you something." She looked terrified, and my heart sank as I nervously replied, "Okay." Without pause or hesitation, she muttered, "I think I'm pregnant." Then silence. Nothing. Just quiet. From both of us. We both looked away from each other like two kids who were too awkward or uncomfortable with ourselves to be seen. "Wait . . . how?" I asked like an idiot. "Are you sure?" She looked at me, "I took two tests, so yeah . . . I'm pretty sure." (If only I had remembered the pilot of *Jane the Virgin,* I would have remembered that false positive pregnancy tests are extremely rare.) We were 100 percent pregnant.

Then came her tears, but they weren't happy tears. We were in many ways in a state of shock—and also mourning. We were mourning the life we thought we were going to have. And for Emily, as a woman who was now thirty years old, in the entertainment business, it felt like a lethal blow not only to her career but also to one of her life dreams. You see, like gynecology, the entertainment industry has a way of making women feel geriatric after thirty-five. We continued to let the feelings come, allowing ourselves the space to feel all we were feeling, knowing that despite the shock, we were also deep down (way, way down) both excited. We had talked a lot about parenthood throughout our dating journey and first year of marriage. We both wanted it. We just wanted it later and on our terms—you know, when we were a little more "ready." I've always loved that saying, "The quickest way to make God laugh is to make plans." Or, in our case, not to use protection.

After the initial wave of trembling, the aftershocks kept rolling in. Until we found out Emily was pregnant, the inner work I had been doing was leisurely—there was no sense of urgency to figure out my shit. It was almost as if I were subconsciously telling myself that "my shit" was a box that didn't need to be checked off until we were going to have kids. What mattered more at that point in my life was making sure that I checked off all the boxes that needed to be checked off as a man—the boxes the world and other men and women wanted to see checked off. Once those were checked, then I could work on myself. So, in my mind, I still had time to grow up, to become a man, to get ready to become the dad I always wanted to be.

But all of a sudden, the time had come, and I was completely frozen by the fact that I was not ready. How the hell was I supposed to parent a child and not mess them up when *I* still felt so messed up? How the hell was I supposed to parent a child when, in so many ways, I still felt like a child myself? How the hell could I ever be enough of a dad when I didn't even feel like I was enough of a man?

That moment we found out Emily was pregnant, what had previously been an *invitation* for me to take the journey from my head to my heart quickly became a *demand* to take the journey. Sure, I could have just gone about my life as if it was no big deal since she was the one whose life was really about to change. After all, it was her body the baby was in, and often men can get away with not being too affected by parenthood until the baby is born. But that's not the life I want or have ever wanted, and that's not the kind of man I want to be.

A few days before Emily found out she was pregnant, I was in my car and felt this really strong urge to pray. This wasn't really normal for me, as I'm usually either on a call or listening to music or a podcast or something, but I remember feeling really off. I had been thinking about my life and just felt this huge imbalance where I felt like I was perceived by others to be selfless, when in reality I felt like nothing I was doing was good enough, and that up until that point in my life, I felt like I had been more selfish than not. So I prayed. And I prayed hard, much harder than I usually do. It was a strange prayer, as nothing out of the ordinary had happened that day to trigger it. But there I was, driving in Los Angeles afternoon traffic, begging God for the strength and the assistance to become selfless. Well, what better way to learn true selflessness than parenthood? Prayer answered, and pro tip: be careful what you ask for.

Just like every other aspect of this journey, I was surprised at where it led me. Initially I would have thought that I would be tackling a chapter on being a dad with a real look into the whiplash that is parenting and maybe offer some tips, tricks, and hacks I've learned along my relatively short parenting path. But this journey took me on a different route. It took me down a path of remembering my own childhood with my dad, and from there it took me to his childhood with his dad. Had we been able to go farther back in time, I know it would have taken me farther down the generational line, because just as the scripts of manhood get passed down from generation to generation, so do the pressures and the wounds of fatherhood.

My Dad the Superhero

In many ways my father was ahead of his time when it came to parenting. He showed his emotions, constantly doted on my sister and me, and was intensely present in our lives. He would cuddle with me every night until I was about ten years old, stopping only because I probably felt like I was too cool to cuddle with him. Or maybe I just learned that my friends weren't cuddling with their dads. I don't remember exactly when we stopped being physically affectionate, but I do know that at some point a wall was built between us, and as a thirty-six-year-old man, I still crave that physical touch and affection from him. I don't know if it's for fear of being judged or if it's not manly or something, but I know for damn sure one day I will give anything to have the chance to hold and be held by him again. That's why it's so confusing to me that I find myself putting up this weird invisible wall and not letting him completely in when I know he so badly wants to be. It's like this invisible barrier of masculinity that I didn't ask to be put up, that I know he doesn't want up, yet somehow we both are trapped behind it. It's something I am actively working on breaking through at this very moment because the last thing I believe we need in this world is more walls. Let's build bridges instead. Especially between fathers and sons.

I was five years old when I started playing soccer, and throughout the next thirteen years my dad rarely, if ever, missed a game. Not only did he not miss a game, but he would sometimes even come to practices. He was my biggest fan, recording every moment, cheering me on after victories, yelling at the refs from the sidelines when they made a bad call, and building me back up after a loss. As I mentioned before, my dad was at the forefront of the product placement industry, but what no one knew is that he would often represent companies I liked just so he could come home with all the new Nerf guns before they were released or get Diadora to hook up my soccer team with new uniforms.

Anything and everything—that's what he did to show me he loved me. It was pretty magical. And it still is. My dad is affectionate, kind, sensitive, and present (especially when his face isn't buried in his phone, just like his son). We had and have such a beautiful relationship, especially from the outside looking in, that it was easy to forget that like many superheroes, my dad was—and still is—human.

Generational Kryptonite

My dad, Samuel Victor Baldoni, was born in 1948 in South Bend, Indiana. His dad, my grandpa Loui, was a well-respected state senator and passed away just a few years before I was born. The reason my dad's middle name is Victor is because on Election Day in November 1948, my grandpa was elected to the senate, and that Friday my dad was born. He was the victory baby. My grandfather came to America from Italy in 1912 when he was eight, landing in Ellis Island with his little brother and sister and his mom. His dad, my great-grandfather, had come over earlier, found a job in Indiana, and had been sending money back to Italy to bring the family over. During this time in America, Italian immigrants were experiencing widespread discrimination, prejudice, and even violence. Because of this, my grandfather grew up under the pressures of feeling like he had a lot to prove to the people around him. He was hardworking, well-spoken, and confident. He cared deeply about making sure that everyone in his life felt good and taken care of, and he always tried to maintain the family image of being happy and put together. I would love to be able to ask him today what that pressure was like for him. How much of that was who he *really* was at his core, and how much of it was a role he felt he had to play because of who society told him he could and couldn't be as an Italian immigrant?

I think both the pressure my grandfather felt as an immigrant in public service, along with the traditional scripts of what it meant to be a man back then, manifested in how he parented my dad and his other children. My grandfather worked hard to provide for his family. As a result, he worked long hours and barely, if ever, made it to one of my dad's wrestling matches. I don't believe it's because he didn't think it was important; but he probably felt that with everything he was dealing with as a provider, protector, and public servant, going to my dad's matches wasn't a priority. I'm also guessing that his dad never went to anything he did considering he was an entire ocean away trying to create a new life for his family, so who knows if it ever registered for him that his absence would hurt my dad.

It won't come as much of a surprise to hear that my grandfather wanted my dad and his siblings to assimilate and grow up as Americans and not as Italian American immigrants. He didn't want them to face the same discrimination and stereotypes that he did. They had to be "real" Americans, and I can only assume he observed that "real" Americans were much less expressive of their emotions than those "ethnics" from Italy. Add to that my grandfather being a senator, and the pressure to protect the image—the family's image, the positive image that they had created as immigrants—was doubled.

Protecting the image became increasingly more difficult as my dad grew up and was, as my aunts and uncles have told me, a "wild child." In fact, I learned that more than once my dad was escorted home by my grandfather's police officer friends for all sorts of trouble he was getting into. The stories they tell of my dad make him sound more like a Kennedy than a Baldoni, but I guess that comes with the territory of having such a well-respected dad in a small town. Had he not been the son of a state senator, I imagine he would not have been dropped off at home. It was a privilege that perpetuated the message that the image was more important than the reality: we can't disclose our family struggles, our humanity, because we have to been seen a certain way to be accepted or for my grandfather to be reelected. But it wasn't just a message my grandfather was sending to his children; it was a message that he had been sent, and one that he would hold himself to until he passed away.

As I was preparing for my TED Talk, I decided I wanted to learn more about my grandfather in an effort to help me understand my dad, and in turn myself. One night, my aunt Susie told me that shortly after my grandfather had lost reelection in the senate, he had fallen on hard financial times. He was around sixty, and my dad and aunt were in elementary school. The car factory he had worked at since he was young (Studebaker) had abruptly filed for bankruptcy and was moving to Canada. They laid off hundreds, if not thousands, of employees in the process—all local hardworking, blue-collar folks. My grandfather was in upper management and was offered a job so long as he would relocate his family to Canada.

He had overcome tremendous adversity to get to where he was, and while he had worked for Studebaker for forty years, he couldn't justify the hurt it would cause the family to pack everything up and relocate. Not only was his family in South Bend, but his friends and constituents were too. So he turned it down, because with the Baldonis, family comes first. But little did he know that when he turned the job down, he would lose his entire retirement because there was no federal protection. It was tragic, and he was left with nothing. At one point he even ended up working nights as a janitor to make ends meet and keep the lights on for his family. That's right, from senator to janitor. While my grandfather struggled financially during that time, despite having helped countless people in his town, he himself was too proud to ask for help, and thus this slight detour in his story was left out of the history books of my family. I can only imagine the heaviness of his heart and the loneliness he must have felt as he suffered in silence with no one to talk to or turn to. How does a giant among men ask for help from the very people he dedicated his life to helping? I don't know if my family thought it would be embarrassing or insulting to talk about when thinking of him and all he accomplished in his life, or if they just conveniently forgot. Either way, in my eyes, as someone who never got the chance to meet him, talk to him, and hear his story, hearing this not only made me respect my grandfather more but also helped me understand myself and some of the issues that I struggle with today.

It was so typical of my grandfather's generation to suffer in silence, never reaching out for help, never showing weakness. That is, my grandfather—and virtually all the men of his generation—struggled mightily to be "man enough" by all the traditional measures. At the time they probably would have spoken of it as their "duty" to provide and protect, to keep their nose to the grindstone, and all that. Some virtues there, sure, but I'm struck now at how utterly lonely their lives must have been to feel that they had to do everything on their own. I would do anything to be able to meet my grandpa Loui. To hug him and talk to him. To thank him for all he did for our family and for his courage to start fresh in a new country and start a family. But also to let him know that I love him regardless of any of that. I love him for who he was to my dad, to my nana, to my aunts and uncle and the community. I'd want him to know that who he was as a man was not just enough, it was more than enough . . . no matter what job he had or what was in his bank account at the end of his life.

I recently sent my dad a text asking him if Grandpa Loui said "I love you" to him as often as he says it to me. His response kind of shocked me. He said that he doesn't remember his dad ever telling him he loved him. My grandpa said he was proud of him, and he told my nana that he knew my dad would be successful, but he never told my dad that he loved him. Ugh. That hit me hard.

Suddenly so much of my dad's behavior makes sense to me: the intense drive for success. The nonstop work and idea generating. The wheeling and dealing and hustle. He is relentless in his pursuit to stay financially secure and relevant, even now in his seventies, which is exactly what he may have felt my grandpa wasn't at his age. It all makes sense. My dad has been living out his life to earn my grandpa's unrequited love, while also trying to give me everything he didn't get from his dad. I just wasn't able to see it until now.

Many of the ways my dad was parenting me were the exact opposites of the way he was parented. On one hand, this is awesome. It's how every generation gets better and improves on itself. It's how cycles of abuse and traumas are stopped and how we make progress as a collective species. But I believe that true healing has to occur first, otherwise even though we are making different choices than our parents did, our childhood wounds find their way in through cracks we can't see or that we didn't know were there in the first place. As an example, my grandpa didn't tell my dad he loved him, so my dad told me every day. His dad didn't go to his sports events, so my dad came to every single one of mine. As awesome as it was to know that I could always look to the sidelines and see my dad, underneath it all, I feel like my dad was trying to heal a wound from his childhood by overcompensating in mine. He was trying to heal a sadness he felt as a child by overextending himself to ensure I never felt the same sadness. Otherwise he wouldn't have put so much damn pressure on himself to show up at literally everything. If he missed something, he would feel terrible and beat himself up, and that's a pressure that, as an adult now, I wish I could have relieved him of. He was trying to convince himself that he was enough by doing everything he could to make sure I knew I was enough. Damn. If he only knew just how enough he already was. How enough he is.

At face value, that doesn't sound problematic. But the issue lies in the fact that while my dad was trying to heal a wound from his childhood, he was wounding himself as an adult, and unintentionally wounding me in the process.

I keep wondering how many of us have that same story, the story of a loving father who was compensating for the fact that he was never told he was loved by being so affectionate, patient, and just "present" in the lives of his kids. Or of the opposite. As I said earlier, I am one of the lucky ones. My dad was healing his wounds by overcompensating and actually showing up for me and telling me he loved me all the time, but unfortunately the vast majority of men are raised by fathers who come from generations and generations of wounded and emotionally unavailable men who then pass on that same woundedness to their kids. Expressing love and saying "I love you" to many men, especially baby boomer men, is like speaking a foreign language. They may feel it, but unfortunately, they often don't have the tools or emotional capacity to express it. So they show it the only way they know how, by working hard, by not complaining, by providing for their families and keeping them safe, as that's how they were taught to show their love. And while there is nothing wrong with that, there is also so much more to be felt and shared and experienced as humans. So while my dad may have made a different choice, it's not the choice that's often made. But things are changing. I'm starting to see more and more men be open, loving, and expressive with their children. It's becoming the new norm, and men everywhere are deciding they will be the ones to end that tradition of inexpressiveness, that they are going to be the ones to take off that stifling male armor. It's happening, and I can't wait to see what comes of it.

While there is hope, so many men I know still ache, wanting to hear those words from their father's lips just once. "I'm so proud of you, son." "I love you, son." Or just to be held in his arms one last time without saying anything. How many unresolved painful relationships between fathers and sons continue to play out every day that will never get a chance to be healed? And how many men didn't grow up with fathers at all and would give anything for a moment like that? I think that's why when we see complicated father/son relationships play out onscreen, it's one of the few places in our lives where we allow ourselves to secretly cry.

Speaking of films that make men cry, have you ever seen *Field of Dreams*, the movie in which Kevin Costner builds an entire baseball diamond in his backyard because he hears a voice that tells him to? "If you build it, they will come" has become one of the more well-known lines in movie history. And while the entire premise is kind of ridiculous, the movie is magical and a guaranteed sobfest for almost any man. It's basically about generational trauma and a son finally getting a second chance to heal while simultaneously healing his dad. The whole thing culminates in a gorgeous scene where almost nothing is said, and you just see these two men playing catch together as the sun sets. I rented it the other night because I hadn't seen it in a while, and when the ending hit, I completely lost my shit. As I was crying, I looked over and noticed Emily wasn't—even though she cries at everything. At first, I didn't understand why it wasn't ripping her heart out like it was mine, but then I realized of course she wouldn't cry at this movie. It's a movie made for men, and it portrays a uniquely male experience between a father and a son. It just makes me wonder how many grown men still ache for a moment of reconciliation with their dads and would do anything to hear the words " I love you" just once, even as their fathers lie on their deathbeds. So many men die with unexpressed love in their hearts, and I think in watching redemption stories, it hits our hearts in the soft spot where our armor can't protect us.

The Superhero's Fall from Grace

Even for a man who had decided, on his own, to change things, to love and show love differently than his father, there are tough costs. My dad was a progressive father: present, emotionally aware, and unafraid of affection. Yet he was silently crumbling under the weight of keeping it all together. On the outside, he was so present, but on the inside, without support, without anyone to really lean on, the weight nearly brought him down.

There were times in my childhood that were difficult because of choices my parents made, and also because of how life just works or doesn't work (as is the case for all families). There were a few periods when we really struggled financially, but it wasn't something that was ever really talked about because no matter what was happening there was always enough of whatever it was that we wanted or needed. I never really understood it as a kid, but as I got older and started asking questions it became easy to see that my dad was just doing what his dad taught him: protecting us and our image. As a child and teenager, I knew that things were hard. I often intuitively felt like something was a little off, but it was never talked about. My dad was a hero, and every hero has certain things they just don't talk about.

Looking back, it was almost textbook: he had to protect the image that everything was okay and that he was the father who took care of everyone and made sure everyone felt good and was happy. From an early age I subconsciously could sense the conflict between the image our family projected and the reality of what our family was going through. There were multiple times when my dad would take two flights after meetings in LA just to make it home for one of my games. He would be exhausted, operating on little to no sleep, but he would be there. Not because I needed him there—I mean, of course I wanted him there—but I have to believe that a part of me would have accepted that he was out of town for work and still felt secure in his love. But come hell or high water, he would be there, and I think it's because he had put this pressure on himself, this otherworldly pressure on himself to show up every time because his father didn't.

So much of who my dad is and how he parented my sister and me was rooted in unconditional love and support, but I also think it's important to look at how he was also parenting from a place of woundedness.

Growing up, I was never privy to any of his wounds. I wish I had been. I wish we could have had the kinds of conversations where he could share his fears, the things he was worried about or scared of. I wish I had known then the parts of him that were imperfect, heard him talk about his shortcomings, or witnessed him own and accept his flaws so I would grow up knowing that, like him and everyone else, it's okay to be flawed; it's perfectly human to be imperfect. But how could he have done all of that? All he knew of fatherhood was passed down from his father. He was simply doing his best with what he knew at the time (and, I must say, he's done a pretty damn good job). But while we may have been Italians who showed emotions, we were also men who didn't know how to show vulnerability.

It wasn't until my early thirties that I was able to know a little bit more information about the dark times that our family walked through. It wasn't until I started this journey in myself and started getting curious about my own behavior and tendencies, and then asking questions about my dad's behavior and tendencies, that I began to scratch the surface of the extreme burden that my father shouldered. While I wish I could say that I met this new information with grace and understanding, initially I mostly felt resentment. It's actually an issue we are still working through and learning to hold space for. I resented the fact that while my dad never lied to me, he did this thing we do as men where we don't tell the whole truth.

When I was younger, during the times when we were struggling financially, even though it wasn't discussed, I quietly resented *my mom* for it. Mothering isn't rewarded and holds no social capital in our society. So in the eyes of a young teenage boy, I saw my dad working tirelessly while observing that my mom didn't carry any of the financial burden. I unconsciously blamed her for spending the money my dad made because I saw how hard my dad was working while failing to notice how hard she was working. This is messy and unfair on many levels, but I realize now that my dad took on the role of handling our finances while keeping my mom in the dark.

Interestingly enough, I've recently learned that my sister holds similar resentments as a thirty-year-old woman that speak toward her socialization as a woman, and the effects of being raised by a dad who worked and a mom who didn't (according to society's standards). Like most men, my dad kept my mom out of it not to hurt her but because that's what a man should do: provide and shoulder the burden so his family doesn't have to. He didn't want her to have to work, yet he also didn't want her to worry. At the same time, even though mothering doesn't get counted as part of our economic output, all the work she did in the home allowed him to work as much as he did outside the home. Capitalism is an impossible system without women's unpaid labor. While mothering doesn't pay financially, it's quite literally the job that keeps the world moving forward. It's simultaneously the hardest and most thankless job on the planet yet one of the most important.

I believe that my dad had to keep up the image of being the superhero, the breadwinner, the man of the household, the man the world told him he needed to be. That was the image he was trying to live up to, and I also think that was, in many ways, the image my mom had been socialized to believe she wanted to have in a husband. So like hundreds of millions of other women and mothers in America and around the world, my mom got stuck doing the hard and too often unappreciated work of running the family while also allowing herself to remain naive regarding our family's financial struggles. This then perpetuated the problem by putting even more pressure on my dad, who continued to internalize it all and didn't share with my mom what he was really going through. And if we connect that back with what we know about marriage, I think this in many ways deprived them of the chance to be truly open and vulnerable with each other during that season of their life.

So looking back, my anger was actually misplaced. It wasn't *his* money, it was our family's money, as he and my mom were partners and coparents. They were co-CEOs of our family, and while I know it's a two-way street, I do believe that as men we could do a better job of helping the women in our lives feel supported and appreciated as partners.

Through therapy I've been able to learn that much of my resentment as an adult toward my dad stemmed from feeling like everything could have shifted had he just let others in—me, my mom, my sister, his family, and his friends—and allowed us to see the parts of him that were hidden under the weight of his armor. It's also thanks to therapy that I've begun to see that I am actually repeating those identical behaviors and patterns in my own life and desperately want to stop. I never thought I would say this, but for better or worse, I have become my dad.

If only he had had the tools to sit me down and take himself off of that superhero dad pedestal, and let me into his weaknesses and mistakes back then, there's a good chance I could have avoided a few of the land mines I have stepped in. But I'm also uncovering another truth: the resentment I have recently been working through came from becoming a father myself and seeing that I was also guilty of perpetuating the message that our image needed to be protected. I can't be mad at my dad for passing down to me the script he was given; after all, he was and is an amazing dad, and he made massive improvements in his fathering style compared to my grandpa. And yet to let it go, I have to allow myself to feel it. I have to be okay with resentment and with the frustrations and limitations that come with shouldering the weight masculinity puts on so many of us—our own dads included. But more than anything, I also need to focus on the positive ways we as a society are improving generationally because there is some beautiful work and progress happening today, and to minimize that would be to undermine all the men (and women) who have been working so hard to make that progress.

The Progress of Presence

One of the areas where tremendous progress is being made is in the active role men and fathers play in the birthing experience. My aunt Susie told me that my grandpa wanted to be in the delivery room when she was born in the 1940s, but the hospital refused to allow him in—even though he was a senator. Instead, he had to sit in the "fathers' waiting room" like the other dads, pacing up and down, drinking crappy coffee, and waiting with a stack of cigars with pink and blue ribbons, ready to hand them out when he was told the sex of the baby. In the 1940s and '50s, virtually no men were in the delivery room when their wives gave birth—that was the law and what was considered to be the norm. If anything it was probably weird to want to be allowed in the delivery room (and don't get me started on the way that women were forced to deliver babies back then . . . that's a whole other conversation. If you want your blood to boil, just research the way we as men created a medical system that classified birth as a sickness, and how we literally would strap women down and perform procedures without consent). But there is hope! There is so much progress and forward momentum, as today, if the couple is married, nearly 95 percent of fathers are in the room, cutting the cord, sharing as much as possible, holding that baby skin to skin, and even more importantly, holding space for their partner. That's an inspiring and hopeful percentage.

When I was getting ready for the birth of our firstborn, Maiya, my dad told me that the moment he watched me come into the world was one of the most profound and spiritual moments of his life. He loved when my mom was pregnant and loved how mindful and careful she was about anything and everything she put in her body—something I would see Emily repeat during both our pregnancies. Growing up I would always hear the stories about my mom's cravings for super weird things that should under no circumstances ever be eaten together, and how my dad would run out to get her everything she needed at all hours of the night. Her go-to cravings while pregnant with me were for creamed pickled herring, which is generally reserved for Jewish funerals and not the easiest to come by, and chocolate cake with buttercream frosting. My dad, being the resourceful man he is, would always find a way to fulfill my mom's desires, regardless of where or when she craved something. He would rub her feet and take care of her every need and was a very present and connected partner the whole time. My mom had really wanted to have an unmedicated, vaginal birth, but after thirty-six hours of intense labor it was clear I wasn't coming into this world that way. So she chose to have an epidural and eventually delivered me via C-section. Luckily, my dad had taken a special class that allowed him to be in the operating room; otherwise he wouldn't have been allowed to be in the room with her. When I finally entered this world, my dad was the first one to hold me, immediately wrapping me up and bringing me over to my mom, who of course couldn't move because of the epidural and surgery. He held me up to her face and put us cheek to cheek. She describes that moment to me as the moment she fell in love and even to this day regards it as one of the happiest moments of her life. My dad tells me just being there to see me come into this world and take my first breath, cut my cord, and facilitate that experience for my mom cemented his belief that there had to be a God.

When Emily told me she wanted to explore the possibility of having a home birth, I remember having this initial protective reaction that made me want to scream "Helllll NOO!" I had never thought of a home birth as a viable, modern option, and all I could think of was how risky it could be not just for her, but for our baby too. It's like without even knowing anything about it, every part of me was already in protector mode. If there was even the slightest risk to my family, I wasn't having it. As I leaned into my reaction and got curious about it, I realized that my entire life I had looked at birth through the lens of not only the way I was birthed, but also the way I had seen birth portrayed. As a result I subconsciously assumed my child would be born in a hospital and probably even in the exact way I was born, by C-section and a surgeon. If I came into the world that way and I was safe, then that means it must be the safest way, right? I think we can all see the false narrative I had created here.

As men, and really as humans, there are just certain things that throughout our lives absolutely never cross our minds, and in my experience, the method our partners choose to give birth is one of them. Of course, I'm sure there are some men who have thought about it prior to marriage, but I was not one of them, which is why it's a bit surprising to learn that there are countless books and documentaries, classes, resources, and Facebook groups all about giving birth at home. It was as if a whole world existed that I was just then being exposed to.

Even though my mind wanted to react quickly and harshly to my wife's idea about exploring home birth as an option, I knew way better than to say anything definitive, let alone a definitive no. At the end of the day, I think it's important for men to recognize that while we are partners, spouses, coparents, whatever title you choose, a pregnancy involves 100 percent of her body and therefore it is 100 percent her choice. For the sake of importance and clarity, let me say it again: it's her body, therefore it's her choice. Of course, that doesn't mean that we as partners don't have a space for input and our opinion, but it does mean that it's not up to us to decide how our wives or partners give birth. In the end, our role should be to be of service, support, research, and help however we can. The birthing process for a woman is more than likely the most intense thing they will ever go through, and they are the ones carrying the baby, not us—they are the first protector of our child, not us. We must learn to trust and honor their intuition and instincts by not inserting ours in a dominant way—especially as it relates to *their* bodies.

After Emily first told me she was thinking about home birth, I had every possible scenario playing in my head like a horror film. I even knew of a man who fought with his wife about it and the only way he would be on board with a home birth was if he could hire a private ambulance to sit outside the house just in case there was a problem. As men we are conditioned to believe that it is our job to stay in control, fix a problem, and protect our loved ones; and a birth is completely out of our control regardless of where it happens, but it feels even more out of control if it doesn't happen in a hospital. My fear kept me from listening to Emily's intuition and trusting her.

Going into that first meeting with the midwife, I was nervous. There are so many variables and things that can go wrong during a birth, and I was already madly in love with this little girl who was growing in my wife's belly, so I just wanted to make sure both of them would be safe. Now keep in mind, my mom was an energy worker and a feng shui master, so I am no stranger to what some might call the "hippie-dippy" stuff. When it's about the safety of your wife and unborn child, however, it feels a bit different. I wanted science and facts, so of course I was calmly freaking out on the inside when we walked into our first interview with our prospective midwife. But those emotions went away within minutes as she told us that the first and most important rule of home birth was not to be attached to birthing the baby at home. The top priorities of a home birth are always the safety of both Baby and Mama. Wow. She must have known how I was feeling, as I'm sure in her thirty years of midwifery she's had plenty of nervous and skeptical dads like me walk into her office just waiting for her to say the "wrong" thing. To her credit she knew exactly what I needed: facts and science. She explained the process, how crucial the weekly appointments were, how paramount physical and emotional preparation were for the both of us (but especially Emily), and how important the role of the father was in the process. I felt included, I felt seen, and more than anything I felt that my wife and our baby would be safe. So with an open heart I dove in, as it was what my wife wanted, and the more I understood her why, the more I realized it was what I wanted too.

Regardless of the demands at work, I showed up to almost every midwife or doula appointment over the next six months because it was important for me to be there physically. I asked the producers to move scenes and schedules around so I could attend the appointments—and not just for my wife but for myself too. I remember getting funny looks when I would ask the assistant directors not to schedule me so I could attend the twenty-six-week checkup. It was clear they weren't used to men asking for this sort of thing, and while that's understandable, it also felt kind of sad. These are the appointments when we get to hear our baby's heartbeat, see how big she is growing, we get to find out what fruit she is the size of, and what physical or sensory qualities she is developing. If we can't get excited about showing up for that, and holding the hand and heart of our partner who is literally giving her body for this life and has been nauseous and unable to eat anything for weeks, then what will we show up for? Why would we think being there for a school play or a recital would be any different? I think showing up is a muscle, and like anything, it needs to be developed. The work of becoming a father doesn't begin when our babies are born; it begins the moment we find out our partner is pregnant.

I share with my friends or expectant fathers I meet through my work the idea that it's important that they remember this is our experience too. We men are in the movie . . . we just aren't starring in it. You will only have one first pregnancy. It's one of the reasons Emily and I decided to say WE were pregnant instead of saying SHE was pregnant. It gives me as her partner agency and accountability in this massive life moment. It also emotionally and spiritually connects me to her physical experience and prepares us for parenthood. But even in that, the mistake many of us make is that we don't stop to ask ourselves how we are feeling about it. We don't stop to check in with ourselves emotionally and see what's coming up for us. Instead, we bury ourselves into what we've been socialized to do: provide and protect. And yet that doesn't make the fear go away, the feelings of inadequacy and wondering if we are really ready to even become dads at all, the worry of being able to provide for another life, to protect another life, the feelings that come up when navigating all the changes that are happening in your partner and in your relationship. Maybe hormones are causing her to have extreme highs and lows, maybe depression is setting in, maybe there are physical complications, and maybe we are feeling the spark of the relationship waning. I just wish we as men could find a way to be honest with ourselves about how hard it can be for us without taking away or diminishing how hard it is for our partners. I'm not saying we are victims by any means, nor should we act like it, but the pressures and stresses are real and deserve to be talked about. Like any feeling that remains unexpressed, if we aren't able to talk about them, they will get bigger and will one day become too much to hold. It's healthy to acknowledge the pressures and stresses we feel when it comes to becoming a dad. It doesn't make us weak or ill prepared. It doesn't make us bad partners or bad parents. This shit is normal! The only thing not normal about it is that we don't talk about it, so each guy feels like he is the only one struggling with it.

For example, if you think I didn't have issues having sex knowing our little baby was inside my wife, then you think way too highly of me. Every guy thinks about it. What if I hurt the baby if I push too hard? Just the thought of knowing there's a baby in there isn't sexy either. And that's okay! All of the feelings and emotions and fear that come up for men during pregnancies and birth are okay and deserve to be expressed and normalized. The key becomes finding a safe place to express them, and that safe place should start with anyone BUT our partner. This is something we can and should be leaning on the men in our lives for. Our partners are on their own intensive journey as their bodies and minds are changing and shouldn't be asked to hold our fears and feelings as well. But male friendships can hold us. Therapists can. Mentors can. And by reaching out and sharing our experiences, we help normalize the feelings that arise with pregnancy—both positive feelings and the ones we may be ashamed or afraid to share.

The Strength of Flexibility

My cousin Aaron lives in a small progressive town in Washington and is a personal development coach (aka life coach). He's made it his life's purpose to use the deep personal work he has done on himself to help others overcome their own limited belief systems and achieve their dreams. He is a bit of a self-development junkie and takes his own weekly therapy sessions and personal growth seriously. He's also the type of guy who loves to be in control, so if you go on a trip with him, he's often the one to make the plan, but just know that if he does, you better stick to it, as he isn't a fan of curveballs. Well, one curveball Aaron didn't see coming despite all of his deep internal work was just how triggering his wife's pregnancy and the birth of their child were going to be for him.

When Aaron and his wife, Erica, found out they were pregnant, they FaceTimed Emily and me to surprise us and ask about our experience with home birth. We were the first of our friends or family to have a baby, and we were very open about our experience in hopes that we could be helpful. Erica is deeply spiritual, and the idea of a peaceful home birth was something that really resonated with her, but Aaron wasn't so sure it was for him and was attached to the idea of having the baby in a hospital. As it turns out, Aaron didn't get the memo that he wasn't the center of their birth story—his wife was.

Over the next six months, for one reason or another Aaron missed many of the midwife appointments. Work had been stressful as he was trying to grow his "life coaching" business via social media, and he was admittedly nervous about supporting the family. He read some books on birth and parenting, but overall he was so focused on himself, going inward, and helping his clients that he forgot to truly be a supportive partner to his wife.

When Erica went into pre-labor, some weird shit started to happen with Aaron. His patience was almost nonexistent, and he started acting strange. He kept leaving the house and coming back and seemed like he was distracting himself with his work in a borderline obsessive way. He also went from being hesitant regarding a home birth to being oddly attached to the idea of having the baby at home—even more so than his own wife. Multiple times through the very long birth, when Erica felt exhausted and wasn't sure she could go on, he made comments to her about needing to have the baby at home, reminding her she should "stick to the plan," while forgetting that the most important rule of a home birth was not being attached to having one.

At one point, Erica called us midcontraction in tears asking us to call him because he had been gone for a few hours and she was worried he would miss the birth of his own baby. So not only is she holding the pain and pressure of pushing a human out of her, she's also having to hold her husband's fragile masculinity and reaction to it. I'm not going to lie—I was furious. And if I could have snapped my fingers and transported myself to Washington, I would have been happy to give him some free life coaching of my own while dragging his ass back to his wife. As it turns out, Aaron had disappeared because he had a client who evidently needed an emergency session. That's right. He left his own wife who was in labor with his child to be there for a client who was having a "crisis" about his career. Now look, this is a delicate subject, as his job helping his clients navigate emotional moments in their lives is important—but when your wife is in labor, it might be a good time to take your own advice and tell your clients you are unavailable.

Many men don't realize just how triggering births can be. A lot of us, whether consciously or not, have some undealt-with wounds and trauma that show themselves in times of change or during emotional turning points in our lives. For Aaron, the wounds and fears that were triggered manifested in his complete lack of awareness, his irritability, and the use of his job to cope with his own unhealed issues. I wish Aaron had reached out ahead of time to us, his family, and other guy friends to share his feelings or ask for advice. I wish he had confided in one of us that he was feeling anxious and on edge. And I wish he had taken his own advice and decentered himself and prioritized what really mattered in the moment. But he didn't, and like many of us men he kept it in until it was too late, almost ruining one of the most important moments of his life: the birth of his son.

After a full twenty-four hours of intense labor and holding not just her pain but also her husband's, Erica gave birth to their baby boy in a beautiful C-section at their local hospital, and thankfully Aaron came to his senses and was right there by her side. He later told me that he wasn't proud of how he handled the birth and wanted me to use his story as a cautionary tale to make sure men don't underestimate the demons that could be hiding in their closet.

I give this example because it was the first time I saw in my own family just how much a massive experience such as birth could throw off a guy who did so much deep internal work and seemed to really understand his own trauma. And while his actions may have not been ideal, I have tremendous compassion for him because the truth is, his models of masculinity failed him. The rigid nature of his masculinity and planning failed him. Even more importantly, the rules and pressures of masculinity failed his wife, through him.

I am reminded of something else my dear friend and mentor Marvin taught me before he passed away. One day while he was teaching me to meditate in what he called "tree pose," he started talking about masculinity and how important it was for us men to be flexible. As I stood there, legs shoulder width apart, my arms bent to form a circle with both sets of my fingers touching each other (as if I were hugging a tree), he kicked behind my knees to make sure there was a slight bend in them. He tapped my shoulders to make sure they were relaxed and not stiff, and then using two fingers in a way I've seen only kung fu masters do, he pushed me and caused me to sway back and forth. "Good!" he said as he told me that "as men we must learn to be flexible and not rigid, we must understand that while our instincts are to be stiff, we, like the tree, will be more susceptible to the winds in the storm if we are rigid."

I wish I had learned earlier in life that there is strength in being malleable and bendy. How different life would be if we took the approach of a palm tree at times, and dug our foundational roots so deep—by opening up our hearts—that it gave us the freedom and permission to move through life open and flexible, without the need to control everything, especially other people, and without the need for everything to be perfect or go according to plan. As I have begun to practice this principle by being mindful of my rigid tendencies and behaviors, I have experienced firsthand the freedom and happiness that come with flexibility. This again reminds me of the physical parallel of flexible muscles. To have true, sustained strength in a muscle, it must be flexible. (I'm still working on the flexible muscles part.)

Maiya's Birth Story

For would-be fathers out there: having now been through the births of both of our children, I can tell you that preparing for the birth of your child is very similar to the way you would prepare for a marathon, or for a championship game. Or at least I think it should be. As every great athlete knows, races and championships aren't won on the day of, but in the weeks and months leading up to them. Even filmmakers say movies are made in prep, not on set. It's about doing the work *before* the big event as if that work is the actual event. It's the hundreds of hours of stretching, training, eating well, and getting your mind in the right place. The difference is that our preparation for the day our children are born rarely involves anything physical, so it can be easy to forget we need to do it.

When I was younger, I always thought of birth like how we

see it on TV shows and in movies. I thought that one day my wife would just look over to me with that look on her face and tell me her water broke. I would then panic to find everything we needed and speed to the hospital, hoping we didn't get pulled over along the way. We would arrive and I would flag down the nurses and doctors and yell, "My wife is in labor!" They would come running out while I coached her through those big deep breaths, and as soon as we reached the hospital room, she would deliver the baby right then and there.

It's pretty amazing to think just how much we've been programmed by the media and how influential it is in our lives. One of the exciting things about being alive now is that we have access to so much information, and with that, we have the opportunity to truly educate ourselves instead of following the scripts and traditions that have been passed down to us for generations. In no way was this more evident for me than when Maiya was born, because, of course, it was nothing like they show in the entertainment business, and it was more than anything I could have imagined.

I watched my wife train her mind and body for Maiya's birth in a way that I have never seen anyone train for anything. She walked five miles a day, stretched, and did breathing techniques; she monitored everything from the food she ate to the content and media she was consuming. She even became a Reiki master. Emily created this safe haven—this cocoon of sorts—around her, and I was in awe of her preparation and discipline. She went full-on Yoda. It would have been easy to say that I didn't have any work to do to prepare because I wasn't the one laboring, since men are often taught that our only job is to be there, to be supportive. But too often when we think of support, we only think of being there, showing up, making sure we don't miss it, and, as we see in the media, being a hand to squeeze and a person to curse at during contractions. Too often we think of support as a passive presence, but watching Emily prepare so actively was an invitation for me to do the same.

So how could I be an active birth partner for my wife and my daughter?

The answer: service. Support without service is passive, but support with service is active. Emily had a thirty-six-hour labor, and my role was to serve her in whatever capacity was needed. At times that meant making sure she was hydrated by offering her coconut water, making her a small smoothie, or just giving her honey so she had sustained energy, breathing alongside her, offering pressure to the small of her back to counter the pressure from labor. I also found it so beautiful that some of the positions that relieved her pain the most were eerily similar to the positions we were in when we made the baby in the first place. Other times my support meant crawling in the kiddie pool along with her to hold her up amid all the various fluids that were floating in the water with us, being a physical brace for her body as she warriored on through those massive contractions. My job was basically to remain physically, emotionally, and mentally sharp, searching for and seizing any opportunity to actively support her—to serve her.

Where did I learn that this was my job, my role? After all, I was the same guy who, not that much earlier, was thinking that doctors and nurses would come out to the parking lot to get my laboring wife. I learned by listening, but not listening to just anyone and everyone. I learned by listening to women: women who had given birth, women who were doulas and midwives, women who were friends, and the woman who was my wife. Men aren't talking about this, and I think a lot of it is because we don't realize that it's our experience too, that we can play an active role. We may not be the star of the team, or in the lead role, but we still have a job to do, and it's an important one. We all have the chance to be the Scottie

Pippen to our Michael Jordan, and let's not forget that Scottie won six championships too.

Over the months leading to the birth, I decided that I was 100 percent going to be right there, between Emily's legs to catch my daughter. Toward the end of her labor, while she was pushing and I was in position, I noticed that I had a split-second thought wondering if I actually wanted to be front and center to see Maiya be born. There are so many scenes where the man does all he can to remain as far away from that view as possible, and I'd be lying if I said I hadn't heard those proverbial stories about men passing out as they watched their baby come out, or saying that they could never look at their wife's vagina in the same way again. So there absolutely was a moment (albeit a very brief one) when I questioned myself and wondered if that would be me too. In the Bahá'í writings we are told that to understand death we have to look at birth. In the womb, babies have all they need as they are existing and developing. Then one day the baby leaves the womb and goes through a tunnel to finally be greeted by all the people who had been preparing for her to enter this world—her loved ones who had been communicating with her, loving her, and waiting for her. It was this concept of birth in my faith that has and continues to be such a massive part of my life and that helped me snap out of that momentary questioning and reminded me what a privilege and gift I was being given to be the first person she saw when she opened her eyes and experienced light in the outside world for the first time. To be the first voice she heard as her ears experienced what the world sounds like outside of the womb. To be the first feeling of physical touch she would experience on her warm, brand-new baby skin. All of this far outweighed any fleeting superficial concern that seeing the full power of my wife's vagina would affect our sex life. So I kept ahold of Emily's hand as I took a front-row seat to watch (and film) Maiya's head slowly begin to appear. As she crowned, I touched her head, I sang to her, and I prayed over her as she emerged into this world. There wasn't a grossed-out thought in my head. It was pure bliss. My dad was right: witnessing this pure magic only reaffirmed my belief in God. When she was finally born into my hands, I whispered a special prayer into her ear through my tears, placed her on Emily's belly, sat back, and marveled at the miracle, the magic, the moment I had the absolute honor to witness.

In those moments, watching my newborn daughter's new body wiggle on the body of her mama, I had this epiphany—this deeply held belief—that one day, hopefully long after I am gone, my little girl will go through another tunnel, leaving this material world for her next great adventure in the spiritual world. Where again I will be right there, waiting for her on the other side. With tears running down my cheeks and the sparkle of joy in my eyes. Greeting her alongside her mother with light and love, my terrible singing voice, open arms, and open heart. "Alláh-u-Abhá," I will say. "You did it. We've been waiting for you. We are so proud of you. Welcome home, my angel." It's all cyclical, and one life's end is really just another beginning.

While there is no one-size-fits-all to birth, and while each story is unique, I do believe that as men we need to do the intense heart work to prepare, to the extent that we can (knowing nothing can fully prepare us), to be able to be of service to our partner and to our child.

Nothing could have prepared me for those moments.

No manual, no how-to book, no documentary.

But I do know that learning how to open my heart, how to be an active support, an active partner, allowed me to experience the full spectrum of birth in a way I wouldn't have been able to otherwise.

Newborn Baby, Newborn Father

When Maiya was born, I was playing a new father on TV. Luckily, she came during the end of our summer hiatus, but I remember being absolutely whiplashed by the emotions, and the sleep deprivation, that I felt in those early months. I also had, and continue to have, a tremendous amount of "dad guilt" as I feel that despite my effort, I never really gave myself a chance to just be a dad and a husband. It was almost like as soon as I found out we were pregnant, my drive to succeed and provide went into hyperspeed, and I wasn't even aware it was happening.

About four months after Maiya was born, I was in an interview promoting season one of *Jane the Virgin,* and the person started to tell me how they already knew I was going to be the best dad because I'm in tune with myself, spiritual, and *blah blah blah.* Then immediately after praising what kind of father they perceived me to be, they asked, "So, what are your tips for new fathers?" I gave some bullshit answer about sleeping when the baby sleeps, and supporting your partner, and how it's all so magical even though it's exhausting. It was one of the many times that I didn't tell the whole truth. On the one hand I didn't really know how I was feeling about everything because I honestly never allowed myself the space or the time to check in, and on the other I was on autopilot and wanted to protect the image.

What I really wanted to say, a few months into fatherhood, when asked for those tips was this: I HAVE NO IDEA!! Everyone visits and showers your family and new baby with adoration and praise. Meanwhile you're trying to figure out how to support your wife, who just pushed a baby out of her vagina, while trying to remember how the doula taught me to make the very specific placenta smoothie recipe that can help with postpartum depression. (*Wait! I'm just supposed to take a chunk of this organ that was inside of you and blend it with acai?!*) All the while, you're trying to figure out how to hold your tiny human daughter so her bobbling head is supported, and put on her diaper the right way so that her poop doesn't blow out of it, and then wipe the right way so that her poop doesn't go in her vagina, and also document and film everything because you don't want to miss a moment, while not breaking under the pressure of knowing you have a new mouth to feed and you have to make money. But that's all normal, right? Or is it? Because everyone just keeps saying: "This is incredible!" "This is amazing!" "You guys must be so happy!" "Those were the best times of my life!" "You'll never get those precious moments back!" And while the truth is that yes, yes, yes, it is incredible, it's also SUPER FUCKING INTENSE, and nothing in life is ever just one thing. It can be incredible, and it can be crazy and hard and tiring and scary and difficult, but none of those things take away from the beauty and magic that is becoming a father. We must learn that happiness and sadness can coexist and that things can be amazing, but they can also be confusing and scary and a ton of other things—at the same exact time. We must learn that it's okay not to be okay.

But instead of acknowledging and admitting what I was feeling, without even realizing it, I projected the image that we had our shit together—that *I* had our shit together. And yes, sure, to a certain extent maybe we did in many ways have our shit together. Yet the idea that I was some sort of unicorn of a man who somehow just knew how to handle everything, give my wife what she needed, give my little baby what she needed, and show up and save the world every day—much like the men in our family had been doing for generations—just wasn't true. I was and still am figuring it out, day by day, step by step.

Generational Healing

One of the coolest things I have learned in this process is that just as the damaging messages and limiting scripts can get passed down from generation to generation, so can the healing. While my dad and I are both incredibly new to this process of practicing vulnerability, recently we have been leaning into these uncomfortable conversations—the ones full of uncomfortable feelings and exposing repressed realities—and we are discovering something that is so much bigger than our masculinity. We are discovering our humanity.

A few months ago, for the first time in my life, my dad reached out via text and said, "Son, I miss you and I feel distant from you. Can we get coffee soon and just talk?" Prior to this part of our relationship, we were both held captive to the image of the strong, silent type. There were parts in both of our lives where we felt comfortable being vulnerable, such as crying watching movies, showing emotion when we're happy, telling each other and our friends that we love them. But it was almost like there was a big NO TRESPASSING sign between us anytime we felt raw in front of each other about other real stuff, such as feeling distant or inadequate in our relationship. Having this sign up also made me feel like a hypocrite, as I was inadvertently being branded the "emotionally open/vulnerable guy" while feeling emotionally stuck when it came to the most important and meaningful relationships in my life outside my marriage. So in many ways while I had been practicing showing up as I am and being vulnerable, I have learned the hard way that when it comes to my dad and my family, it's a different story. I show up just like he does: strong and put together.

It's ironic—painful sometimes, gratifying at other times—that the people you love most are also the ones who test you the most.

For me, it's easy to be brave and open in front of strangers and friends, but it's much harder to be 100 percent authentically who I am in front of those who really, *really* know me. Ironically, I have also found that it's way easier to lose my cool with those I love, and who love me, the most. Sometimes it might be because I feel safe enough to feel all my feelings, but more often than not, it's because I have been repressing my deeper feelings—the ones below the anger—and the pressure from holding them in builds and builds until eventually it has to be released. But by the time it's at a breaking point, by the time I'm at a breaking point, how those feelings end up getting expressed can hurt the people I love. I rarely, if ever, saw my dad get angry, and if he did, he would often immediately be filled with sorrow and make sure that we felt loved. But as I've grown to become a man, I've found that while I can at times have superhuman patience with the world, and even my own family, no one is superhuman and eventually the dam will break, often when I least expect it. As men we are socialized to believe that feeling at all is a sign of weakness and that the only socially acceptable feeling we are permitted to feel is anger or rage. But if we actually stop to think about why many of us lose our shit, or break in moments when we should have the power to keep our cool, especially with the ones we love the most, we will realize that it's only because we haven't given ourselves the space or the time to actually feel what's underneath it all. And what's underneath the anger is often some form of sadness, anxiety, or if we're being honest, a feeling of inadequacy. So the next time you feel that anger or rage bubbling inside you, and you feel like you're going ninety miles per hour but you're not in the driver's seat and you want to explode, take a breath and remember that nine times out of ten if you really check in, you may find that your anger is actually informing you about your deeper feelings of tiredness or sadness or not feeling seen, loved, or appreciated. By acknowledging *those* feelings as they build, we can release them before we explode. In my faith, we are told that for world unity to be established, it must first be established in the home. I find this profound in so many ways, but in large part because of our inability to show up with and for the people who test us the most. If we can show up fully there, then we can show up fully anywhere.

For most of my twenties, my conversations with my dad were mostly about superficial things or about business. The exceptions were the two times I was getting my heart broken and I was completely raw and crushed. Both times my dad was there for me and showed up in huge ways. It felt really good to have no walls between us, no constructed bullshit barriers between our hearts. To be able to simply just BE with him and my mom was an amazing feeling despite the pain I was in. But it also makes me wonder why we have to go through extremes to let people in. Why does it take an event to allow the ones we love most to see us? Whether it's heartbreak or mourning (which are very similar), or crises and catastrophic events, it seems to take extremes to bring us men together to knock down those barriers. It reminds me of the great Rumi quote "Your task is not to seek for love, but merely to seek and find all the barriers within yourself that you have built against it." I used to think that related to romantic relationships, but now I can see how it applies to all relationships, to all of humanity.

Recently my dad and I have just started a new kind of ritual, hanging out to "just talk," and little by little we are getting closer, which to many who know us might seem odd as they would already consider us to be close. But we Baldonis know that there is a difference in seeming close and being close. I am discovering that I have never felt closer to my dad than I do in the moments when I see him for the human he is, when I see myself in him and in turn see him in me. I've begun to see him as a young boy who watched his dad provide and protect, I see him as a teenager being escorted to his front door by the police, and I see my grandpa looking at him with disappointment. I see my dad as a scared new father, holding me in his arms and having no idea what to do or any clue how he is going to provide for me and my mom. By knowing him more fully, the anger and frustration I had with my dad turn into compassion because what I once thought were his flaws and weaknesses, I'm now realizing are the very things that make him human. So when I see my dad as a human—not as a dad who has to teach his son everything perfectly or prove to him and everyone else he is enough as a man, not as a man who has to act a certain way to be man enough—it's then that I realize that my dad, the superhero, didn't need to fall from grace. Instead, my dad, the superhero, needed to fall *into* grace and show me that his fall is the thing that actually makes him the kind of superhero I always needed, the kind of superhero I can grow up to be for my own kids.

Show Me Your Heart

As I have started going into battle with the barriers I put up in my own heart and dissecting some of these topics with my dad, what's been coming out is a new type of parenting that neither my dad nor I got to experience in our childhood. To add another Rumi quote to this chapter, one of my favorites of all time is "The wound is where the light enters you." Leonard Cohen later sang in his masterfully beautiful and haunting song "Anthem," "There's a crack, a crack in everything / that's how the light gets in." Additionally, Bahá'u'lláh in the Bahá'í writings says, "My calamity is my providence, outwardly it is fire and vengeance but inwardly it is light and mercy."

I am seeing the meanings of these quotes in such profound ways as they relate to my own journey with masculinity. As an example, I have this song that I wrote for Maiya and Maxwell. It's called "Show Me Your Heart," and it's become their favorite song to sing. I wanted to find a way early on with my subpar music skills to teach them that they had a heart. It's super simple and it goes like this:

Show me your heart.
Show me your heart.
I'll show you, you are my heart.
When the world seems dark, you are
  the light.
When times get hard, just smile inside.
Because you.
You are my heart.

The point of the song is that it's all about knowing where your heart is and knowing that our hearts cannot be separated from who we are. Recently Emily and I thought we would take it a step farther and create a little ritual with both of them and teach them a little more about their hearts and, more importantly, that their heart is the strongest muscle in their body. Now after we sing the song, I whisper in their ears these simple words that Emily and I came up with together:

The strongest muscle in my whole body is my heart.
I love my body. My mind. My heart and my soul.
I love God, I love Bahá'u'lláh, I love myself, and I am enough.

And now each night before they go to bed, both kids take turns performing what was once a simple affirmation and has now become a mantra. It has some pretty fancy choreography and everything. It's been so much fun to see Maxwell walk around the house singing "Show Me Your Heart" and showing his grandpa that his heart is the strongest muscle in his body, and although sometimes he changes the word "heart" to "penis" or "poo-poo," it's still a way of daily reminding him and his sister that as two-year-old boys or four-year-old girls, as grown men or as grown women, we must practice incorporating our heart and feelings into our sense of self as much as we incorporate our muscles, heads, shoulders, knees, and toes into it.

One day my parents were at our house and Maxwell was singing our song, and it was the first time my dad had heard it. Maxwell ended up teaching it to my dad that day. So here we are, three generations of Baldoni men, all singing this ridiculously simple yet insanely meaningful song together. When I looked over at my dad, I could tell he was doing everything he could to keep from crying, which is a normal occurrence in the Baldoni household these days. It's in these moments that I feel the impact of the multigenerational healing that's happening when we remind each other, and invite each other, to show our hearts.

What does showing my heart look like as a dad? Well, right now it's as simple as making an effort to be fully present whenever I am with my family, to put down my phone when my kids need me instead of making them repeat "Daddy!" over and over again until the black box I'm holding between me and them finally gets out of the way. This happens too often, and I'm feeling guilty about it. I hate that my kids are competing with my phone. But this is part of the journey, and as we have talked about before, awareness is the first step. The truth is I am also working too damn much, and I have this bad habit of coming home and still not being disconnected from my work. Like many men, I carry my days home with me, and even when I look like I'm present, many times I'm not.

So how do I fix this? First, by being compassionate to myself in the same way I'm learning to be compassionate with my dad—and by just putting my damn phone down and playing! By dancing, being silly, goofy, and using my imagination with my kids instead of using it only when I am working and wanting to create change in the world. Here's the deal: if I can't do it at home, with my own family, how am I going to do it anywhere else? Also, showing my heart looks like showing my playful side. As adults—hell, even as teenagers and preteens—it's easy to feel wildly uncomfortable being silly, but kids are hilarious, and if you let them, they will teach you how to have simple fun again. It's like that popular internet meme says, "No matter how badass you think you are, if a toddler hands you a toy phone, you answer that shit." So I'm putting down my phone and picking up their toy phone.

Showing my heart also means listening to them, apologizing to them when my tone is a little too harsh and my patience is short, and sharing with them (in terms that they understand) when I am having a hard day or feeling a big emotion. It means learning to sit with my own emotions so I can be with theirs. Showing my heart means doing the work—going on the journey—to be able to parent from a place of wholeness instead of woundedness.

Showing my heart means showing my humanity, knowing that I do not need to fear my humanity. Showing my emotions, struggling, and asking for help don't make me any less of a man. They simply make me more of a human.

CHAPTER TEN

ENOUGH

Waving the White Flag

A foundational part of this book, and my journey, has been taking the messages that society has given us and trying to reframe them in a way that actually benefits us. It's the same principle that my TED Talk was based on. Are you brave enough to be vulnerable? Are you confident enough to listen? Are you strong enough to be sensitive? Are you adventurous enough to dive into the deep waters of your shame, into your behaviors, your thought patterns, and the stories you carry that hurt like hell? Are you hardworking and courageous enough to take the journey from your head to your heart?

I needed this type of challenge. I needed to relate my emotional health to my physical health, to think of the heart work as the hard work, as being just as important as a workout in the gym—if not more important. Even if I was reframing the traditional messages in a healthier, more holistic approach, I unknowingly still needed every aspect of this journey to be centered around that same traditional principle of masculinity, that deep-seated desire to be man enough. That is, until I discovered that below the deep-seated desire, there is a more fundamental need.

You know that phrase about sweeping shit under the rug, creating an illusion that your house doesn't have dirt in it? This journey feels a little bit like that to me in the sense that, for so long, I was subconsciously sweeping all these messages under the rug. And to begin this journey, I had to lift the rug and examine the dirt that had collected there for years. (It's worth noting here again that dirt and shit make a great fertilizer for things to grow.) So I'm sifting through all this shit. I'm covered in sweat and dirt and tears. I'm doing the work to get to the bottom of the pile somewhat anticipating that underneath it all is some sort of reward or trophy or at the very least a damn participation ribbon that reads "Man Enough."

And yet there is only the bare floor. So I rip up that too, desperate to discover that I am man enough. Now look, I am not a contractor or a builder, but I have seen enough HGTV to know that there are several more layers of flooring to get through before you reach the foundation. And then of course after the foundation comes the ground, the original empty space of earth that your house was built on.

There was no "Man Enough" trophy there either.

But you know what I discovered underneath the messaging, the dirt, the layers of flooring, the foundation? I discovered that what I had mistaken for a desire to be man enough was actually a fundamental need to belong.

At my innermost core, I do not need to be man enough. At my innermost core, I don't even desire it. Because what I need—in the same way I need food, water, and shelter—is a sense of belonging. So while I spent this part of the journey, and the better part of this book, reframing the traditional messages of masculinity to be more inclusive and holistic, I'm ending the book by doing what arguably may be the most unmasculine thing. For all intents and purposes I'm right in the middle of the battle, and I'm going to do what I've been told men never do.

I'm surrendering.

I'm waving the white flag.

Not because of defeat, but because it's time to be done playing the game by a set of rules that keeps everyone from winning. I know now what I didn't know when I started this journey: I don't need to seek out, sort out, reframe, fight for, or work to establish that I am man enough; I need to accept that I am, and that I always have been, enough. I know now that while my battle may have been against the messages of masculinity, the real war has been the war I waged against myself, and I am so tired of fighting that war.

Removing the Armor

I was taught never to quit, to fight for what I want, what I believe in, to endure. I was taught to believe that "good enough isn't enough" and that second place is the first loser. More. Harder. Faster. No pain, no gain. Winners never quit. Give me the long, grueling hours on a set, in the editors' room. Give me the lack of sleep and the exhausting mental work of perfectionism. Give me the pain and the sweat of an intense workout, give me the resistance, and let me fight back. These I know how to do. But surrender? It just feels so . . . *passive.*

It's almost as if I took off the armor, stood in front of the mirror, looked at myself, and thought, *Now what?* There has to be more. This can't be it. Where's the hustle? Where's the hard work? When you've been conditioned to believe that your productivity is a measure of your worth, doing what feels like nothing then indicates your lack of worth. But this was the whole point, right? To uncover that who I am, underneath all the armor, is simply enough.

Robert Fisher's *The Knight in Rusty Armor,* which should be required reading in school and which I first read in a three-day intensive therapy retreat with my family, tells the story of a heroic knight known for slaying dragons and rescuing damsels in distress, who is on a mission to become the greatest knight in all the land. He has become so attached to the armor he is known for that he never takes it off, despite his wife's pleading to see who he really is. Eventually his wife threatens to leave and take their son with her if the knight doesn't take his armor off. But the problem isn't that he doesn't want to take it off; it's that he actually doesn't know how to take it off—and no one else does either. So he goes searching for help. He goes on a journey through the woods, searching for a path and guidance from others, like Merlin the magician, to help remove the armor, only to find that while on his journey, the armor keeps getting heavier and heavier. At one point he even forgets the purpose of his journey and why he had left home. He encounters many challenges, including dragons, all of which are metaphors for the various battles we fight as men on our journey to becoming more full humans. Eventually he faces his deepest, darkest fear and finally lets go of all the things he had been holding on to, all the things he thought defined him. He had to be willing to detach from and unlearn all he thought he knew, including who the world wanted him to be and who he thought he was. And it is the release of his guilt, judgments, and excuses that allows him to cry the tears of joy that eventually melt away his armor.

Just like every part of this process, my journey has been a continual unfolding as opposed to a one-time revelation. It's not as if I took off the armor and never put it back on again. In fact, I go days and months with the armor still on—sometimes it's the full suit; other times maybe it's just the helmet or the chest plate. But the difference now is that I return again and again to that full-length mirror and taking inventory and removing whatever pieces of armor I have consciously or subconsciously put back on. Now, while part of this practice has entailed literally standing in front of the mirror, I use that more so as a figurative way to illustrate this ongoing coming back to myself. While everyone's path will look different, as there can't be and shouldn't be a one-size-fits-all approach to this work, here are some of the other things I have found that work for me: going to therapy, prioritizing my mental health, daily affirmations, prayer, moving my body, breath work, check-ins with my male friends, reading books, and (when I am crunched for time) reading and repeating quotes that resonate with me. Here are a few I am leaning on currently:

> "The cave that you fear to enter holds the treasure you seek."
> —JOSEPH CAMPBELL

> "Little by little. Day by day."—'ABDU'L-BAHÁ

> "The wound is where the light enters you."—RUMI

> "O SON OF SPIRIT! Noble have I created thee, yet thou hast abased thyself. Rise then unto that for which thou wast created."—BAHÁ'U'LLÁH

I also find that engaging in spiritual practices such as prayer, readings, weekly study circles, and service all help bring me back to that place of contentment where I'm less distracted by the messages of the world and more in tune with the messages of my heart.

It's easy to see then that while the act of surrendering may not be the sweaty, dirty, laborious work that I had come to value most, it is definitely not passive. To continually show up for yourself, to get to know yourself, to remove the armor, to literally change your thought processes and brain pathways is some of the most important work I have ever done. There is a different kind of stamina needed, a different kind of endurance needed, for a journey that has no finish line. A journey that has no external validation, no awards, gold stars, or trophies. It's a journey that begins and ends with me, but in no way is it a journey that I have to take alone.

One of the greatest lessons I have learned on this journey is that I don't have to go at it alone. In fact, I think that one of the more harmful myths of masculinity is that we have to do it alone—we need to be the Lone Ranger, the superhero, the man who has it all together and doesn't need anyone else. But guess what? I need people. I need to be in relationships with other people who are on this journey, to hear their stories and witness their vulnerability, their shame, their longing, and their belonging. I need to know that while it is a very personal journey, it is also a communal one—that while we each have our own battles to fight and to surrender to, we are not just doing it for or with our own selves; we are also doing it together and for the greater good. I no longer want the unwritten rule to be that we go at it alone, that we have to navigate success, failure, marriage, divorce, fatherhood, sickness, and all of life's events on our own. I want it to be that we share our experiences, as men and as humans, from an honest and vulnerable place, that we send the elevator back down so that generation after generation, we begin to improve and stop making the same damn mistakes. Instead of passing scripts down to our children, I want the unwritten rule to be that we exchange our ideas and our stories with them, so that one day they can do the same for their children. Instead of every man for himself and the old teaching the young, we open ourselves to the truth that the young have a lot to teach the old as well. I want a world where learning, questioning, curiosity, and growth are a part of the mainstream narrative.

How many of the greatest stories of our collective culture have this theme: you go on a journey to find your self only to realize that it was there all along? Or that in a time of crisis, it's our friends and family who pull us through, that mean more to us than all the money and fame in the world? It's a crucial part of every great storytelling arc because it is the very thing that makes us human.

One of my best friends, Ahmed, once told me that one of the original meanings of the word "human" in Arabic is *insan*, which translates in English to "insane." Now, while it has many meanings and translations, one of the more accurate translations is "they who forget." So to be human quite simply means to forget. For me that means that the real journey is in the remembering: remembering who we are, who created us, our purpose, and our worth.

This book and this journey as a whole have been such an incredible healing and remembering process not just for myself but for my family and close friends as well. The journey has invited my wife and me into deeper conversations that have only increased our intimacy, attraction, and connection to one another. It has impacted my children as I am learning to be more present in the now with them, and it has rippled out into my relationship with my parents and sister so we can finally start really living like all that matters is that we are "rich in love." This journey has even inspired my mom to tear down her walls and start going to therapy so she can heal the parts of her that need healing. But with all that said, by no means have I arrived, nor am I sure there is even a place to arrive at. I say that because when I gave Emily this last chapter to read, she looked at me and said, "Wow, baby, this is really good. But I think you need to read your own book." Well, she's right and I do. So just know as you read my words that they are just that: words. It's actions that matter more than anything. Just because someone you follow, or look up to, wrote a book or is considered an "expert," it doesn't mean they have it all figured out. It doesn't mean that they have arrived in some way or that they are on the other side, or even that they always succeed in taking their own advice. It just means they have learned enough and are willing to share their learnings in an attempt to help, but please remember that true learning never ever stops.

By continuing to lean into this notion that I am enough, it is inevitably an invitation for others to do the same, but more than that, it is an invitation for me to continue doing the same. And let me be clear: others in my life have given me that same invitation by doing their own work. Nothing touches my heart more than the work I'm witnessing my own father do at seventy-two. I'm watching as my dad for the first time in his life is realizing that all these years he has had his own suit of armor he didn't even know he was wearing, and despite his age, he is making a Herculean effort to remove it—little by little, day by day. He does this by telling me what he is working on, by reaching out and making an effort to talk about things that don't have to do with work and all the comfortable things we've always fallen back on. He's trying to put his phone down around his grandkids, he's actively listening and hearing what is being said around him, and he is really showing up. He is fighting the battles within himself that keep him from experiencing his son and his family in the most intimate of ways, and he is learning how to surrender. And just like the knight in rusty armor, I've had a chance to witness firsthand my dad crying tears of joy that have melted away the armor he's been carrying around without knowing it for his entire life.

I Am Enough

More than anyone else in my life besides my wife, my children have been a consistent and persistent source of joy, inspiration, and wisdom on this journey. I mean, think about young children for a minute. They have no concept of social norms, and as their eyes begin to open to socialization, it is, at first, very limited. They express themselves fully because they literally cannot regulate their emotions. They like what they like and don't like what they don't like, even down to the infuriatingly normal phases of picky eating and protesting sleep. Children have no armor. And if we are honest, their lack of armor creates some of the best memories.

Just yesterday I was playing with my kids in the pool. We had a few friends over, and without warning my two-year-old son jumped out, took off his swimsuit, ran to the nearby hedges, spread his legs, leaned back, and started to pee. It was his first time peeing standing up, and he excitedly yelled, "Look, look! I'm peeing like Daddy! I'm peeing like Daddy!" Then without warning, my daughter ran over next to him, took the same position, and peed the same way (with surprisingly good aim) while also yelling the same thing. We all had a great laugh and I high-fived them both, got a little pee on my hands, and told them how proud I was of them. These are the moments that mean the world to me, and these are the moments—as weird as they are—that remind me of what it was like when I was their age and had none of my armor on.

Now think of us as parents or grown-ups in a child's life. If we're lucky, or if we're doing it well, we encourage children's innate worth all the time. We tell them they can be whoever they want to be, like whatever they want to like, and pee however they want to pee, because who they are at a foundational, cellular level is good and is enough. (Of course, we are human, and we aren't executing this perfectly, but if we are consciously parenting, we are aware of how much our support and affirmation of who they are, as they are, are needed.)

In other words, we aren't picking apart young children the same way we pick apart our own selves. We aren't demanding that they be more successful, confident, and brave; we aren't demanding that they have a stronger body to earn our love. To me Maiya and Maxwell's ordinariness is enough. Everything about them is enough. And every time I affirm that in them, it is an invitation to affirm it in myself.

If I am encouraging my children to be themselves, then I need to be myself.

If I am encouraging my children to like what they like, then I need to like what I like.

If I am encouraging my children to believe that who they are, as they are, is enough, then I must also believe that who I am, as I am, is enough too.

Sadly, there are a lot of us, a lot of men, who are still waiting, at age thirty or forty or fifty or older, to have their worth validated just once by their parents, particularly by their father. Just once. They've heard those lines over and over again, about not being tough ENOUGH, or strong ENOUGH, or fast ENOUGH. Or they've heard that they were "too" something—too soft, too weak, too much of a crybaby, a mama's boy. Well, enough of "enough"!

Or maybe I should say it this way. You know how we say "enough is enough"—well, maybe that phrase was right the whole time, but we've just been using it wrong. Maybe enough is enough because what we are and who we are ARE enough. Maybe we don't have to strive and work so damn hard all the time to fulfill someone else's idea of what "enough" is. It's been here the whole time, just waiting for us to take off our armor to be able to see it. How many of us use the word "imperfect" to describe ourselves? Well, we were right all along. I'm perfect.

I was once a young child, unarmored and liberated. I would yell, like my kids do now, about how smart and brave and kind I was. I was more than content climbing trees, coloring, and making pretend movies with a broken camcorder. There was a time when I couldn't even fathom the concept of needing a certain job, or looking differently than I did, to be enough. There was a time when I didn't have to give a second or third or fourth or fifteenth thought to whether I was enough, when I didn't have to remind myself to be nice to myself. There was a time when it wasn't even a question because I loved myself. Because that's how God created me. Not just as enough, but also as more than enough. The younger we are, the easier it seems to be for us to remember it. But the older we get, the easier it is to forget. And I guess that's what makes us human.

So I'm making an effort to remember, and right now I'm doing that by surrendering the war I have waged on myself, to get back to that time, to that Justin—the one who knew that he was enough, not because of anything he did, but because of who he was.

Of course, it looks different to me now than it might for a child (although I am convinced that blanket forts, hide-and-seek, and trampolines are always good starting places for, well, anything), but the principle remains the same. My job doesn't determine my worth. My confidence, or lack thereof, doesn't determine if I belong. The size of my muscles or my penis doesn't equate to how much of a man I am. The amount of sex I am having or not having doesn't mean I am more or less worthy of love.

There are no prerequisites for worthiness. There are no boxes I have to check or rules I have to follow before I can be enough. I already am simply because I am.

Dr. Brené Brown describes it this way: "Don't walk through the world looking for evidence that you don't belong, because you will always find it. Don't walk through the world looking for evidence that you're not enough, because you will always find it. Our worth and our belonging are not negotiated with other people. We carry those inside of our hearts."

For me, *that* is why I am so damn committed to undefining my masculinity and to taking this slow and long journey from my head to my heart. It is in making that connection with my heart that I make the connection with my worthiness. The messages of masculinity will tell me over and over again that I need to be better or different, that I need to conform to be worthy. They'll tell me to acquire more success, confidence, muscles, women, social status—you name it, I will always need more. But my heart? My heart will simply say, "I am enough," over and over again.

. . . and You Are Too

If you take one thing from this book, let it be this: **you are enough**—not man enough, not woman enough, not fill-in-the-blank-identity enough.

You are human enough.

Right now, in this exact moment, whoever you are, wherever you are, no matter what you are dealing with, how much you are hurting, how much you are holding or who is holding you . . . you are enough.

While this truth may be at the end of the book, it is the beginning of the journey—one that is simultaneously very personal, and one that we must take together. It is a journey that involves the need for systemic change, but it is a journey that starts within our own stories, our conditioning, our awareness, our conscious and subconscious thought patterns . . . our hearts.

I'm not going to give you a list of next steps or hand you a map and say, "Follow these directions." I wish I could. I wish I could offer you a handbook and a GPS and confidently send you on your way. I wish I could say exactly the right thing or write the perfect metaphor that speaks to you the most. I wish I could know precisely what you need to be encouraged, inspired, and fueled for this journey. Maybe you need a loud, boisterous coach breathing down your neck, challenging you to do the work, or maybe you need a soft-spoken invitation to it.

In the same way, I am not going to tell you to abandon all it means to be a man in this world, but I am also not going to tell you not to. This is your journey; this is the work—your work—to know yourself. For some of you, your journey might look like mine, and you'll need to reframe the traditional messages in a more holistic way to make this feel like a journey you can take. You'll need to settle into those parts of you that are traditionally masculine and use them to encourage you to dip your toe into the other parts of you that you've been cut off from. Others might have been waiting for permission this whole time, so you'll just throw off the armor and feel so fucking liberated right off the bat. Some of you may want to pick up that self-help book that keeps popping up in your life, while others will need to put down the self-help books that you've been reading for what feels like your whole life. Some will head to therapy, while others will commit to risking vulnerability the next time your friends get together to watch a game. Someone might decide to finally put down that bottle, or close that browser, and search for an AA or SAA meeting near him, while another may realize that just because he doesn't hit his wife doesn't mean he isn't hurting her. There is no one way to do this; it is not this end of the spectrum or the other end, nor is it the middle.

And because there is no one way, no perfect plan, path, or road, the greatest adventure you will ever go on begins and ends with you.

There are 7 billion people on this planet, each one on a similar adventure every second of every day. So despite how lonely it may feel at times, you are not alone. The adventure that remembering your worth and your enoughness will take you on is all a part of our human experience. The only thing absolutely universal about the journey from your head to your heart is that you and I, and all of us, are worthy enough to take it.

ACKNOWLEDGMENTS

I believe that true creativity thrives and flourishes in community. Art and inspiration may come through each of us as individuals, but they are not of us. These ideas are not our own; they come through us to be of service to the collective WE, to the greater good. And it's through the collective inspiration of community that I believe that art truly thrives. I cannot think of one accomplishment or piece of art I have ever made solely on my own. Every good thing in my life, every goal I have ever hit, film or story I have told is the result of hundreds and thousands of people who have shaped and influenced my life in large and small ways for as long as I can remember. For every person like me, fortunate enough to find some success in whatever field they are in, or to have a publisher deem their thoughts worthy enough to be shared with the masses, or who find themselves with their name or face on the cover of a book, remember there are hundreds of people who carried them, held them, taught them, shaped them, challenged them, and inspired them along the way—people who may never be publicly acknowledged or rewarded for their efforts. So, I write this today filled with gratitude that I am standing on the shoulders of spiritual and creative giants who have loved and nurtured me and made any trace of success in my life possible. If it were not for the people listed below, the people in my community, my tribe, my family, then this book would not exist, as left on my own, I would not have seen myself as enough to either write it or finish it.

To my wife, Emily. My love. My friend. My rock. My helpmate and companion in both this world and the next. I don't know what I did to deserve your grace, patience, compassion, and radical empathy. Thank you for holding me up while also holding up our entire family, and yourself, as I crumbled time and time again writing this book. You are a marvel and my personal hero. You know exactly how I feel about you, so I don't need to write any more. "If I love you, I need not continually speak of my love—you will know without any words."—'ABDU'L-BAHÁ

To my mom and dad, I am the best of both of you. While at times I know this book could be hard to read, I want you to know that it is and was your unique combinations of being free thinkers, optimists, spiritual gurus, and entrepreneurs that created my relentless search for all that is good and true in myself and in the world. I could write multiple books on all the things you did that were amazing and the ways you taught me to love and exist. But this, my first book, had a specific purpose, and I can't thank you enough for giving me space to feel and process all the big, small, and hard things I have worked through on my journey to being enough. Thank you for raising me to be human, to be kind, to use my heart, to be seeker of truth, and above all, to love God. I am so grateful and proud to be your son. And Mom, thank you for being my first educator and for the millions of tiny sacrifices you made for me over the course of my life that no one will ever know about and that you never got praise for. But most importantly, thank you for introducing me to Bahá'u'lláh.

Sara—my strong, empathetic, kind, magnetic sister. While you may not be in this book much by name, you are tattooed on my heart and will be for life. I have so much to learn from you and your wild free spirit. Here's to moon dancing, gardening, and howling under the moon together in this next phase of our life and siblinghood.

Will Youngblood—my friend, brother, and amazing assistant. I don't know how you do it and I can't thank you enough for putting up with me. I don't know what I would have done without you these last few years. Thank you for your integrity, your intuition, your heart, your faith, your protection, your positivity, and for believing that all things are possible. You are an incredible man and human and you deserve the world. I'm honored to be in the trenches with you.

To Fari, our beloved nanny, friend, and real-life angel. Your kindness, patience, and gentleness is unmatched. Thank you for being of service to our family and making it possible for us to serve others. At times your contribution to our lives, and this world, may seem invisible or go unnoticed, but please know that your work is perhaps the most important work of all, as you make all other work possible.

To my editor, Gideon Weil. Thank you for your superhuman patience, your belief, and being such a champion of this book and my story. Thank you for trusting me and also giving me space to feel all I was feeling as I rewrote and rewrote and rewrote long after I was supposed to. I will forever be grateful for your partnership and holding my hand through this strange, wild, and therapeutic process.

To my powerful, kind, intuitive, loving, and firm hand, my agent and friend, Johanna Castillo. You believed I had a book in me long before I ever thought I did. If there is anyone responsible for all of this, it is you, my dear. Thank you for demanding that I give this book all of me in the way that it deserved all of me. Thank you for not letting me quit and back out of it no matter how many times I tried, and for finding me and this story its perfect home in HarperCollins. You are a force to be reckoned with, and I am so grateful for your intuition and mentorship and for never giving up on me.

Noelle René—this book simply doesn't exist without you. Thank you for the last eighteen years of steadfast friendship and love. Thank you for being one of the first people in my life to ever truly see me. All of me. The beautiful and the broken—at a time when no one else could. Your sensitivity is your superpower, and I can't thank you enough for being by my side all these years and being patient with me as I tried on all the different masks of masculinity while knowing I would eventually find the perfect fit without one. Thank you for coming along on this journey with me and reminding me of what I have to offer when I couldn't see it, for helping me find my voice when I wasn't sure if it was there. (Thank you to Casey and Elden too!)

To my incredible and brave HarperOne family: Judith Curr, you are a visionary and a force for good in this industry. Thank you for taking a chance and believing in me and this message. Thank you to Paul Olsewski, Sam Tatum, Laina Adler, Aly Mostel, Lucile Culver, Ashley Yepsen, Terri Leonard, Suzanne Quist, William Drennan, Adrian Morgan, and the whole team at HarperOne who each played a massive role in bringing this book to life and into the hands and hearts of so many around the world.

To the selfless, insanely talented, brilliant, and kind humans and friends who gave their time and energy in helping shape this book and, in turn, my life. I am so grateful:

Michael Kimmel, thank you for everything. I have learned so much from you and will forever be grateful for your friendship and inclusivity as I began this journey into the wild world of masculinity.

Liz Plank—you man-loving masculinity-wizard you. Thank you for your friendship and for caring about this book and this message almost as much as, if not even more than, I do. Your passion for helping men and changing the world is contagious, and I am so grateful to be able to call you a friend.

Glennon Doyle—you popped into my life when I needed you the most. You made me feel seen and gave me the strength to keep going when I was doubting myself the most. Thank you for seeing me and believing in this message. May this inspire more men to be able to love, support, and appreciate the Untamed among us.

John Kim—you angry awesome former miserable f#*!. I love and appreciate your honesty, your friendship. Thanks for pushing me to go deeper when I was skimming the surface.

Ted Bunch—your commitment to men and to the safety and lives of women is awe inspiring. Thank you for your friendship and your tireless work to make this world a safer, more just, and more equitable place.

Masud Oulafani—you are a spiritual and artistic force. I appreciate you, brother!

Brad Reedy—thank you for pushing me to go deeper in both my life and in this book. And thank you for introducing me to *The Knight in Rusty Armor* and helping me finally see the weight of the armor I had been unknowingly wearing and carrying all these years.

Layli Miller Muro—thank you for always finding the time to mentor me and for your invaluable perspectives on justice and spirituality. I will forever be a supporter of the Tahirih Justice Center and the work you do to save the lives of immigrant women and girls.

Farhoud Meybodi—I love and appreciate you, brother. Iron sharpens iron and I will always appreciate you seeing me and pushing me to go deeper, and to expose the parts of myself that I might be ashamed of. Thank you for being a Wayfarer, for putting so much of yourself into that first season of *Man Enough*, and for never letting me settle for mediocrity.

Jamey Heath—I love you deeply. You are basically single-handedly responsible for the recognition of my white privilege and I am still in awe of the fact that you love me as much as you do, because if I were you, I honestly would have given up on me a long time ago. Whenever I need mentorship, guidance, or the truth, you are my first call. Not Rainn or Andy or Travis—you. And I put that in writing because I know that rubbing that in their faces is slightly more important to you than anything. That is my gift to you. I love you. Now please go eat shit immediately, you Executive Man.

Rainn Wilson—you are a weirdo and I love you to death. Thank you for being my Bahá'í brother, my mentor, and my phone-a-friend when in need. You are responsible for all of my success, and I'm okay if people can't tell if I'm serious or joking when I say that, because I can never tell if you're serious or joking.

Travis Van Winkle—one of my best friends in the world. Thank you for breaking up with me via email when we were twenty-three, and thank you for wanting to be friends again with me at twenty-five. I have learned so much about myself and masculinity from our brotherhood. We have been through so much together these last sixteen years. I hold our friendship so near and dear to my heart and appreciate you more than you could ever know. If it weren't for you, so much of the goodness in my life, along with this book, wouldn't exist. Oh, and thanks for confessing your unrequited love for my wife in your best man speech. Nice touch.

Andy Grammer and Adam Mondschein—my spiritual brothers. Thank you for always being there for me and for seeing me. You showed up when I needed you the most, told me the hard truths, and changed my perspective on brotherhood. I will never forget those months I slept on your couch and the spirit and faith you reinstilled in me. And Andy, thank you for that month you slid $500 under my door when you knew I couldn't pay rent. I love you deeply. Now go make a TikTok.

Ford Bowers, your knowledge of our faith is awe-inspiring. I appreciate you and your contribution to this book and my life.

Samantha Emmer-Fink—you are a lifesaver. Thank you for your boundless energy, optimism, and giant heart. I have no idea how you do it; you are such a gift to our family.

Labid Aziz—had you not joined the Wayfarer family, I couldn't have given this book the time and attention it deserved. Thank you for your heart, support, vision, and commitment to personal growth. You are enough, my brother.

Kay Hubbard, thank you for your friendship, forgiveness, transparency, and vulnerability in letting me share the story of our friendship. I don't deserve the amount of kindness and grace you have shown me. I love and appreciate you.

To all the friends and experts who have been a part of *Man Enough* and influenced my journey and relationship with masculinity, there are too many of you to name but each of you impacted my life and taught me so much about myself. May God bless you on your journey as you continue your deep heart work in both public and private, and may you all know just how enough each of you are.

Steve Sarowitz—thank you for coming into my life when I least expected it and being the best business partner and spiritual brother I could ever ask for. This is just the beginning.

Cyrus Sigari—you were the first to invest in me. Thank you for running that Iron Man and raising money so that I could start this work. And thank you for making me go all in on *Man Enough*. I'm still not going to fly in your helicopter.

Mina Sabet and Pat Mitchell from TED Women—thank you for thinking that my thoughts were valuable enough to be included on the TED stage and for not letting me back out each time I tried. And Mina, thank you for making me change outfits and wear the blue sweater and not my ripped-up T-shirt just before I took the stage.

Payam Zamani—thank you for your friendship and mentorship. For always standing by me and being not just a friend but a true spiritual brother on this journey.

Stefan Sonnenfeld—thank you for letting me use your office café to write during COVID when I had to escape my house. I will forever be grateful for your endless lattes and that fire pit.

Ahmed Musiol—my Muslim spiritual brother, partner, and fellow Wayfarer. I love you. Thank you for always reminding me to make time for the Creator of time. For loving me and helping me see my nobility when I haven't been able to see it myself. For inspiring me to be a better Bahá'í by your devoted practice to Islam, and for modeling through your goodness so much of what I write about in this book.

Jay Shetty—I am in awe of you. You have mastered the art of distilling ancient wisdom in a way that's digestible to the masses and are giving people the tools that can help unlock their own happiness at a time they need it most. Thank you for your friendship, support, and belief in this work. I appreciate you, brother.

Shawn Mendes—you popped into my life when I least expected it and helped me remember that I was enough. Thank you for your sincerity, your purity, and being a relentless student and seeker of the truth. I admire you, brother, and deeply appreciate the way you are inspiring millions to connect to their hearts.

Karamo Brown—my soul brother. Your energy is infectious. Your skin is flawless. And you make everyone around you feel like they are enough. You have such a gift with words, and I feel so blessed to know you. Thank you for being there for me and joining me on this Man Enough journey. Please send me your skin-care routine.

To the entire Wayfarer family—you represent all that is good in our industry. Thank you for joining me on this journey, for your massive hearts, and for your commitment to telling stories that move the soul and help us remember what truly matters.

Cori Valois—you saw past the restless, distracted student and believed in me when I didn't believe in myself. Thank you for seeing what I couldn't see in high school and believing I had wings I didn't know I had.

Marvin Brock—my spiritual brother who is reading this from the next world. I love you. Thank you for teaching me the importance of steadfastness and flexibility. "Is there any Remover of difficulties save God? Say: Praised be God! He is God! All are His servants, and all abide by His bidding."—THE BÁB

Christopher Aiff and Zach Sobiech—may the entire world know your names. Meeting the two of you altered the course of my life. You didn't know each other in this world but I have a feeling you are best friends where you are now. I learned so much about what it means to be a man and human from both of you. You showed me how beautiful and fragile life can be, and how fortunate I was to find someone I wanted to share my life with. Thank you for guiding me, and never leaving me alone on this journey. "This is revolutionary friendship. It started in my heart, and it's living in my soul."

Lisa Fuxler—my sister. I think you are the shit. Thanks for making Emily laugh until she pees herself and being such a strong force for good in her life.

To my mother-in-love, Bettan—thank you for raising such a strong and powerful woman in Emily and instilling in her such immeasurable grace and kindness. And for always supporting me despite my very un-Swedish fast-paced lifestyle. You are the best mormor and I love you so much.

And to Roland Fuxler. Even though we didn't get to meet in this life, I know our hearts have met and we are deeply connected. Thank you for raising your little girl with wonder and inspiration and for helping to guide her to me. You will forever be an integral part of our life and our love story. This book is also dedicated to you.

And finally, to my two beating hearts that exist outside of my body. Maiya and Maxwell. Your daddy loves you more than you could ever imagine. The hardest part of writing this book has been feeling like I was letting you down by being so close yet so far away. I want you to know that you will always come first in my life, and I will not choose my work or my service to the world over you. May you always remember that your heart is the strongest muscle in your body, and that you are and will always be enough. I love you thisssssss much and in all the worlds of God. Now please go to sleep so your mommy and I can have some alone time together.